Accountant's and Lawyer's Concise Guide to Tax Saving Opportunities

Accountant's and Lawyer's Concise Guide to Tax Saving Opportunities

F.S. NOURALLAH CPA, Ph.D.

Prentice-Hall, Inc. • Englewood Cliffs, N.J.

Prentice-Hall International, Inc., *London*
Prentice-Hall of Australia, Pty. Ltd., *Sydney*
Prentice-Hall of Canada, Ltd., *Toronto*
Prentice-Hall of India Private Ltd., *New Delhi*
Prentice-Hall of Japan, Inc., *Tokyo*
Prentice-Hall of Southeast Asia Pte. Ltd., *Singapore*
Whitehall Books, Ltd., *Wellington, New Zealand*

"This publication is designed to provide accurate and authoritative information in regard to the subject matter covered. It is sold with the understanding that the publisher is not engaged in rendering legal, accounting, or other professional service. If legal advice or other expert assistance is required, the services of a competent professional person should be sought."

—From the Declaration of Principles jointly adopted by a Committee of the American Bar Association and a Committee of Publishers and Associations.

Library of Congress Cataloging in Publication Data

Nourallah, F S
Accountant's and lawyer's concise guide to tax saving opportunities.

Includes index.
1. Tax planning--United States. I. Title.
KF6297.N68 343'.73'052 77-8963
ISBN 0-13-001172-X

Printed in the United States of America

A Word from the Author

Few taxpayers have been left untouched by the 1976 Tax Reform Act, the most sweeping overhaul of the federal tax code in more than 20 years. The changes make it vital for the tax advisor to re-examine suggestions for tax savings and to review everyone's tax situation. In particular, upper-income taxpayers will require careful guidance in interpreting complex new regulations to ferret out the remaining and newly opened-up tax saving opportunities.

This book reduces the highly complicated area of taxation to a crystal clear guide to tax saving opportunities. Instead of dealing with the individual taxpayer as a single, married, or a head of household, a different, unique approach is used. The main source of taxable income is emphasized in order to classify taxpayers into groups according to their business activities.

For each group of individuals having in common one major source of income and business activities, numerous suggestions for minimizing their tax bills are offered.

This new approach to tax saving opportunities deals with the taxpayer as an employee, a self-employed, a landlord, a farmer, an investor in stocks and bonds, a partner in a partnership, an owner of a corporation, a seller of a home, a seller of a property under an installment method, or an investor in a depreciable business asset. A more meaningful relationship between the individual, his source of income, and his opportunities for income tax saving is clearly defined.

Furthermore, this book looks at the practical relationship between the federal income tax and the unified gift and estate tax. Each individual is concerned about his annual income tax bill as well as the possible inheritance tax on his estate in case he dies leaving any material amount of wealth to his family and beloved ones.

Therefore, the approach adopted in this book is that in order to implement a tax saving idea for an individual, both the effect on his federal income tax and expected estate tax liability should be considered very carefully.

F. S. Nourallah

About the Author

F. S. Nourallah is a Texas Certified Public Accountant and principal of his own public accounting firm in El Paso. For the past 18 years, he has been teaching, writing and practicing in the taxation area. He has written numerous professional articles and has also served as a tax manager, educational consultant and lecturer to various groups of practicing accountants.

He received his Ph.D. in accountancy from the University of Illinois (Urbana) and is presently professor of accounting and taxation at the University of Texas at El Paso.

CONTENTS

TAX SAVING OPPORTUNITIES FOR EMPLOYEES (con't)

TAX SAVING OPPORTUNITIES FOR FARMERS (con't)

TAX SAVING OPPORTUNITIES FOR OWNERS OF CLOSELY HELD CORPORATIONS (con't)

TAX SAVING OPPORTUNITIES FOR INVESTORS IN STOCKS AND BONDS (con't)

ESTATE TAX SAVING TECHNIQUES (con't)

THE GIFT TAX AND GIFTS TO FAMILY MEMBERS (con't)

Chapter 1

TAX SAVING OPPORTUNITIES FOR THE SELF-EMPLOYED

1.1. Hiring a Family Member

If you hire a teenage child (in 1976), you can pay wages up to $2,700.00 without the teenager (or the employee) incurring any income tax liability.

Gross Wages	$2,700.00
Less: low income allowance (for a single)	1,700.00
	1,000.00
Less: personal exemption	750.00
Taxable income	250.00
Tax rate	14%
Tax before credit	35.00
Less: credit against tax	35.00
Income tax liability	0

Therefore, hiring the taxpayer's own child (a family member or a friend) at an annual salary up to $2,700.00 will not result in any tax liability to the child, while the parent will claim the salary paid as a business expense.

1.2. Tax Saving Devices upon Sale of a Going Business

The sale of a business may result in a large income tax bill. Special care should be exercised in stating the sale price. When a business is sold the tax effect will depend on the nature of property sold. Any amount received from selling inventories and accounts receivable is completely taxed as ordinary income. The sale of goodwill results in a long-term capital gain. However, the sale of a depreciable business asset is subject to the recapture of depreciation rules (under Sections 1231, 1245 and 1250).

When a proprietor sells his business he should negotiate the sale carefully, since for tax purposes he will not be selling the business as a whole, but, each individual asset separately. The total sale price of the business can be agreed upon in advance, but a certain part of the total price is to be allocated to each separate property. For tax saving purposes, observe the following:

1. If you fail to allocate the total sale price between the various assets sold, the IRS, or the Tax Court will make the allocation; but most likely to your disadvantage.
2. Establish support for the allocation of a larger amount to the sale of assets producing a long-term capital gain.
3. Keep good records to support the computation of the sale price of each individual business asset.
4. A self-employed professional can make a partial transfer of goodwill when admitting a partner to his practice.
5. Copyrights are not capital assets if they were created by the taxpayer's personal efforts.
6. Patents held by amateur or professional investors are given the long-term capital gain treatment.
7. The seller of a sole proprietorship should try to allocate a larger portion of the sale price to goodwill, unexpired cost of prepaid expenses, land, machines, buildings, fixtures and leases.
8. The seller should try to allocate a smaller portion of the sale price to inventories, accounts receivable and covenant not to compete.
9. On the other hand, the buyer of the business should try to allocate a larger portion of the price to prepaid expenses, inventories and accounts receivable. A smaller portion of the purchase price should be allocated to non-depreciable assets such as land and goodwill. A medium portion should be allocated to machines, buildings, fixtures, leases, and covenant not to compete.
10. If the installment method is used for reporting the gain from sale of business, the payments received in the first year of sale cannot exceed

30 percent of the total sale price. The 30 percent is figured on the total sale price less the amount allocated to accounts receivable and inventories. As a result, the sale of accounts receivable and inventories does not qualify for the installment method.

11. If you want a large payment in the year of sale and still use the installment method, sell the inventories and receivables in cash, and separately sell the remaining business properties with a payment not exceeding 30 percent in the year of sale.

1.3. Converting an Ordinary Expense to a Capital Gain

If you sell a property at a gain, and the property was owned for more than six months (more than nine months in 1977, and more than one year in 1978 and later years), half of the gain will escape taxation since it constitutes a long-term capital gain. This type of gain is desirable and you can convert part of the ordinary income from the property to a long-term capital gain. The method of conversion is simple. Before selling a property, repair it and deduct the repair expense from the ordinary income of the property. After finishing the repairs you have a more valuable property which can be sold at a higher price. The increase in the sale price (because of the repairs) is taxed as a capital gain upon the sale or disposition of the property.

1.4. Proceeds from Sale of Goodwill and Covenant Not to Compete

The sale of a business for a price in excess of the current market value of its tangible assets will lead to the creation of an intangible asset or assets. The intangible part can be charged to a goodwill account, a covenant not to compete account, or to both. The seller will treat goodwill as a capital asset and the proceeds from covenant not to compete, as an ordinary income (*Rogers v. U.S.* 7AFTR 2d 1318, 290 F.2d 501). The buyer will treat goodwill as an undepreciable asset and the payment for the covenant not to compete as an amortizable tangible asset (Reg. 1.167 (a)-3). It is to the seller's advantage to allocate a large amount to goodwill, but it is to the buyer's advantage to allocate a large value to the covenant not to compete. The one who fares better is the one who knows about the tax effect and tries to protect his interest through a proper allocation of the total sale price, or bargains for a lower or higher sale price of the whole business in order to reflect a tax disadvantage or savings because of the price allocation.

1.5. Tax Benefits of a Sale-Leaseback Arrangement

A taxpayer may acquire tax and financial benefits from a sale-leaseback arrangement. The principal financial and tax effects of a sale-leaseback are the following:

1. Through sale of property the business is provided with more liquidity which will be reflected in an increased working capital.
2. The rent paid under the leaseback agreement is fully deductible.
3. If the asset is already fully depreciated, the sale-leaseback will result in deducting rent as a substitute for the lost depreciation.
4. If the property is a building, the owner will not be allowed any depreciation for land value. On the other hand, in a leaseback agreement the amount of rental charges reflects the value of both the building as well as land.
5. If the property has declined in value, the sale will lead to a loss deduction.
6. If the property has increased in value, then the depreciation claimed on it does not reflect the correct amount of business deduction (since depreciation is based on original or actual cost).

Before entering a sale-leaseback agreement (Code Sec. 514; Rev. Rul. 55-540, 1955-2 CB 39) watch for these financial and tax pitfalls:

1. The sale of property will increase working capital and the increment should be used wisely. Of course, there is no economic benefit from increasing idle working capital.
2. After completing the sale, the leaseback will result in periodic cash payments for rent. The effect on future cash position should be anticipated.
3. The sale-leaseback arrangement should not be between related parties (Sec. 1239; 1.1239-1).
4. The leaseback should be for a period less than 30 years (to avoid problems with the IRS).
5. The terms of the leaseback should be stated on an arm's-length basis, reflecting the fair rental value of the property.

1.6. Tax Saving Ideas Before Buying a Business Asset

If you buy a business asset, try to put together all of the following tax saving ideas:

1. Make the purchase under an installment plan in order to deduct any interest on the unpaid balance.

2. Check the qualification for the investment credit, first year additional depreciation, and the use of an accelerated method of depreciation.
3. If the asset has components, allocate the cost between the various components and select an estimated useful life that fits each part.

1.7. Travel and Entertainment Expenses While Away from Home

Travel and entertainment expense while away from home, constitutes an important and often large business deduction which should be handled with special care. To protect your claim for travel expense deduction, remember the following:

1. If the journey is inside the U.S., the primary purpose of the trip should be for business. If part of the trip was used for pleasure, the cost of that part is not deductible.
2. If the trip is outside the U.S. and lasts not more than one week, you do not need to allocate part of the cost to business and the other to pleasure, because the primary purpose of your trip outside the U.S. is for business.
3. If the trip is outside the U.S. and lasts over one week, you need to show that more than 75 percent of the time was used for business purposes in order to deduct all the travel expenses. However, if the trip lasts over one week and more than 25 percent of the time is spent for pleasure, then you need to apportion the total cost between business and pleasure. (To figure total days of the trip, exclude the day of departure and include the day of return. In figuring the percent of time used for business activities, count both the day of departure and day of return).
4. Attending foreign conventions after December 31, 1976, is subject to new rules (Sec. 602 of the 1976 Tax Reform Act). Starting in 1977, a taxpayer may deduct the costs of attending only two foreign conventions in any year. Therefore, if a taxpayer attends more than two foreign conventions in one year, he (or she) may select the costs of two trips only for which he (or she) is entitled to claim deductions. It helps to log the time and expenses and attend at least two-thirds of the business activities scheduled during the convention. Also, the new rules for deducting costs of attending foreign conventions require a statement from the organization that sponsored the convention verifying the amount of time spent by the taxpayer at seminars and other business-related functions.

According to the rules applicable to travel expense (Sec. 162 (a); 274; Reg. 1.274-4), it pays to make a trip outside the U.S. within a one-week period because you can avoid the apportionment rules.

1.8. Travel Expense Investigating a New Business Venture

If you incur a travel expense investigating the opportunity to invest in a new business venture and the new deal does not go through, you cannot deduct the travel expense as a business expense unless you were already in a business connected with the field of activity of the new venture you were investigating. To avoid losing the deduction of a travel expense, use one of the two following ways:

1. Check the relationship between your present business and the new business requiring travel. The two businesses should be related. Also, your present business activities should be substantial enough to support the travel.
2. Establish a corporation with a minimum capital investment. Charge the corporation with the travel expense. If the result of traveling is not a successful acquisition of a new business, you can still deduct the expense in the books of the corporation.

1.9. Business Gifts and Giving Income-Producing Properties

You can deduct as business expense gifts to any individual, if the total cost of gifts made to one individual for his personal use during the year does not exceed $25 (Reg. 1.274-3). If an item costs $4 or less and bears the name of your business, it will not be counted toward the $25 limit per individual per year. If you make a gift to an employee, you can deduct it as a business expense provided it does not cost over $100 and that it is given because of safety achievement or length of service. Using business gifts as a means of reducing taxable income is popular, but should be used only after understanding the dollar limitations placed on business gifts.

Another type of gift which will affect taxable income is the distribution of income-producing properties between family members. Instead of reporting all income on one tax return and paying tax at a high rate, give income-producing properties to those family members with no or little income. This will result in shifting income from high to lower tax brackets (for more details about gifts to family members see Chapter 17).

1.10. Deducting Expenses of an Entertainment Facility

If you use an entertainment facility more than 50 percent for business purposes, you can deduct a proportionate share of its cost as a business expense. Entertainment facilities include a wide variety, such as a club membership, lodge, yacht, swimming pool, tennis court, apartment, hotel suite, etc. If you can show that you use the entertainment facility more than 50 percent for business purposes, deduct a proportionate share of depreciation, rent, dues, repairs, insurance, maintenance, wages and utilities as a business expense. Then deduct all of the cost related to interest expense, taxes and casualty losses on Schedule A as itemized deductions without apportionment. An initiation fee to join a club is not deductible since it is considered a capital (or non-recurring) expenditure, although the annual dues are considered as expense of an entertainment facility. Therefore, through your business you can enjoy a wide variety of business deductions, if you are careful enough to prove time, cost, and purpose. Count the total number of days the entertainment facility was put into use each year. More than 50 percent of those days should be for business use. If in a specific day the facility was used for both business and personal purposes, that day counts as a day of business use. Keep an accurate record of the cost of each entertainment facility. Make specific references to the business purpose of the use of the facility (Reg. 1.274-2 (e); 1.274-5).

Retroactive to January 1, 1976, if a vacation home is used by the owner for more than two weeks a year or more than 10 percent of the annual rental time, deductions for depreciation, utilities and maintenance are not allowed to exceed rental income. If the vacation home is rented out less than 15 days a year, the owner would not have to report the income, but would not be allowed any business deductions either. Notice that the 1976 Tax Reform Act does not disallow deducting interest, property taxes and casualty loss as itemized personal deductions even if a vacation home is not rented. Also, since the deduction for depreciation, utilities and maintenance is connected with rental income from the vacation home, it pays off to concentrate the rental income in certain years and maximize the deduction for those years. On the other hand, for the years reporting low rental income, the deduction for depreciation, utilities and maintenance is limited to the rental income, while property taxes, interest on mortgage and casualty loss are claimed separately as itemized personal deductions.

1.11. Deducting Auto Expenses

The use of a truck or car for business purposes results in a major business deduction, and you should try to make the best out of this deduction. The deduction for a business auto should be figured twice: (1) Under the actual cost method, and (2) under the optional estimated cost or standard method. Under the actual cost method, add up the cost of gas, oil, lubrication, repairs, washing, parking, tools, license plates, insurance, garage rent, interest, depreciation, etc. (In the year of purchase try to claim the 20 percent first-year additional depreciation and the investment credit.)

Under the optional method you can deduct 15c per mile for the first 15,000 miles and 10c per mile thereafter. Also, under the optional method you can deduct in addition, as an auto expense, all parking and toll fees (Sec. 274 (d); 1.274-5 (b) (1). If you use the optional method, claim as an itemized deduction on Schedule A all the interest expense related to the purchase of the auto (for gasoline tax, you can deduct as an itemized item only the tax related to the personal use of the auto). You can shift from the actual cost to the optional method from one year to another without approval of the IRS. However, in each year you use the optional method, you should reduce the cost or basis of the auto by depreciation figured under the straight-line method (this is needed mainly to compute the gain or loss on the auto upon its final sale and is needed in case of shifting back to the actual cost method).

1.12. Contributing to a Retirement Plan

Any tax planning for a self-employed is not complete unless it explores the area of retirement plans. There are various types of retirement plans and various ways of funding. The most popular type is the self-employed retirement plan also commonly called "HR-10" or "Keogh" plan. The self-employed retirement plan can be used by a proprietor or a partner in a partnership. It allows a maximum yearly contribution of the lesser of 15 percent of earned income, or $7,500. A similar contribution percentage (but not amount) should be adopted for each eligible full-time employee with three years or more of service. The minimum contribution to the plan is the lesser of 100 percent of earned income, or $750. If the self-employed controls more than one business, he should establish one plan only for all his businesses. An owner-employee can contribute (and also his eligible employees) an additional 10 percent of his earned income or $2,500, whichever is less, but the additional contribution is not a deductible business expense. Only the interest from the additional contribution is allowed to accumulate tax free. The money accumulated in the retirement plan account can be invested in various ways. A popular method of funding is to deposit the money in a bank, with the bank as trustee. (Sec. 401 (a); 501 (a)).

A self-employed who is not covered by a retirement plan can set up his own retirement account (Individual Retirement Account) and deposit up to 15 percent of his earned income, not exceeding $1,500 per year (there is no guaranteed minimum). If both spouses are working and neither one of them is a member of a qualified pension or profit-sharing plan, HR-10 plan, tax-sheltered annuity, or a retirement plan for government employees, then both can establish an individual retirement account. This can give both of them, on a joint return, an annual deduction of up to $3,000. The earnings of an IRA accumulate tax free. When distribution is made from IRA (after age 59 1/2), the amount received will be taxed as ordinary income. The 1976 Tax Reform Act allows a husband or wife not covered by a company pension to contribute up to $1,750 or 15 percent of earned income, whichever is less, and to set up a jointly-owned retirement account. Or the worker can contribute up to $850 to a personal account and the same amount to one owned by the worker's spouse.

If the taxpayer has more than one job, or he is both an employee and a self-employed, he can benefit from more than one retirement plan or set up more than one Individual Retirement Account. However, the limit for his deductible contributions under all the plans remains up to 15 percent of his total earned income, not exceeding $1,500 per year ($1,750 if his spouse is unemployed). There are no provisions in the Employee Retirement Income Security Act of 1974 for making added contributions under an Individual Retirement Plan (while the Keogh plan allows the added voluntary contribution).

For tax saving purposes, it is important to delay contribution to the retirement plan to the last possible date and yet treat the payment as a deductible contribution. A contribution to the self-employed retirement or Keogh plan is considered timely if made any time up to the point when the federal income tax return is due, including extensions. However, a contribution in cash should be made to the Individual Retirement Plan during the taxpayer's taxable year.

1.13. Maximizing Tax-Free Income

To save tax, the following items of income should be examined carefully since they represent tax-free income:

1. Annuity income that represents returns of original investment in an annuity (Sec. 1.72-1(b); 1.72-2(b)).
2. Recovery of bad debt where no prior deduction took place.
3. Accident and health insurance proceeds.
4. Compensation for personal injury.
5. Compensation for damages to character.
6. Casualty insurance proceeds (limited exemption).
7. Disability and death payments.
8. Social Security benefit payments.
9. Gifts, bequests, or inheritances.
10. Interest on tax-exempt state or local bonds.

11. Income received under a legal dispute that has not been settled as yet.

1.14. Proceeds from Business Interruption Insurance

It is common to carry business interruption insurance or use and occupancy insurance. It pays for loss of profits and reimburses overhead loss incurred in case of fire or any other event that may interrupt normal business activities. Two types of business interruption insurance can be acquired although each of them leads to entirely different tax results.

The first type of business interruption insurance will tie the insurance proceeds to an estimated profit loss. Such proceeds are completely taxable to the recipient as ordinary income (*Oppenheim's, Inc. v. Cavanagh,* 90F. Supp. 107, 39 AFTR 468; Rev. Rul. 55-264, 1955-1 CB11).

The second type of business interruption insurance is called "valued" form of use and occupancy insurance. The proceeds under the valued form are specified as a fixed amount for every day the use and occupancy of a building is prohibited. If the proceeds from the insurance policy are measured by a fixed periodic amount (and not by lost profit), then the amounts received are considered as proceeds of an involuntary conversion. Under the involuntary conversion rules such proceeds will be taxed as capital gain and not as ordinary income (*Piedmont-Mt. Airy Guano Co.,* 3BTA 1009; *Miller v. Hocking Glass Co.,* 80 F2d436, 16 AFTR 1448; Treasury Department booklet "Tax Guide for Small Business" (1976 ED.), p. 162).

1.15. Applying Accumulated Dividend Toward the Cost of Additional Insurance

A good insurance coverage is important to every business and businessman. When an insurance company pays dividends to a policyholder, such distributions are not taxable since they are regarded as reductions in insurance premium or cost (Treasury Department Booklet "Tax Guide for Small Business" (1976 Ed.), p. 112). However, if the insurance dividends are left to accumulate, any interest on such accumulation is taxed as ordinary income without regard to whether such interest on accumulated insurance dividend is actually received in cash or accrued only. To avoid the tax on such interest use the following simple solution:

> Request the insurance company to apply any accumulated dividend toward the cost of additional insurance. In this way, you

can use the income tax saved to cover part of the additional insurance cost.

1.16. Interest Paid Under a Minimum Deposit Life Insurance Plan

As a general rule, an individual taxpayer cannot deduct as an expense the payment for life insurance premiums. Also, as a general rule, any interest paid on a loan used to pay the life insurance premiums, is not deductible. A life insurance policy with premiums paid through borrowed money (usually the collateral is the cash surrender value of the policy) is called a minimum deposit life insurance plan. Since August 6, 1963, a limited deduction is allowed for interest paid under a minimum deposit life insurance plan (Sec. 264; 1.264-4 (b)). The annual interest expense deduction under such a plan is allowed if it is $100 or less, the plan to borrow the cash surrender value of the policy is for business purposes (or unforeseen loss of income or large expense such as a large medical bill), and no part of 4 of the first 7 annual premiums is paid out of borrowed money.

The interest deduction from a minimum deposit life insurance plan is not a major deduction (since 1963), but still claiming up to $100 per year can help reduce the overall income tax bill.

1.17. Effective Use of the Net Operating Loss Deduction

A net operating loss occurs when total allowable deductions are greater than gross income. First a net operating loss is carried back to the third preceding year. If any loss remains, it is carried to the second preceding year, then to the first preceding year. If any loss remains, it is carried forward to the following seven years. When the following seven-year period is over, any remaining operating loss which is not used, will be lost (Sec. 172 (b) (1); 1.172-4). A good method to avoid losing any part of the net operating loss deduction is to adopt the following:

> Carry the operating loss backward and carry it forward until you reach the seventh following year. Before the end of the seventh year, compute the net income for that year and compare it with the remaining balance of unused net operating-loss deduction. If the income of the seventh year is not large enough to cover all remaining loss balance, then try to pre-collect income. Even if you offer a special discount to your business customers, it pays off to use every possible way to encourage a faster collection of both earned, as well as, unearned income (e.g., due rent, as well as rent for a future period).

1.18. Switching to the Last-in-First-Out Method of Inventory Valuation

In a period of inflation a switch to the last-in, first-out, method of inventory valuation will lead to an increase in the cost of goods sold and a decrease in taxable income. This tax saving loophole applies to sole proprietorships and partnerships as well as corporations. It does not matter whether the size of the business is small or large (Sec. 1.446-1 (e)).

1.19. Timing the Constructive Receipt of Income

Two methods of accounting are available for income tax purposes. The first method is the cash method of accounting. Under this method, income is recognized when it is actually received or put under the unconditional use of the taxpayer (which is considered as constructive receipt). Also, all business cash disbursements made during the year are deductible expenditures unless the payment is considered a capital expenditure. The second method is the accrual method of accounting. Under this method, income is taxed in the year it is earned and expenses are deducted in the period in which they belong. If a taxpayer is engaged in more than one separate business, he can use a different method of accounting for each distinct business. An application to change the accounting method used (on Form 3115) is needed in order to change the method of accounting (Sec. 1.446-1 (e) (2)).

A main principle in tax planning is the timing principle. According to it, income is timed to fall in "low income" years instead of "higher income" years. Expenses and deductions are timed in order to be claimed in "higher income" years instead of "lower income" years. The use of the timing principle will depend on the method of accounting used for the determination of taxable income. If the cash method is adopted in the last part of each tax period, reduce your income collection effort and speed up the payment of expenditures. If the accrual method is adopted in the last part of the tax year, delay the billing for services performed and increase your commitment for expenditures (i.e., delay sending bills to customers and request the creditors and suppliers to bill you for any products and services). Shifting income and deductions from one tax year to another should be given special consideration by the taxpayer. Timing analysis should be made in the last part (e.g., last month or two) of each tax period. The decision to shift an item should be based on a full understanding of both the total tax situation (i.e., forecast or expected taxable income for the whole year) and the special nature of the expense or income item which may be subject to shifting.

1.20. Income Averaging

Sections 1301-1305 provide a major tax break through the provisions of income averaging. In the 1969 Tax Reform act, income averaging was made available to any taxpayer with a current year taxable income in excess of 120 percent of the average taxable income for the last four years. Income averaging benefits apply to a wide variety of situations, such as a business man with a very profitable year, a professional with a large contract or bonus, a housewife who returns to work, a winner of a large lottery prize, etc. The income averaging rules cannot be used in the following two cases:

1. A penalty distribution from a self-employed pension (HR-10) plan.
2. A distribution from a trust in excess of distributable net income where the throwback rules related to an accumulation trust apply.

Income averaging benefits are available only to self-supporting individuals. To be self-supporting, an individual must have provided 50 percent or more of his own support in the last four years preceding the current tax year. This will prevent a student with little or no taxable income until his graduation from using the income averaging method.

1.21. Expenditures That May Result in Both Business and Non-Business Use

As a general rule business expenses are deductible on an income tax return, while personal or non-business expenses are not deductible. However, in practical life, there is a wide variety of expenditures that may result in both business, as well as non-business, use or benefit. Any self-employed taxpayer may find it advantageous to dress an item as a business expense while benefiting from the expenditure, at least partially, on a personal basis. A list of expenditures which may be used for both business, as well as personal, purposes may include:

1. Business telephone.
2. Services of assistants or employees.
3. Office supplies.
4. Office magazines and newspapers.
5. Memberships to clubs and associations.

6. Business travel and attendance at meetings.
7. Business entertainment.
8. Entertainment facilities.
9. Business cars.
10. Office and business equipment (e.g., calculators, typewriters, etc.).
11. Business gifts.

1.22. Deducting Educational Expenses

Educational expenses are not deductible if the education is for the purpose of obtaining a new position, advancement in a position, or to fulfill educational aspirations (Sec. 162-5 (b)). Also, educational expenses to meet requirements for qualification or establishment of new trade or business are not deductible. On the other hand, a businessman or a professional person can deduct as a business expense, education expenses incurred for maintaining or improving skills required in his present trade or business. The expense of attending business or professional conventions is deductible.

In general, to deduct an educational expense the taxpayer should show that the purpose of the expense is maintaining or improving skills required in trade, business, profession or employment. If the classes are located within the city or area of the taxpayer's work, he may deduct the cost of one-way commuting from work to classes. If the classes are outside the city or general area of the work, the cost of the two-way trip is deductible. Besides travel and transportation expense, the taxpayer may deduct as educational expenses any tuition and fees, and cost of research and typing. A professional or self-employed will deduct his educational expenses with his other business deductions (i.e., as a deduction for adjusted gross income and not as an itemized deduction).

1.23. Qualifying for the Child Care Tax Credit

Retroactive to January 1, 1976, the deduction for child care became a credit deductible directly from income taxes. Therefore, a taxpayer may use the standard deduction and still claim the child care tax credit. The maximum credit is $400 for one dependent and $800 for two or more dependents. The tax credit is figured at 20 percent of child care expenses up to a maximum of $2,000 expenses for one child (or a spouse or dependent incapable of self-care) and $4,000 for two or more children. For example, Robert and Karen Brown earn $21,000 of gross income and pay a house keeper $2,400 to take care of their three-year-old son Richard.

Robert and Karen Brown could itemize their deductions or claim the standard deduction and still lcaim a tax credit of $400 (or 20 percent of child care expenses up to $2.000)

The following items may be reported under employment-related expenses:

1. Child care
2. Disabled dependent care expenses
3. Disabled spouse care expenses

In order to qualify for deducting the above-mentioned employment-related expenses, the following four main requirements should be met:

1. The taxpayer must have been gainfully employed during the period the expenses were incurred. Married taxpayers must show that one works full-time and the other is a part-time worker or a full-time student (unless disabled).
2. The taxpayer maintained a household that included one or more qualifying individuals.
3. The expenditures must have been necessary to enable the taxpayer to be gainfully employed, and
4. Relatives may be hired if Social Security taxes are paid on their baby-sitting income and the relative is not a dependent of the taxpayer.

Gainful employment includes working for others, employment in your own business or partnership, and an active search for gainful employment. In the case of hiring your spouse in your business (in order to report both parents as gainfully employed and eligible for the child care deduction) observe that the period of gainful employment must correspond to the months in which expenses were paid. Also, substantially full-time employment means employment for at least three-fourths of the work week.

The tax advisor should assist the taxpayer in qualifying for the child care tax credit. The self-employed should claim the credit against the tax liability and not as a deduction for a business related expense.

1.24. Maximizing the Benefit from Tax Credits

A self-employed taxpayer may qualify for a wide variety of tax credits against his income tax. The following credits against tax should be considered carefully in order to maximize the benefit from them:

1. An investment tax credit is allowed for investment in certain depreciable business property. For the period beginning January 22, 1975, and ending December 31, 1980, the credit rate is 10 percent of the cost of such property. The investment credit may not exceed $25,000 plus 50 percent of the tax liability over $25,000.

2. A tax credit equal to 20 percent of wages to employees undergoing training under a Work Incentive Program certified by the Secretary of Labor, can be claimed. The credit is 20 percent of cash wages paid or accrued to employees under a W.I.P. during the first 12 months of employment (Form 4874 should be used to claim this credit). The 1976 Tax Reform Act raised the credit ceiling to $50,000 plus half the employer's taxes above $50,000.

3. Any foreign source income subject to a foreign country tax is entitled to a tax credit, if this foreign source income is subject to a U.S. income tax. The foreign tax credit can be claimed (on Form 1116) under the "overall" method only. The 1976 Tax Reform Act ended the use of the per-country method of claiming the foreign tax credit.

4. A special tax credit was introduced by the Tax Reduction Act of 1975 and is called the earned income credit. A self-employed (as well as an employee) can claim a maximum credit equal to 10 percent of the first $4,000 of earned income. Above the first $4,000 of earned income, the credit is reduced by an amount equal to 10 percent of adjusted gross income over $4,000. Therefore, at the $8,000 adjusted gross income level, the entire credit is eliminated. For 1976 and 1977, the earned income credit is equal to the greater of $35 per individual personal exemption or 2 percent of the first $9,000 of taxable income. For 1976 and 1977, the earned income tax credit is available to a taxpayer who maintains a household for a dependent child who is under 19 (or a student). Also, the credit is available to taxpayers with adult disabled dependents.

5. The buyer of a new home, constructed or under construction before March 26, 1975, qualifies for a tax credit equal to 5 percent of the purchase price, not to exceed the maximum of $2,000.

6. A tax credit of 50 percent for a political campaign contribution is allowed. However, the maximum credit is $50 for joint returns and $25 for single returns and those married taxpayers filing separately (an alternative is to claim the political contribution as an itemized deduction and deduct up to $200 on a joint return).

7. Retroactive to January 1, 1976, a child (or dependent) care tax credit is allowed. The maximum credit is $400 for one dependent and $800 for two or more dependents.

8. The 1976 Tax Reform Act introduced a tax credit for the elderly. Any individual who has attained the age of 65 before the close of his taxable year is eligible for the credit. The initial credit is 15 percent of $2,500 for single and married couples where only one spouse is 65 or over. The credit base is $3,750 for married couples filing jointly and both spouses are 65 or older. In the case of a married individual filing a separate return, the credit base is $1,875. The tax credit for the elderly is subject to

9. The new jobs tax credit should not be overlooked by any employer. For tax years beginning in 1977, the new jobs tax credit is 50 percent of the amount by which an employer's FUTA (Federal Unemployment Tax Act) wages paid during 1977 exceeds 102 percent of FUTA wages (i.e. $4,200 per employee) paid during 1976. For tax years beginning in 1978 the credit is 50 percent of the amount by which FUTA wages paid during 1978 exceeds 102 percent of FUTA wages paid during 1977. If the new jobs tax credit exceeds the employer's income tax liability for the year, the excess can be carried back to the three preceding tax years and carried over to the seven succeeding tax years. The carry backward may result in a needed cash refund.

10. An additional credit for hiring handicapped individuals is allowable for tax years beginning in 1977 or 1978. The amount of additional credit is 10 percent of FUTA wages (i.e. up to $4,200 per year) paid to new employees who are handicapped individuals. Only wages paid during the first year period after the beginning of the individual's rehabilitation plan are taken into account.

1.25. Deducting Interest Expense

In general, interest expense is deductible whether it is incurred for business or personal purposes. Interest connected with business is claimed as a deduction for adjusted gross income, while interest incurred as a non-business expense is claimed as an itemized deduction (or deduction from adjusted gross income). In tax years beginning after 1975, the deduction for non-business interest would be limited to $10,000 plus the taxpayer's net investment income ($5,000 for marrieds filing separately). If the taxpayer is on a cash basis, interest is usually deductible in the year of actual payment. However, the 1976 Tax Reform Act requires cash method taxpayers to deduct prepaid interest over the period of the loan. In the case of a taxpayer on accrual basis, the interest expense is deductible in the year the liability is incurred. Therefore, under the 1976 Tax Reform Act, both cash and accrual method taxpayers are treated equally in the area of deducting prepaid interest expense.

For tax saving purposes, a widely used technique is to claim prepaid interest expense by a cash basis taxpayer in a year when his taxable income is high. Although the deduction of prepaid interest is allowed under Code Section 163, the deduction is not without limit. The Internal Revenue Service considers a prepayment of interest as "materially distorting" income, if it is prepaid for more than 12 months beyond the end of the taxable year. In case of property under construction, and unimproved and unproductive real property, the taxpayer has the choice of deducting interest and carrying charges during the period of construction, or capitalizing such items (this election applies also to real property taxes) (Treasury Department booklet "Tax Guide for Small Business" (1976 Ed.)

p. 23). Before making the election, the effect of charging interest to current income or to a capital account should be decided after estimating the present, as well as future, level of annual taxable income. If future income is expected to be higher than present income, it would be advisable to capitalize such interest expense. The 1976 Tax Reform Act came to the aid of the Internal Revenue Service by requiring a cash method taxpayer to deduct prepaid interest over the period of the loan. Therefore, the tax advisor should be careful about the pre-'70, pre-'76, and post-'75 interest deduction rules.

1.26. Deducting Charitable Contributions

An individual taxpayer can claim as charitable contributions deductions up to 50 percent of his adjusted gross income. The maximum deduction allowed for contributions of capital gain property is 30 percent of adjusted gross income. Any excess contribution over the maximum allowed ceiling can be carried forward for a period of five years. Since the maximum allowed contribution deduction can represent a substantial deduction, charitable contributions should receive special attention.

A contribution in cash will lead to an immediate cash outflow or sacrifice. Also, cash has only one value and a contribution in cash must be reported at its face value. A contribution of property is more desirable for tax saving purposes. No gain is realized on a charitable contribution of appreciated property. In certain cases (e.g., gifts of tangible personal property used by the charity in its exempt function), the deduction is computed on the basis of the fair market value of the property. This combined effect of not paying any tax on the appreciation (or increase in value) of property and claiming a deduction for the full fair market value of the property contributed, makes it favorable for tax purposes to donate an appreciated property. On the other hand, no loss is recognized on a charitable gift of property. Therefore, it may be advisable to sell property whose value is less than its basis, to realize the loss for tax purposes, and then make a gift of the proceeds or give another property which appreciated in value. If the property whose value is less than its basis is for personal use, no loss from its sale is deductible for tax purposes. Therefore, personal use assets (such as books and used clothing) should be donated to charitable organizations claiming their fair market value (since they normally would not be appreciated in value).

1.27. Deducting Moving Expenses

A self-employed may deduct moving expenses in the same way as employees (Sec. 217 (a), (f); 1.217.2 (f). See **2.18** in Chapter 2.)

Chapter 2

TAX SAVING OPPORTUNITIES FOR EMPLOYEES

2.1. Giving a Loan to a Friend or Relative

If you make a loan to a friend or relative and the loan becomes worthless, the bad debt is considered a non-business expense. As a non-business expense such a loss is treated as a short-term capital loss (Sec 166). To deduct a short-term capital loss you need to have a capital gain sufficient to match it. Otherwise, each year you can deduct out of ordinary income up to $1,000 until the loss is completely written off. However, in a very easy way, you can change the loan to a friend or relative into a business loan. Then as a business debt, if it becomes worthless, you can deduct all of it against your ordinary income in the year of declaring it uncollectable. All you need to do is not to make an out-right loan to the friend or relative, but rather arrange the loan with your personal endorsement or guarantee through a bank or third party. A non-corporate guarantor or endorser who pays the debt of the principal may deduct as a business bad debt the loss sustained upon that person's payment of the obligation, if the following requirements are satisfied (Sec. 166 (f); 1.166-8):

1. The borrower's obligation to the creditor was worthless at the time of payment by the guarantor.
2. The proceeds of the loan were used in the trade or business of the borrower. To satisfy this requirement the guarantor or endorser should request the borrower's use of the loan in an activity related to his trade or business.

2.2. Timing the Payment of Deductible Items

Most employees adopt the cash method of accounting for income tax purposes. Under the cash method an expense is deductible only in the year of actual payment. For example, if a taxpayer borrows $4,000.00 on August 10, 1975, at an interest rate of 10 percent per year, and makes no interest payment in 1975, this taxpayer cannot claim any interest expense deduction on this debt for 1975. However, what he should do is compute the interest on this loan in the latter part of December, 1975, then acquire a new loan and use its proceeds to pay off the interest on the first loan. Timing the payment of deductible items should take into consideration the level of taxable income. More deductions should be timed to fall into a high income tax year. Deductions claimed in the year of actual payment include medical expenses, property taxes, sales taxes on home improvements, interest expense, charitable contributions, union dues, cost of working uniforms or clothes, employment-related travel and entertainment expenses, professional books, etc.

2.3. Taking Advantage of the Net Operating Loss Deduction

A net operating loss occurs when total allowable deductions are greater than gross income. A common misconception is to relate the net operating loss deduction to businessmen or self-employed taxpayers only. An employee also can take advantage of the net operating loss deduction. A casualty or theft loss sustained by an employee (or any other individual taxpayer) on property held for personal (or non-business) use is treated as an allowable deduction for purposes of computing the net operating loss (Sec. 172; 1.172-3). For example, a salaried employee who lost his home in a fire accident can claim the non-business casualty loss (minus $100) as a deduction against his income. If his income is less than the total allowable deductions (including the non-business casualty or theft loss), the net is called a net operating loss. Like any other net operating loss, it qualifies for the three-year carryback and seven-year carryover. A net operating loss carryback may result in a tax refund and the receipt of needed cash.

2.4. Purchasing a Split-Dollar Life Insurance Policy

An employee (especially with a family to care for) should check with his employer about the possibility of purchasing a split-dollar life insurance policy. Under such a policy, the employer will pay the portion of the annual premium that represents the annual increase in the cash surrender value of the policy and the employee pays the balance of the annual insurance premium. The employer is co-beneficiary for the total amount of the cash surrender value. The family of the employee is co-beneficiary for the balance of the life insurance proceeds. The tax effect on both the employer and employee can be summarized as follows:

1. *Effect on Employer:*

(a) Amounts paid by the employer are not deductible and the proceeds from policy cancellation or in event of death are not taxable.

(b) The statement of financial position of the employer will look better, since it shows the cash surrender value of the policy.

(c) The employer will gain loyalty from the employee and the employer can select any employee for the plan.

(d) The employer can terminate the policy at any time and recover all the investment in the policy.

(e) When an employee reaches retirement age, the employer can use the cash surrender value to finance a retirement plan.

(f) No I.R.S. approval is required (Rev. Rul. 64-328, 1964-2 CB 11; Rev. Rul. 66-110, 1966-1 CB 12).

2. *Effect on Employee:*

(a) The employee is taxed on the value of benefits received each year under the split-dollar policy since they represent compensation for services. However, the beneficiaries of the employee are not taxed on the proceeds from the policy.

(b) During the first several years of the policy, the employee will pay some premium. After that, the payment of the employee will decrease quickly and throughout most of the life of the policy the employee will pay very little or no premium. The split-dollar insurance plan will give the opportunity to a younger employee to acquire greater and more expensive life insurance at lower cost.

To show the tax effect of a split-dollar life insurance policy on both the employer and employee, assume an employer buys $100,000 accelerated 10-payment life insurance policy for an employee, age 40. The premium is $7,600 a year. In the first year, employer pays $6,900 (increase in surrender value) and the employee pays $700 ($7,600 less $6,900). The cost of one-year term protection on $93,100 of insurance ($100,000 less $6,900) is $550. Since the employee paid more than $550, he has no taxable income this year. Let us assume further that in the fourth year the employer pays $7,400 (increase in cash surrender value) and the employee pays $200 for insurance protection ($7,600 total premium for the year less $7,400 paid by the employer. The cost of one-year term insurance protection is $520. The amount of $320 ($520 less $200) must be added to the employee's gross income as a compensation for services.

2.5. Timing the Payment of Medical Expenses

You should spend at least $300 per year for medical insurance. The first $150 is completely deductible if you itemize your personal deductions. The remaining balance of medical insurance premiums will be added to your medical expense. Timing your medical expenses in order to claim them as an itemized deduction should also be considered. Certain medical expenses are urgent and cannot be postponed, such as surgery and irregular medical examinations. But a large variety of medical expenses can be postponed and timed to fall together in a certain year, such as dental work, eye examinations and glasses, regular checkups, etc. If the taxpayer has a family, all major medical bills can be scheduled for the entire family to occur in certain tax years.

2.6. Payments to Beneficiaries of a Deceased Employee

The first $5,000 of payments to beneficiaries of a deceased employee are deductible by the employer and not taxable income to either the employee or his beneficiaries (Sec. 101(b)(1); 1.101-2). This exclusion applies also to the first $5,000 paid to the beneficiaries of a deceased employee under a stock bonus, pension, profit sharing or annuity plan, if all payments are made within one tax year of the beneficiary. To take advantage of the exclusion, the following items should be considered carefully:

1. The employer is not legally obligated to make the payment under the terms of an enforceable employment contract.
2. The employer is not connecting the payment with services or accrued salary.
3. The total exclusion is $5,000 without regard to the number of employers the deceased employee may have had at the time of death.

2.7. Meals and Lodging Furnished to the Employee

If the employee pays for his own meals and lodging, such payments are nondeductible on his tax return because of their personal nature. However, the value of meals and lodging furnished to the employee for the convenience of the employer is not taxable income to the employee and at the same time is deductible by the employer as a business expense (Sec. 110; 1.119-1). Therefore, an employee can approach an employer requesting a salary cut (or using an expected salary raise) in exchange for free meals and/or lodging. To achieve this tax saving be sure to satisfy the two following rules:

1. The meals are furnished on the business premises of the employer, and
2. The employee is required to accept lodging on the business premises of the employer as a condition of his employment.

Notice that neither a self-employed nor a partner (in a partnership) can enjoy this tax saving device.

2.8. Supporting the Deduction for Travel Expense

Travel expense to attend a meeting or seminar is deductible if the trip is primarily related to the field of activity of the employee (Sec. 62(2)(B); 1.62-1(e)). To support the deduction, observe the following bookkeeping rules:

1. State in writing the date of departure from home and the date of return to home.
2. Keep the receipt for the registration fee to attend the seminar or meeting.
3. All expenditures of $25 or more should be supported with a receipt or paid bill.
4. Keep any written communication with your employer regarding the trip to attend the seminar.
5. Make entries at the time (or near the time) of the expenditure in a book or diary or statement of expense. Do not estimate the cost of meals and lodging; instead, state the exact amounts. If you use your car for transportation, keep an account of the actual cost, or you can estimate the cost using the number of miles traveled. If you deduct transportation expense on an estimated basis, you can deduct 15¢ per mile for the first 15,000 miles and on top of that deduct any toll and parking fees.

2.9. Use of Auto for Business Purposes

If your employer requires the use of your auto for business purposes, figure the auto expense twice: (1) under the actual cost method, and (2) under the optional or estimated cost method. If the employer reimburses you for the use of your auto, calculate your auto expense deduction (on actual or standard mileage basis) and, after that, deduct the employer reimbursement in order to arrive at your business deduction. If the employer reimburses you at the rate of 15¢ per mile and your actual auto expense is less than that, the difference between the two does not need to be reported as taxable income. It is tax free. This special exemption applies also to a stockholder-employee and should be fully used whenever possible. To generate this type of tax-free income, it is better for a stockholder-employee to use his personal car for business purposes instead of using his corporation car (if his reimbursement is at the rate of 15¢ per mile; or the reimbursement exceeds his actual auto expense).

The employee should keep a record of the date, number of miles, place and purpose of auto use. If reimbursement of expense is equal to actual auto expense, the employee may omit reporting both on his tax return.

2.10. Maximizing the Deduction for Car Expenses

No prior IRS approval is needed for a change from the method of itemizing car expenses (i.e., deducting the actual expenses) to the method of claiming a standard deduction of 15¢ per mile for the first 15,000 miles and 10¢ for each additional mile. You may switch from one method to another from one year to another year, but if the switch is made after the business car is fully depreciated, the maximum standard deduction per mile is only 10¢ (even for the first 15,000 miles) (Treasury Department booklet "Tax Guide for Small Business" (1976 Ed.), p. 104). Notice that, in order to use the standard mileage rate, the following requirements must be observed:

1. Not more than one car is simultaneously used in connection with trade or business.
2. The taxpayer claiming the standard mileage must own the car, and not use it for hire (e.g., for a taxi).
3. If in prior years the actual method was used in claiming car expenses, depreciation was claimed under the straight line method only.
4. If depreciation was claimed in prior years, the additional first year depreciation was not elected for the car.

2.11. Credit for Tax on Gasoline and Oil

If you purchase gasoline and lubricating oil for off-highway use (e.g., for mowers, boats, chain saws, etc.), you can claim a credit against your income tax of 2¢ per gallon of gasoline and 6¢ per gallon of oil (Sec. 39). This credit is more important than an ordinary deductible expense. One dollar of a deductible expense will reduce taxable income by the amount of one dollar, while a dollar of a tax credit will reduce the liability for tax by a similar amount. This credit for tax on gasoline and oil for off highway use should be considered separately from state and local taxes on diesel and other motor fuels. A state and local tax on motor fuels is deductible only if the taxpayer-employee is itemizing his deductions. For example, a taxpayer used 340 gallons of gasoline and eight gallons of lubricating oil in operating his motor boat. He can claim a gasoline tax credit of $6.80 (340 x 2 cents) and a lubricating oil tax credit of $0.48 (8 x 6 cents) (he may use Form 4136 for computing the gasoline and oil tax credit).

2.12. Contributing to a Retirement Plan

After 1974, anyone not covered by a qualified retirement plan (corporate or Keogh type), may claim retirement benefits through either:

1. An individual retirement account (IRA),
2. An individual retirement annuity, or
3. Retirement bonds.

The most popular method is to set up an individual retirement account. Contribution to the IRA can be up to 15% of compensation or earned income not to exceed $1,500 per year, without a guaranteed minimum (in case of a Keogh plan the minimum is earned income or $750). If the wife of the employee also works and qualifies for an IRA, she can also set up her own retirement account. Therefore, for a husband and wife the total combined deductible contribution can be up to $3,000 per year. The 1976 Tax Reform Act allows a husband or wife not covered by a company pension to contribute up to $1,750 or 15 percent of earned income, whichever is less, and to set up a jointly-owned retirement account. Or one spouse can contribute up to $850 to a personal account while the same amount is contributed to another account owned by the other spouse. Notice that a contribution in cash should be made to the IRA during the taxpayer's taxable year. If the employee has more than one job, he can benefit from more than one retirement plan or set up more than one retirement plan or set up more than one IRA. The limit for his total deductible contribution always remains up to 15 percent of total earned income, not to exceed $1,500 per year.

Amounts contributed to the IRA (within the specified limits) are tax exempt. Interest earned on money in an IRA is also not subject to tax. However, after retirement at age 59 1/2 or older, any amounts received from an IRA are taxed in full as ordinary income. No contributions to an IRA are allowed after the age of 70 1/2. Notice also that the annual contribution to the IRA is part of compensation for services and is subject to the F.I.C.A. tax.

2.13. Payments Received from a Wage Continuation Plan

If the employer adopts a wage continuation plan (also called a sick pay plan), both the employer and employee will benefit since any payment under such a plan is exempted from the Social Security tax, if both the employer and employee meet the reporting requirements specified in Code Sections 31.6001-5 and 31.6001-1(d). It is better to adopt the wage continuation plan in writing, covering one or more employees and keeping a record of payments made under the plan (Sec. 105(b); 1.105-2; *Chism's Est. v. Comm.,* 12 AFTR 2d 5300). Besides the exemption from the Social Security tax, the employee may qualify for the sick pay exclusion. If a wage continuation plan is adopted, the covered employee or employees should be notified. Notice that under Code Section 31.6001-1(d) an employee should retain the duplicate copy of the Form W-2 furnished by his employer for four years after the tax is paid or after the due date of the tax, if he receives any payments from a wage continuation plan.

For years beginning after December 31, 1975, an employee is not allowed the exclusion for sick pay unless he meets these requirements:

1. The taxpayer is under 65 years of age.
2. The taxpayer is totally and permanently disabled. Permanent and total disability means the individual is unable to engage in any substantial gainful activity by reason of any medically determinable physical or mental impairment which can be expected to result in death or which has lasted or can be expected to last for a continuous period of not less than 12 months (Sec. 105, of the 1976 Tax Reform Act).

The new sick pay exclusion is up to $100 per week ($5,200 of sick pay each year). However, the exclusion is reduced on a dollar-for-dollar basis by adjusted gross income over $15,000. For example, Mr. Richard Jones reported an adjusted gross income (including disability income) of $16,000 in the year 1976. His maximum sick pay exclusion is $4,200 or $5,200 less the excess of his adjusted gross income over $15,000. Therefore, when a taxpayer reports an adjusted gross income equal to or in excess of $20,200, he will not be entitled to any sick pay exclusion.

2.14. Claiming a Deduction for an Office at Home

Claiming a deduction for an office at home is no longer dependent on having an employer requesting the use of the home as an office as a condition of employment. At present, such a deduction can be claimed by employees as well as the self-employed. If it is helpful in your line of business to use part of your home as an office, then you can deduct items such as office supplies, dues and subscriptions to magazines, telephone expense, heat and light expense, repairs and maintenance expense, insurance, cleaning and wages of domestics, depreciation of office area, depreciation of furniture and fixtures used in the office, etc. In order to deduct any part of a common expense (i.e., an expense used for the entire home) such as heat and light, one of two methods of apportionment can be used. The first method is to compare the number of rooms used as an office with the total number of rooms in the entire house. The second method is to compare the number of square feet used as an office with the total number of square feet in the entire home. After determining the ratio, apply it to the dollar amount of the common expense in order to determine the deductible part of the expense.

To support the deduction for an office at home observe the following (Treasury Department Booklet "Your Federal Income Tax" (975 Ed.), p. 105):

1. Establish the regular use of part of your home for employment or business related purposes. An incidental or occasional use of part of his residence for business or employment-related purposes does not entitle the taxpayer to a business expense deduction.
2. Specify the portion of the home used as an office in terms of number of rooms or square feet of space.
3. Maintain records that will support the computation of the various expenses and their apportionment between business and personal use.

2.15. Taking Full Advantage of Tax-Exempt Income

Certain types of income are completely exempt from tax or are subject to tax according to special limitations. The following sources of income are usually exempt from tax and should be explored in order to take full advantage of their special tax status:

1. Accident and health insurance proceeds.
2. Advances from employer which are repayable.
3. Compensation for personal injury.
4. Compensation for damages to character.
5. Casualty insurance proceeds (limited exemption).
6. Cost-of-living allowances paid to U.S. employees stationed outside the United States.
7. Deferral of college or university tuition and receipt of a fellowship or scholarship grant.

8. Disability and death payments.
9. Employment agency fee paid directly to the agency by the employer.
10. Social Security benefit payments.
11. State unemployment compensation.
12. Veterans benefits.
13. Workmen's Compensation Act payments.
14. Gifts, bequests, or inheritances.
15. Interest on tax-exempt state or local bonds.
16. Meals and lodging furnished by employer for employer's convenience.
17. Military reserve allowances.
18. Employer payments to beneficiary of deceased employee, up to $5,000.
19. Railroad Retirement Act pensions.
20. Relocation payments.
21. Rental allowance for clergymen.
22. Car pool receipts (to the extent they do not exceed the expenses).
23. Group life insurance premiums on up to $50,000 coverage paid by the employer.
24. Insurance interest included in payments to surviving spouse up to $1,000 per year (Sec. 101 (d); 1.101-4).
25. Reimbursement of employee out-of-pocket expenses.

2.16. Income Tax Credits Available to an Employee

An employee may qualify for a wide variety of tax credits against his income tax. The tax advisor should check the requirements for each credit and recommend possible actions in order to meet the requirement. The following credits against tax should be examined thoroughly:

1. Earned income tax credit available to low income taxpayers under the Tax Reduction Act of 1975. This credit is 10 percent of the first $4,000 of earned income and after that, the credit declines until it is completely eliminated when adjusted gross income reaches $8,000. The 1976 Tax Reform Act extended the earned income tax credit through December 31, 1977. For 1975, the earned income credit was available only to a taxpayer who maintained a household for a dependent child who was

under 19 or a student, and for whom he could claim a personal exemption. For 1976 and 1977, the credit is also available to a taxpayer with adult disabled dependents and to a taxpayer who maintains a household for a child who is under 19 or a student, even if he can not claim a personal exemption for the child.

2. A tax credit of $30 for each personal exemption (except the exemption for old age and blindness) was available for the year 1975. The 1976 Tax Reform Act changed this credit to a taxable income credit. It applies to 1976 and 1977 and an individual taxpayer can take a credit equal to the greater of $35 per individual personal exemption or 2 percent of the first $9,000 of taxable income.

3. Retirement income credit of 15 percent on the retirement income of up to $1,524 or a maximum credit of $228.60. The 1976 Tax Reform Act changed this credit to a credit for the elderly. It applies to taxpayers age 65 or over, and the 15 percent credit base is $3,750 for married couples filing jointly, where both spouses are eligible for the credit ($2,500 in the case of a single individual). However, the maximum credit base is reduced by one-half the amount of adjusted gross income above $7,500 for singles, $10,000 for marrieds filing jointly, and $5,000 for marrieds filing separately. Therefore, a single taxpayer loses the credit for the elderly when his (or her) adjusted gross income reaches $12,500 ($15,000 of adjusted gross income for marrieds filing jointly and only one spouse is 65 or over; and the limit is reached at $17,500 of adjusted gross income for marrieds filing jointly and both spouses are 65 or over).

4. Political contributions can be claimed as an itemized deduction (up to $100 or $200) or one half of the political contribution is allowed as a tax credit up to $25 ($50 on a joint return).

5. Tax credit for any excess withholding of Social Security taxes, especially if the employee had two or more employers during the tax year.

6. A purchaser of new housing constructed or under construction before March 26, 1975, qualifies for a tax credit of 5 percent of the purchase price up to a maximum of $2,000.

2.17. Deducting Employment-Related Expenses

An employee can deduct up to $400 per month ($4,800 per year) as employment-related expenses (mainly for child care and disabled dependent or spouse care expenses). The 1976 Tax Reform Act changed the dependent care deduction to a tax credit. For more details about this major item see **1.23** of Chapter 1.

2.18. Deducting Moving Expenses

Moving expenses can be deducted whether they are connected with a new employment or a transfer to a new place of work. The deduction for moving expenses covers the following:

1. Moving household goods and personal effects (with no dollar limit).
2. Travel, meals and lodging on the way to a new residence (with no dollar limit).
3. Travel, meals and lodging from the old residence to search for a new residence and return (after obtaining new employment and subject to dollar limits).
4. Meals and lodging for up to 30 days in the general area of the new job site while waiting to move into the new residence (subject to dollar limits).
5. Expenses of selling the old residence, purchase of new residence and any expenses of settling the old lease and acquiring a new lease. Cost of selling the old residence that may be claimed as moving expense includes real estate agent's commission, escrow fees, expenses of advertising the property for sale, preparing the deed, other legal services related to the sale and "points" paid by the seller to obtain an FHA mortgage for the buyer, and any state transfer taxes on the legal fees, title costs and appraisal fees. When selling and/or purchasing a home, these related expenses may be claimed as moving expenses. If they are claimed as moving expenses, then they cannot be used to reduce the sale price of the old residence or increase the purchase cost of the new residence. Notice that deductible sale, purchase and lease expenses are subject to dollar limits.

The total deduction for items (3), (4) and (5) cannot exceed $2,500 (increased to $3,000 for tax years beginning after 1976). The deduction for house-hunting trips and temporary living expenses cannot exceed $1,000 (increased to $1,500 for tax years beginning after 1976). For tax saving purposes, the total $2,500 limit (or $3,000 new limit) should be observed carefully. If the cost of selling the old residence and acquiring a new residence results in a total indirect moving expense above the $2,500 (or $3,000) limit, any cost which is not claimed as a moving expense should be used as an adjustment to the sale price of the old residence or to the basis of the new residence.

Another item of special interest to the tax advisor is that if an employee is reimbursed for his moving expenses, he may elect to claim them in the year of payment or in the year of reimbursement. Using this election wisely will lead to some tax manuevering if there is a difference between the total deduction for moving expenses and the amount of reimbursement by the employer, and if the year of paying moving expenses differs from the year of reimbursement. For example, a taxpayer incurred deductible moving expenses of $4,850 in the year 1975. His employer reimbursed him $2,400 in the year 1976. The taxpayer may elect to claim the difference between the $4,850 and $2,400 as a deductible moving expense for either 1975 or 1976.

Notice that the employer withholds income tax and Social Security on only any excess of reimbursement over the employee's deductible moving expenses. For example, an employee's deductible moving expenses amount to $6,200 and his employer reimbursed him for $6,850. The employer should withhold income and Social Security taxes on $650 only ($6,850 less $6,200). For years beginning after December 31, 1975 military personnel may deduct out-of-pocket moving expenses even if they do not meet either the 35-mile test or the 39-week (in the new location) test.

2.19. Avoiding Taxable Income When Selling to Yourself

An employee should avoid making taxable income selling to himself. An insurance salesman, a real estate salesman, or a stockbroker, for example, will be taxed on money made selling an insurance policy, real estate, or securities to themselves if their employers charge them the price they charge the public and routinely send commission checks to those salesmen. Any commission from selling to yourself should not be received in cash and consequently reported as an ordinary income. Instead, the commission should be claimed as an adjustment (or a decrease) to the cost of acquiring the related item or property. When an employee buys a property from his employer for less than its fair market value, the difference between the purchase price and the fair market value of the property is taxable income to the employee. A better alternative is not to purchase the property directly from the employer. Instead, request the employer to sell the property at the special low price to a third party. After that, the employee will purchase the property from the third party at a price equal to its cost to the third party. In this way, the employee will not be subject to the rules of "bargain purchase by employees" or have to report a taxable income from any commissions or discounts.

2.20. Deducting Educational Expenses

An employee can deduct his education expenses if they are incurred to maintain or improve skills required in his job, or required in order to meet new requirements of his employer or the law (Sec. 1.162-5(c)). Education expenses include amounts paid for tuition and fees, books, supplies, lab fees, typing, travel and transportation expenses. Teachers can deduct any expense incurred to qualify for a teaching certificate to teach in another state. Teachers can also deduct any education expense related to a change from one subject to another or from one type of duties to another. Employee education expenses are claimed as itemized deductions, while related travel and transportation expenses are claimed as deductions for adjusted gross income. An employee who works as an outside salesman has no choice and should treat all education expenses as deductions for adjusted gross income. If an employee attends training programs or conventions in a location away from home, he may deduct travel, meals, lodging, and registration fees.

An important factor in deducting away-from-home expenses is whether they were primarily for personal purposes or whether any personal activities were incidental. An important factor in determining whether a certain trip is primarily personal or primarily to obtain education is the relative amount of time devoted to educational, as compared with personal, activities.

Chapter 3

TAX SAVING OPPORTUNITIES FOR LANDLORDS AND TENANTS

3.1. Allocating the Cost of a Newly Acquired Property

Depreciation constitutes the most desirable type of business expense to a landlord. While depreciation lowers taxable income, it does not require any outflow of cash, since payment is made when the real estate is purchased. To maximize the benefit from depreciation deduction, you need to start very early, when the real estate is acquired. When a building is acquired, a careful and thorough allocation of cost to each component of the asset acquired is needed (e.g., land, air-conditioning, roofing, pavement, electrical equipment, leases, escalators and elevators, building, etc.). After an allocation of cost is made, it will be used for the remaining expected life of the item and, consequently, affect present as well as future years' taxable income.

When an investment is made in real estate (other than undeveloped land), it pays off to use the services of a specialist in order to allocate the total cost of the investment among the various items acquired. Keep the professional report of the specialist for at least four years because you will need it if the IRS challenges the allocation of cost. The part of cost allocated to the value of leases is frequently investigated by the IRS. If you allocate a material part of acquisition cost to an intangible asset called leases, you had better be prepared to defend your basis of allocation. Of course, the best defense you can use is to show that your allocation is not arbitrary and is based on the written report of a professional expert.

3.2. Depreciating a Residential Rental Property

For a residential rental building, the declining balance method of depreciation can be used. If the residential building was acquired new after December 31, 1953, the 200 percent declining balance can be used. If the residential building is acquired used after July 24, 1969 and its estimated remaining life is at least 20 years, the 125 percent declining balance rate can be used (Sec. 167 (j) (5); 1.167 (j)-(6)). It is important to remember that in order to qualify as residential property, at least 80 percent of the gross income from the building each year must be derived from rentals of residential units (houses or apartments). The 80 percent test is computed each year. For example, if 72 percent of the gross income from a building was derived from rentals of residential units in 1975, the taxpayer may use the 150 percent declining balance of depreciation for that year. If the 80 percent test was satisfied in the following year, the taxpayer may use the 200 percent declining balance for 1976 (if the residential rental property is new). Notice that a change in the method of computing depreciation because of the operation of this test does not require the approval of the Internal Revenue Service (Treasury Department Booklet "Tax Guide for Small Business" 1976 Ed., p. 96). If a real property is converted from personal use to business use, it should be treated as used property.

3.3. Using Accelerated Depreciation

For commercial and industrial real property, the 200 percent declining balance rate can be used for new property acquired between January 1, 1954 and July 24, 1969. The 150 percent declining balance rate can be used for any new real property acquired after July 24, 1969 (Sec. 167 (j) (1); 1.167 (j)-1). For used real property acquired after July 24, 1969, the accelerated method of depreciation is not allowed. Notice that:

1. A used residential property acquired after July 24, 1969, can use the 125-percent declining balance rate.
2. For components of the building, the declining balance method can be used. When the building is acquired, exercise special care when allocating the cost of the acquisition to the various components of the real property. The allocation will, in a sense, determine your depreciation method as well as the maximum depreciation rate allowed.

3.4. Avoiding the Recapture of Depreciation Upon Sale of Property

If you use an accelerated method to depreciate a real property, upon the sale of such property you may pay higher income tax on the gain from sale. This may happen because of the recapture of depreciation rules. To avoid this possibility, be sure to hold a residential property for at least 100 months before selling it (if you did use an accelerated method of depreciation while the property was in your possession). For new or used residential real property acquired after December 31, 1969, the percentage of recapture that applies to excess depreciation is 100 percent until the property is held for 100 full months, then it declines 1 percent for each full month of ownership, with no recapture after 16 years and 8 months (or 200 months) (Sec. 1250 (a) (1) (c) (iii); 1.1250-1 (d)(1)).

There is no recapture of depreciation upon the sale of real property if the straight-line depreciation method is used, unless the property was held 12 months or less. An effective method to avoid the recapture of depreciation is not to make an outright sale of the real property. Instead, exchange it for another similar property. If the exchange qualifies as a non-taxable exchange, then there will be no taxable gain. If there is no taxable gain, no gain can be recognized as ordinary income under the recapture of depreciation rules. (For more details about non-taxable exchanges see Chapter 10.)

3.5. Distinguishing Between Repair Expenses and Improvement Cost

Repairs do not add to the value or utility of the property nor do they materially prolong its life. On the other hand, improvements increase the value of property, make it adaptable to a different use, or prolong its useful life. The cost of repairs to a building is deductible as a business expense, while the cost of improvement should be capitalized and written-off throughout the useful life of the improvement. If you do repairs and improvements work with the same contractor, receiving one bill, the IRS may treat the entire cost as improvement to be capitalized. To avoid this from happening, use one of the following solutions:

1. Request two separate bills from the contractor; one for the repair work and the other for the cost of improvement.
2. Do the repair work at a separate time from the improvement work. If the cost is a part of a general plan of improving or remodeling the property as a whole, all of the cost must be capitalized even though certain portions of the work represent ordinary repair (Treasury Department booklet "Tax Guide for Small Business" 1976 ed., p. 90). To prevent the capitalization of repair expenses, do the repair work at a time when no general plan of remodeling the whole building is in effect.

3.6. Charging a Friend or Relative Rental Below the Fair Market Rental Value of a Property

There is a dollar limitation on the amount of deductible rental expenses if a property is leased to a friend or relative for an amount below the fair market rental value of the property. Any deductible expenses for such property cannot exceed the rental income reported from the property. Therefore, if a relative or related party is charged rent below the fair market rental value of a property, deduct depreciation, repairs and maintenance, utilities, and insurance up to the amount of rental received (only). Separately, on Schedule A deduct the property tax and interest on mortgage as itemized deductions. In this way, the property tax and interest on mortgage deduction will be claimed without dollar limitation.

3.7. Supporting a Claim for a Casualty Loss

Computing a loss from fire, theft, flood, and other casualty is needed in order to figure the recognized (or deductible) amount of casualty loss and the new basis of the related property. The total amount of the casualty loss is equal to the difference between the value of the property immediately before and immediately after the casualty. Establishing the value of the destroyed portion of a property is usually difficult and could be subjected to various estimates. To support your claim for a casualty loss, on a periodic basis take pictures of the interior and exterior of your property. In the case of a casualty loss, these pictures can support a claim for loss for both tax as well as insurance purposes. The cost of taking such pictures may prove to be considerably less than the tax benefits and insurance proceeds in case of a casualty. Notice that after a casualty or theft the basis of property should be decreased by

1. Reimbursements received from any insurance, and
2. Any deductible loss not covered by insurance (Sec. 165 (b); 1.165-1 (c) (4), 1.165-7 (b) (1)).

3.8. Incorporating or Owning Real Estate as a Sole Proprietorship

A major item to be considered by a landlord is whether or not to incorporate or to own real estate as a sole proprietor. From a tax saving point of view, it cannot be said that either incorporation or sole proprietorship will always lead to tax savings. The following major considerations should be regarded before incorporation:

1. Incorporation will usually lead to double taxation. This chance can be reduced by paying a reasonable compensation for the services of the stockholder and by leasing the real estate to the corporation.
2. The effective tax rate on the corporation should be compared with the tax bracket of the incorporator. Income splitting may lead to a final reduction in tax liability.
3. If the landlord keeps the real estate under his own name, a major tax

savings device available to him is to set up a short-term trust and transfer the ownership of the property to the trust. However, in case of death, the value of the trust property will be included in his estate. On the other hand, if the landlord will incorporate and transfer the stock ownership to members of his family, then upon his death, the value of the stock will not be included in his estate.

4. An option can be given to the corporation to buy the property from its accumulated earnings in order to avoid any tax on excessive accumulation of profits.

3.9. Income Items with Full or Part Exemption Status

The following types of income are of special interest to the landlord since they represent tax-free items with full or part exemption status:

1. Compensation for casualty and theft losses (limited exemption).
2. Compensation for involuntary conversion (limited exemption).
3. Improvements made by lessee and not considered as part of rent (Sec. 109; 1.109-1).
4. Option payments made to a seller until option is either exercised or given up.

3.10. Deducting Penalty for Mortgage Prepayment

A mortgage prepayment penalty is deductible as interest expense (Rev. Rul. 57-198, 1957-1 CB 94). Therefore, when a real property is acquired, the buyer should request the right to make any future mortgage prepayment. If a penalty is connected with the mortgage prepayment, a deduction of this penalty against gross taxable income will reduce its unpleasant effect. Notice that although a mortgage prepayment penalty is deductible as interest, any amount designated "interest on mortgage" paid for occupying a home before settlement or arrangement of a mortgage is not deductible as interest and considered, instead, as payment in lieu of rent (Rev. Rul. 58-129, 1958-1 CB 93).

3.11. Selling a Lease Versus Subleasing the Property

A tenant may decide to move to another property before the expiration date of his lease. If his lease has any economic value due to a low rental rate, he will have two main alternatives with entirely different income tax effects to choose from:

Alternative One: To sublease the property and report the difference between the rent he charges the new tenant and the rent he pays to the landlord as ordinary income.

Alternative Two: To sell the lease and report any gain from sale as a capital gain. To use this favorable alternative, two major items should be observed carefully:

1. The written agreement to sell the lease should refer to a buyer and a seller and not to a tenant and a landlord.
2. The new tenant should make the rental payments directly to the landlord.

When a lease is sold, the sale price can be paid as a lump sum or spread over a certain number of payments. Also the type of capital gain or loss from sale of lease depends on the lease's prior tax treatment. If the lease is depreciable and held over six months, the sale is subject to Section 1231 rules (Sec. 1221; 1231; 1.1221-1). However, if the lease is nondepreciable, the leasehold is treated as a capital asset.

3.12. The Cost of Permanent Improvements Made by a Tenant

Improvements made by a tenant are not income to the landlord. They increase the value of the leased property and gain or loss is recognized only upon the sale or disposition of the property (Sec. 109; 1019). On the other hand, the cost of a permanent improvement to property made by the tenant is not deductible by him as a current expense. It is treated as a capital expenditure, recoverable by him either through an amortization based on the remaining period of the lease or by depreciation using the estimated useful life of the permanent improvement, whichever period is shorter.

The cost of permanent improvements made by a tenant on leased property held on an indefinite or month-to-month (or period-to-period) basis is not amortizable, but can be recovered only under a depreciation method using the estimated useful life of the improvements. Notice that if the lease is canceled before deducting the entire cost of improvements, the tenant is entitled to deduct the remaining balance of undepreciated cost, in the year of cancellation. Under Section 178, if the lessee and lessor are "related persons," as defined in the section, the lease is treated as including a period at least as long as the useful life of the improvement. Therefore, for tax saving purposes, writing-off the cost of a permanent improvement made by a tenant is subject to an election regarding the write-off period (lease vs. improvements remaining life). Special areas to watch for are:

1. When the lessee has an option to renew the lease.
2. When the lessee and lessor are "related persons".

3.13. A Lease with an Option to Buy the Property

Under a lease with option to buy the property, the optionee takes current deductions for the full amount of rent paid. On the exercise of the option, the optionee becomes the owner of the property. If the rental payments are high and the option price is low, the optionee has, in effect, deducted part of his total purchase price as current rental expense. Before setting up high rental payments and low option price, or low rental payments and high option price, care should be exercised in examining the full effect of such an arrangement on both the optionee and present landlord.

Under certain circumstances, even with the absence of evidence of a lease with option to buy, the IRS may consider the lease of property as purchase if one or more of the following conditions are present (Treasury Department booklet "Tax Guide for Small Business", 1976 Ed., p. 89):

1. Portions of the periodic payments are used to acquire certain equity or rights by the lessee.
2. Lessee will acquire title to property upon the payment of a stated amount of "rent."
3. Total amount of payments substantially exceed current fair rental value.
4. Property may be purchased at a nominal price at the end of the lease period.
5. Total rental payments plus option price are equal to an amount close to the value of property when it was leased, plus interest and related finance charges.

3.14. When to Use a Sale-Leaseback Arrangement

For different tax and business reasons, sales-and-leaseback arrangements should be taken seriously. An owner of a fully depreciated property may consider selling it and still continue to use it as a tenant after the sale is completed. An owner can also raise extra cash by selling a property, and then arranging to lease it back. The sale-and-leaseback arrangement can serve both the new investor and the old owner of the property. The investor is purchasing property with a built-in tenant. The investor will be entitled to deduct interest, taxes, depreciation and any other expenses related to the property. The old owner of the property will be entitled to deduct all the rental payments under the lease (assuming unrelated persons). Any payments received from the sale price would be non-taxable since they represent part of the total sale price. Only the gain from the sale or disposition of property is taxed and not the total price received from the sale. The attractiveness of a sale and leaseback becomes greater in the following cases:

1. If the property involved is land, no depreciation is allowed to an owner of land. After paying in full the cost of acquiring land, the only possible deduction is for related property taxes. Selling such land and leasing it back will give the old owner a deduction for rent, while the new owner or investor will claim a possible deduction for interest and related finance charges.
2. If the property is fully depreciated, the old owner may reinvest the proceeds from sale in a new property giving him a depreciation deduction. At the same time, all his payments under the agreement for rent are fully deductible too.
3. If the property was acquired by the old owner at a bargain or low cost, and has substantially appreciated in value, selling such property will result in a new (and relatively high) basis for depreciation by the new owner.

Under Reg. 1.1031 (a)-(1) (c) the Internal Revenue Service considers a sale and leaseback of real estate (by non dealers) for 30 years or more as a tax-free exchange. This regulation is directed toward the case of a sale-leaseback resulting in a loss. Such loss will not be deducted (or recognized) if the sale-leaseback is treated as a tax-free exchange. Of course, the trap set by this regulation may be avoided by a leaseback for a period of less than 30 years.

3.15. Using Tax-Free Exchanges

Generally, gain or loss is recognized on the sale or disposition of property. However, the exchange of property held for productive use or investment for property of a like kind, will qualify for a non-taxable exchange (Sec. 1031 (a); 1.1031 (a)-(1)). If the exchange is non-taxable, the tax on the gain from the exchange is postponed. Non-taxable exchanges include a wide variety, such as, a farm for a farm, an apartment house for building lots, an office building for a ranch, a leasehold for 30 or more years for real property, etc.

Non-taxable exchanges can be used to postpone the tax on the gain from an appreciated property, and at the same time boost the claim for depreciation deduction. When a tax-free exchange takes place, a new basis should be figured for the newly received property. Generally, the basis of property acquired in a non-taxable exchange is the adjusted basis of the property traded, plus any "boot" given, additional costs incurred, and gain recognized. Therefore, if the exchange is made with the taxpayer making an additional cash investment and at the end receiving a more valuable property, the effect would be a higher basis for depreciation deduction. Of course when the property received consists of land and building, the basis of each part must be determined separately. If the land-building allocation ratio can be improved as a result of the exchange, there can be a step-up in the basis for depreciation. Therefore, a tax-free exchange can be aimed at the following tax benefits:

1. Postponement of tax on the gain from disposition of an appreciated property.
2. If the taxpayer invests some money and receives a more valuable property, the newly acquired property will be reported with a higher basis for depreciation.
3. If the newly received property has both land and building (or a building with structural components), the new basis should be allocated to the various parts acquired. The allocation of basis can also lead to an increase in the amount of deductible depreciation. (For more details about tax-free exchanges see Chapter 10.)

3.16. Considering a Change in the Adopted Method of Depreciation

An owner of real property may step up or slow down his depreciation deduction through a change in the method of depreciation or/and change in the property's estimated useful life.

1. A change in an adopted method of depreciation requires the approval of the IRS. If the application for change (on Form 3115) is filed during 180 days from the first day of the year of change, the IRS will usually approve such change. Generally, the permission of the IRS is not needed to change from the declining balance to the straight-line method. A change in an adopted method of depreciation resulting from a property qualifying (or not qualifying) as residential rental property, can be made without IRS approval.

2. The useful life of a depreciable property must be estimated before making any periodic deduction for depreciation. The estimate for useful life is based on the period over which the asset is expected to be of service. If there is a mistake in estimating useful life, it should be redetermined. For example, the taxpayer's policy on repairs, renewals and replacements is an important factor in estimating useful life. If the owner changes his policy on repairs and the result is a faster deterioration of the

property, then its useful life should be shortened. Stepped-up use of property is another reason for changing the adopted useful life.

The owner of depreciable property and his tax advisor should keep an eye on the facts of property use and determine whether depreciation should be claimed on a faster or slower basis. Even in the case of entering a binding written agreement with the IRS on Form 2271 as to useful life, deprecation rate and method, and salvage value, the taxpayer has the right to serve a notice proposing the change. (For more details see Chapter 13.)

3.17. Acquiring Property with a Depreciable Leasehold

When a landlord acquires a real property with an outstanding lease, a value may be assigned to such a lease. This assigned value will be written off in future tax years through amortization and by using the shorter of the lease period or the property's estimated useful life. However, a leasehold cannot be depreciated under the declining balance or sum-of-the-years-digits methods. After the acquisition of a leasehold, any amounts received by the landlord for canceling or amending the lease are taxed as ordinary income. On the other hand, any amounts paid by a landlord for the cancellation of a lease are reported as capital expenditures.

Therefore, if the landlord acquires property with a depreciable leasehold, his chance to claim a faster write-off is usually improved since the acquired lease may cover a period shorter than the estimated useful life of the property. For tax saving purposes, it is important to check if a leasehold is acquired whenever a real property under lease is purchased. The purchase contract should allocate a part of the purchase price to the acquired leasehold. Otherwise, the testimony of experts can be used for determining the fair market value of the newly acquired lease.

3.18. Making Special Purpose Improvements

A different method for increasing deductions and at the same time improving the value of real property is to offer the tenants any specially needed improvements. A tenant may need a special purpose addition, cooling, heating, alteration, or replacement, and yet may fear sinking substantial sums of money into it. After the landlord makes such improvements, he may claim depreciation on the cost of the improvement while charging the tenant higher rent to recover the added cost. If the improvements are made for a specific tenant's benefit, the landlord may also claim a depreciation deduction, using the shorter of that tenant's remaining lease period or the estimated useful life of the improvements.

3.19. Selling Property and Qualifying for the Installment Method

The sale of an appreciated real property may qualify as an installment sale, whether or not the seller is a dealer in real estate. The taxpayer should show the contract price, adjusted basis of the property, and total payments received in the year of sale. Also, a record should be made for any payments received on account of such sale. Before accepting an offer to sell a piece of real property, the seller should decide whether or not the installment method will be used for reporting the gain from sale. The installment method may not be used if the payments in the year of sale are more than 30 percent of the selling price (Sec. 453 (b)(2)(a); 1.453-4).

When a going business is sold, including real property and inventory, the sale contract should specify the value assigned to each asset sold as well as the part of the down payment assigned to each asset. If a going business is sold under one agreement, it is customary to relate the cash payment to inventory value and any cash payment left to be assigned to the other assets sold. To avoid any misinterpretation, it is better either to draw one agreement stating the values assigned to each asset sold and to assign the amount of down payment, or to sell the inventory under a separate agreement. Selling the inventory under a separate contract is a good solution since it may result in lowering the cash payments received in the year of sale on the non-inventory items to 30 percent or less of their sale price.

Chapter 4

TAX SAVING OPPORTUNITIES FOR FARMERS

4.1. Avoiding a Loss from Farming Entered into on a Non-Business Basis

Any income from a hobby is taxable and any loss is not deductible. In order to deduct the loss from an activity, the activity should be shown as one entered into for profit rather than as a hobby. Generally an activity will be considered as one for profit if it is profitable for at least two years during the five-year period ending with the current taxable year (Sec. 1.183-1 (a)). In cases of breeding, training, showing, or racing horses, however, the activity should be profitable for any two years during the seven years ending with the current taxable year (Sec. 1.183-1 (c)(1)). It is essential, therefore, to show profit from a property owned for personal or recreational purposes for at least two years during a five-year or seven-year period before being able to deduct any loss from such a property.

If an activity is not engaged in for profit, non-business deductions such as interest expense and property taxes can be claimed only as itemized deductions. If the activity is not for profit, any business deductions are deductible only to the extent of gross income derived from the activity. For tax saving purposes, it is essential to concentrate income in at least two years in order to show a profit twice during a five-year or seven-year period. Concentrating income may lead to the classification of an activity as one entered into for profit and, consequently, allow the deduction of losses suffered in low income years. This tax saving device can be beneficial to a "gentleman farmer," an owner of a house, or any taxpayer with an activity entered into a non-business basis.

4.2. Using a Special Tax Break Under Section 1231

Under Section 1231, if a net gain results from all of Section 1231 assets, then every gain is considered a long-term capital gain and each loss is a long-term capital loss. If the net effect of all Section 1231 assets is a loss, however, then every gain is an ordinary income and each loss is an ordinary loss. A farmer should be aware that the following items qualify as Section 1231 assets:

1. Livestock (but not poultry) held by the taxpayer for draft, breeding, dairy, or sporting purposes. Holding period for cattle and horses is 24 months and for all other livestock, 12 months.
2. Unharvested crop sold with land, if the land has been held over six months.
3. Cut timber on which a taxpayer has elected to report the gain at the time of cutting.

Before the end of each tax year an estimate should be made for the net effect of all Section 1231 assets. By postponing a possible gain and realizing an expected loss, the net effect of all Section 1231 assets could be shown as an ordinary loss which is fully deductible against ordinary income. Timing Section 1231 gains and losses can lead to material tax savings if a review of all possible gains and losses is made before the end of the income tax year. Section 1231 offers a significant tax break if the net effect of all Section 1231 assets is a net loss, while it gives no special tax benefit if the net effect is a gain. The tax advisor should try to use this special tax break by steering the sale of Section 1231 assets toward a net gain in a certain year and a net loss in another year.

4.3. Deducting the Cost of Cattle Feed

The cost of purchasing livestock for draft, breeding, or dairy purposes must be capitalized by both cash basis and accrual basis taxpayers. However, the cost of raising (not purchasing) livestock can be currently deducted against ordinary income by cash basis taxpayers without taking an inventory of their animals. Paying for cattle feed and claiming the deduction in the year of payment, while the actual use of the feed takes place in a different (usually future) tax year or years, constitutes a popular tax shelter. In order to expense the cost of cattle feed the following four tests must be observed carefully:

1. The payment is for feed purchase and not a mere deposit. The price of

purchase is fixed and the buyer is not entitled to a refund or repurchase.

2. The payment for feed is motivated by business purposes. Buying a large quantity at a lower price or buying a large quantity in anticipation of shortage or increased prices, constitutes a good business purpose.
3. Deducting the entire cost of feed in the year of purchase does not result in a material distortion of income. This test has not been adopted by tax courts and only the IRS has been trying to apply it.
4. The payment does not include any compensation for future services to be performed by the managers of the cattle-feeding operation. Such a payment can be viewed by the IRS as deductible only in the years of actual performance of the services.

If the agreement to purchase cattle feed is worded carefully, it can lead to a substantial deduction.

4.4. Avoiding the Recapture of Excess Farming Loss Under Section 1251

An Excess Deductions Account (EDA) must be opened when an individual taxpayer using the cash method has non-farm adjusted gross income in excess of $50,000 and sustains a farm net loss in excess of $25,000. The amount added to the EDA is the excess of the farm net loss for the year over $25,000. After the first year of opening an EDA, each tax year's net loss is added and from it a tax year's net farm income is subtracted. When farm property is sold, an amount of capital gain up to the balance in the EDA will be recognized and taxed as ordinary income (Sec. 1251 (c) (2)). This rule will not disallow the deduction of farm losses but will result in a recapture of an already allowed farm loss as an ordinary income (Section 1251 recapture).

To avoid any possibility of recapture, a Subchapter S Corporation may be used. The stockholder of a Subchapter S Corporation should transfer all his farming activity to the corporation. Since he does not own the farm (the corporation owns it), he will not be required to maintain any Excess Deductions Account. Each year, the net loss of the Subchapter S Corporation is claimed as a deduction by the various shareholders, so that upon the sale of the farm, the gain from the sale (if any) will not be subject to any recapture from a remaining balance in the Excess Deductions Account. For this tax saving device you need to satisfy the following requirements:

1. None of the shareholders is an individual who has a farm net loss on his own. Through a transfer of all farm ownership to the corporation this requirement can be met.

2. The corporation's non-farm taxable income does not exceed $50,000. By creating more than one corporation, this requirement will be satisfied.

A taxpayer also can avoid the Excess Deductions Account and the recapture of already deducted farm losses by adopting the accrual method of accounting, using inventories and capitalizing all costs that belong to future accounting periods (Sec. 1251 (b) (4)). Either a change to the accrual method of accounting, or incorporation of farming activities and election as a Subchapter S Corporation, can lead to an escape of the recapture of excess farming losses under Section 1251.

Section 206 of the 1976 Tax Reform Act amended the farm loss recapture rules. Under the new rules of Section 206, no amount shall be added to the excess deductions account (EDA) of farmers for any taxable year beginning after December 31, 1975. However, the recapture rules under Section 1251 still apply to farmers with existing excess deductions accounts.

4.5. Minimizing the Taxable Income from Timber and Evergreen Trees

Section 631 (a) offers a choice to consider the mere cutting of timber as a sale or to defer the recognition of any gain or loss until actual sale takes place. Timber includes evergreen trees over six-years old when cut down as Christmas trees or for ornamental purposes. This choice can be exercised if the taxpayer owned the timber or a contract to cut it for more than six months before the beginning of the year when it was to be cut, and if he elects on his return, in writing, to recognize the gain or loss at the date of cutting the standing timber (Sec. 613 (a); 1.631-1).

If the taxpayer elects to recognize a gain or loss at the time of timber cutting, his gain or loss is computed as the difference between (a) the fair market value of the timber as of the first day of the taxable year in which it is actually cut, and (b) its cost or adjusted basis to the taxpayer.

If a loss deduction is expected, the taxpayer should use the date of timber cutting as an assumed or fictional date of sale. On the other hand, if a gain is expected, the actual date of the timber sale should be used as the time of income recognition.

Expenditures related to planting and cultivating Christmas trees are subject to their own rules (Treasury Department booklet "Farmer's Tax Guide" 1974 Ed., p. 28). You may deduct as ordinary business expense the cost incurred for shearing and basal pruning of trees, weeding or cleaning, and non-commercial thinning. Expenditures which should be capitalized include the cost of land improvements, such as road grading, ditching, and fire breaks, that have a determinable useful life in excess of one year. If such improvements do not have a determinable useful life, then their cost should be added to the basis of the land and would be recovered when the land is disposed of.

4.6. Expensing the Cost of Replanting a Citrus Grove

Expenditures incurred within four years after a citrus grove is planted must be capitalized. Expenditures incurred in replanting a citrus grove damaged or destroyed by frost, drought, disease, casualty, or pests, however, does not need to be capitalized (Sec. 1.278-1 (b)). Therefore, in the year of citrus grove damage or loss, a double deduction can be claimed by incurring planting or replanting costs before the end of the taxable year. The first deduction is for the damage or destruction of the old grove. The second deduction is through expensing the cost of replanting the citrus grove. The double deduction can bring the total tax bill for the year down if income from other activities is high. Otherwise, only the loss from damage or destruction is claimed in one tax year and the deduction for replanting is claimed in another tax year.

4.7. Allocating the Cost of Acquiring a Farm

If a farmer acquires land and buildings or land and livestock, or fruit orchards with a down payment and the remaining balance is to be paid on future dates, the following tax advantages can be claimed:

1. Depreciation deduction on the entire cost of buildings, orchards, or livestock. Depreciation basis includes both the indebtedness on the property and the cash investment.
2. For buildings, the structural components, e.g., wiring, floors, elevators, etc. should be given their own estimated useful life and each component depreciated separately (to maximize the depreciation deduction).
3. Interest and taxes are deducted against ordinary income even if the land or farm acquired is in a non-productive stage.
4. Gain or loss from the sale of livestock, unharvested crops, or cut timber may get Section 1231 favorable tax treatment. To maximize the benefit from Section 1231, all capital losses from the sale of Section 1231 assets will be realized in one year in order to claim them as ordinary losses and deduct them against ordinary income; whereas all Section 1231 gains from the sale of Section 1231 assets will be realized in another year and reported as capital gains receiving the long-term capital gain favorable treatment.
5. Land and buildings qualify as real property under the non-taxable

exchange rules. Instead of selling a farm and paying tax on a possible capital gain, it can be exchanged with a like property in a tax-free transaction.

6. While certain farm expenditures are deducted against ordinary income, the gain realized from the ultimate sale or disposition is subject to the favorable capital-gain tax treatment. An example of an operating expense is the cost of cattle feed; whereas the sale of livestock can qualify under Section 1231.
7. Cost of clearing land, not exceeding $5,000 or 25 percent of annual taxable income derived from farming, can be expensed at the taxpayer's option. The amount in excess of the lesser of $5,000 or 25 percent of taxable income will be capitalized (Sec. 182; 1.182-1-1.182-6).
8. If part of the dwelling house is used by a hired hand, then the expenses of maintaining the dwelling, including depreciation, should be apportioned. For this purpose, a son or daughter of the farmer is considered the same as any other hired hand if he or she is working for an agreed-upon compensation. If the son or daughter is a minor, however, the cost of maintaining the dwelling cannot be apportioned since a parent is legally obligated to care for a minor child.
9. Soil and water conservation expenditures can be expensed if the deduction per year does not exceed 25 percent of gross income from farming during the tax year. Expenditures in excess of the 25 percent of farm gross income are carried over to the following tax years (Sec. 1.175-5).
10. Cost incurred for fertilizer or other materials for enriching, neutralizing, or conditioning land used in farming can be deducted as a current expenditure without any dollar limitation (Sec. 180; 1.180-1, 1.180-2).

4.8. Developing a No-Basis Herd

Cattle breeding means owning a herd of bulls and cows and producing calves for sale. Usually, about 20 percent of the heifer calves and a few of the bull calves are kept for future breeding. The income of livestock operators is taxed as ordinary income unless the sale of cattle qualifies under Section 1231. If the sale is considered as a Section 1231 transaction, the gain will be reported as a long-term gain and receives a special tax treatment. In order to use Section 1231, the gain should result from the sale of animals used for breeding or dairy purposes.

The provisions of Section 1231 apply to livestock held for draft, breeding, dairy, or sporting purposes. However, the animal must be held for at least 12 months, except cattle and horses which must be held for 24 months or more. The holding period starts from the date of acquisition and not the date the animal was put to draft, breeding, dairy, or sporting purposes. For purposes of Section 1231, livestock includes cattle, horses, mules, hogs, donkeys, sheep, goats, and fur-bearing animals. Section 1231 assets do not include chickens, turkeys, pigeons, geese, fish, frogs, other birds, etc.

A cattle operator is in a position where he can routinely produce long-term capital gain from selling his animals used for draft, breeding, dairy, or sporting purposes after they qualify under Section 1231. For meeting Section 1231 requirement, the holding period must be observed carefully. Notice that an animal held for breeding, but not bred, may still qualify as a Section 1231 asset. For example, the sale of an unbred heifer, because it was found to be sterile or because of sickness or drought, would not prevent qualification under Section 1231. A cattle operator may use the capital-gain rules on a regular basis if he can develop what is called a no-basis herd. This means, raising heifer calves born to his purchased cows and using them as replacements for the purchased cows. Since the no-basis herd cannot be depreciated, its sale will not be subject to recapture of depreciation and at the same time the gain from its sale is reported as a long-term gain under Section 1231, as follows:

	Section 1231 No-Basis Cows	Section 1231 Cows with Basis
Selling price	\$500	\$500
Less: adjusted basis	0	100
Gain	500	400
Less: 50% Capital gain Deduction	250	200
Add back depreciation recapture	0	150
Total ordinary income	\$250	\$350

4.9. Expensing the Cost of an Orchard or Vineyard

Developing an orchard or vineyard will result in deducting the current expenses as they are paid or accrued from the time the seedlings are planted. Until the orchard or vineyard reaches the productive state, all farming expenses are deductible except capital expenditures. Some of the usual items of capital expenditures include the cost of land and buildings, equipment and machinery, fences, water wells, leveling and conditioning of land, purchasing and planting trees, and the cost of clearing land unless the election to treat land clearing cost as an expenditure is exercised (deductible expenditure cannot exceed \$5,000 or 25 percent of taxable income from farming).

Citrus and almond grove farmers are subject to special rules. They must capitalize all of the cost of planting, irrigation, cultivation, pruning, fertilizing, spraying, upkeep, and management fees of the citrus or almond grove if they are paid or incurred before the close of the fourth tax year beginning with the tax year in which the grove was planted (Treasury Department booklet "Farmer's Tax Guide" 1974 Ed., p. 28). If a portion of the grove is planted in one tax year and a portion in another tax year, each portion must be treated separately. A citrus or almond tree is considered planted on the date it is placed in the permanent location from which production is expected. Therefore, the productive period for citrus and almond groves is well defined and all the cost of pre-production must be capitalized, while the farmers of orchards and vineyards receive a better tax treatment.

4.10. Qualifying Farm Investments for the Investment Credit

Farmers should try to take advantage of the investment tax credit. For the period January 22, 1975, to December 31, 1980, the investment credit is up to 10 percent of the cost of certain tangible depreciable personal property. The investment credit may not exceed the tax liability, or $25,000 plus 50 percent of the liability over that amount (Sec. 46 (a), (c); 1.46-1). To qualify for the investment tax credit, the property must (1) be depreciable, (2) have a useful life of at least three years, (3) be a tangible personal property, and (4) be placed in service during the tax year. The following are examples of farm investments that qualify for the investment credit:

1. Machinery and equipment.
2. Cars and trucks may qualify if the estimated useful life is three years or more. The investment credit may be claimed even though the deduction for car operating expenses is claimed under the optional or the standard mileage method.
3. Livestock other than horses acquired after August 15, 1971. Special rules apply in determining the investment credit if substantially identical livestock is disposed of during the one-year period beginning six months before the date of acquiring qualifying livestock.
4. Fences used in connection with raising livestock. Also, fences used to keep livestock and other animals out of cultivated areas.
5. Paved barnyards used to keep livestock out of mud and for loading them onto trucks.
6. Water wells that provide water for raising livestock and poultry.
7. Drain tiles that enable the land to be used for agricultural purposes.
8. Groves, orchards, and vineyards in the productive stage.

9. Storage facilities used for the bulk storage of fungible goods, e.g., grain storage bins, corn cribs and silos. Farm buildings such as barns, stables, poultry houses and warehouses, however, do not qualify for the credit.

4.11. Selling Land and Unharvested Crops

A farmer or a nurseryman who grows crops, other than timber, that have not been gathered and sold during the tax year in which they are planted may, with the Commissioner's consent, report the income using the crop basis method. Under this method, the entire cost of producing the crop will be deducted in the year in which the crop is sold. If a farmer or a nurseryman does not elect the crop-basis method, he may deduct the cost of producing the crop in the year in which they are paid or incurred, without regard to the date of their actual sale (Sec. 1.61-(4) (c)).

A cash basis farmer can deduct all current expenses and not assign any cost of year-end inventories of cattle and crops. A farmer on accrual basis can even use the special rules under the crop-basis method. A farmer may also elect to deduct as current expenses the cost of soil and water conservation, fertilizing and land clearing instead of capitalizing them. The deduction for soil and water conservation is limited to 25 percent of the gross income from farming during the tax year. There is no dollar limit on expensing fertilizing costs. A farmer may elect to deduct as a current expense the cost of land-clearing up to the lesser of $5,000 or 25 percent of that year's taxable income from farming.

If land is held for more than six months and sold, together with an unharvested crop, the crop will be treated, like land, as Section 1231 property. The same rule applies to exchanges and involuntary conversion of land. Notice that if the crop is sold separately, any gain from it will be taxed as ordinary income. But, if it is left unharvested and sold (or exchanged) with the land, the gain will be reported under Section 1231. The general rule is that if the net from all Section 1231 transactions is a gain, then each gain or loss is a long-term capital gain or loss. If, however, the net from all Section 1231 transactions is a loss, then all the gains and losses are treated as ordinary gains and losses. Therefore, it may be rewarding to consider selling the land with any unharvested crop together, rather than selling each one of them separately.

4.12. Pricing Inventories of Crops and Livestock

A farmer may use the accrual method of accounting to report his income. Under this method, inventories at the beginning and end of the tax year, must be reported separately. However, the farmer has a choice to adopt any of the following methods:

1. The actual cost method where the price of purchased animals will be used or the cost of raising crops. If an animal was originally purchased, its cost is the purchase price plus any expense of raising it. If an animal was born on the farm, its cost includes the cost of raising it.
2. The second method is cost or market, whichever is less. The term cost is defined as in (1) above.
3. The farm-price method which may be used for reporting both crops and livestock. Farm-price means the current market value less any expected direct cost of sale, such as a broker's commission, freight or drayage charges and other handling expenses. It is better to use local market prices, rather than prices of a distant market.
4. The unit-livestock-price method which is used for reporting inventories of livestock only. Under this method raised livestock, depending on age and kind, are valued at estimated unit prices. It is customary to classify cattle into calves, yearlings, 2-year-olds, and mature animals before assigning any value to each class. If an animal is purchased, the unit price includes the cost of acquisition plus the cost of raising it. However, if the animal is purchased during the last six months of the tax year, no increase will be made in the purchase price.

For tax saving purposes the following suggestions should be considered:

1. If livestock is held for draft, breeding, dairy, or sporting purposes, the farmer has the option of either including such animals in inventory or capitalizing their cost and depreciating them. If such animals were purchased, their cost should be capitalized and subjected to depreciation. For raised animals held for draft, breeding, dairy, or sporting, however, it is better not to assign any basis through capitalization. For more detail see 4.8 of this chapter.

2. The cost or market, whichever is less, may prove to be advantageous if used for reporting crops inventory, while the unit-livestock-price method may serve well the valuation of livestock inventory.

4.13. Maximizing the Deduction for Depreciation

The deduction for depreciation may constitute a major item. Depreciable farming property includes machinery and equipment, autos and trucks, purchased livestock, fences, paved barnyards, water wells, drain tiles, storage facilities, buildings and their structural components, additions and improvements to buildings, land preparatory and development costs, citrus or almond grove development cost, Christmas tree cultivation cost, and any capital expenditure for the acquisition or improvement of an asset having a useful life of more than a year. Depreciable assets used in farming are eligible for the additional first-year depreciation. The deduction for additional first-year depreciation can be claimed on new or used tangible personal property with a useful life of six years or more. Special consideration should be given to these factors:

1. The additional first-year depreciation can be claimed only in the first tax year a depreciation deduction is allowable on such property.
2. Real property does not qualify for the first-year additional depreciation.
3. The maximum additional depreciation allowance is 20 percent of the cost (without reduction for salvage) of all qualifying property purchased during the tax year not in excess of $20,000 (or $10,000 if a separate return is filed).
4. To maximize the additional first-year depreciation deduction try to spread the acquisition of qualifying property over more than one tax year, if the total cost of acquisitions is expected to exceed $20,000 (or $10,000).
5. If the assets are recorded in separate accounts in the accounting records, each asset may be depreciated under a different method. If several assets are recorded in one account, however, the same method must be used for all assets in that account.
6. The declining balance method may be used to depreciate tangible property (except certain real estate) having a useful life of three years or more and acquired as new or constructed, reconstructed, or erected after December 31, 1953 (Sec. 167 (c); 1.167 (c)-1).

4.14. Sale, Exchange, or Involuntary Conversion of a Farming Asset

To a farmer, the sale or exchange of land, machinery, trucks, barns, sheds, etc., may constitute a significant event. Any property used in farming or the production of rents and held over six months, and any property held over six months that is subject to an involuntary conversion, is called "Section 1231" property. A gain or loss on the sale, exchange, or involuntary conversion of Section 1231 property may be a capital gain or loss, or an ordinary gain or loss, depending on the net from all Section 1231 transactions. In the case of a loss from a Section 1231 asset, the tax advisor should try to report it by itself without offsetting it against gain from another Section 1231 asset. In this way, the net result of all Section 1231 transactions will show a loss, and this loss will be deducted as an ordinary loss. Also, if a gain is expected from a Section 1231 property, this gain should be realized in a tax year when no loss from another Section 1231 asset is realized, in order to show a net gain from all Section 1231 transactions and to tax the gain under the special rules for long-term capital gains.

4.15. Minimizing the Taxable Gain from Sale of a Farm

The sale of a farm will usually include the sale of both non-business property (e.g., personal residence and furniture) and business property (e.g., land, buildings, machinery and livestock). The sale agreement should assign a separate price to each item sold or a separate agreement should be made for the sale of personal (on non-business) property. To minimize the possible tax liability on gain from sale of a farm, consider the following:

1. Postpone the gain from sale of residence under the replacement of residence rules. If the residence will not be replaced, try to report the sale under the installment method.

2. All business property sold, must be classified into:

(a) Capital assets held six months or less;

(b) Capital assets held over six months;

(c) Property (including real estate) used in business and held six months or less (including draft, breeding, dairy and sporting animals if held less than the holding period required under Section 1231).

(d) Property (including real estate) used in your business and held more than six months (including draft, breeding, dairy, and sporting animals if held for the period required under Section 1231).

(e) Property held primarily for sale or which is part of inventory.
After classifying the property sold according to these groups, assign the sale price to the various assets included in each group.

3. If the gain results from a condemnation, try to use the rules related to replacement of property.

4. If you sell under a contract that postpones all or part of the payments to a year after the year of sale, try to report the gain under the installment method.

5. The installment sale of an entire farm for a lump sum under a single contract should be avoided. Sale of a farm generally includes the sale of real and personal property that may be reported under the installment method and inventory items that may not be reported on the installment basis. The down payment and payments received in the year of sale must be allocated among the various property items sold. To avoid any possible problems related to price and down-payment allocation, draw more than one separate agreement. For example, a taxpayer sold his farm, including a residence, on June 1, 1976, and realized a gain as follows:

	Residence only	Farm, not including residence	Farm, including residence
Sale price	$30,000	$90,000	$120,000
Cost (or basis) plus expenses of sale	20,000	30,000	50,000
Realized Gain	$10,000	$60,000	$ 70,000

The $10,000 gain from the sale of residence is a capital gain. The tax on this gain can be postponed if the taxpayer acquires another residence at a cost of $30,000 or more (with in the required period of time). However, the $60,000 gain from the sale of the property used in the farm business is taxed, even though he may invest all of the $90,000 selling price in another farm. Also, part of the $60,000 gain may be taxed as ordinary income under the recapture rules of Sections 1245 and 1250. The installment method may be used if there are no payments in the year of sale, or the payments in the year of sale do not exceed 30 percent of the selling price. The 30-percent test is applied to the part of the sale price attributed to the real property and to the personal property, but not to inventory items.

4.16. Increasing the Amount of the Net Operating Loss Deduction

A farmer is entitled to the special rules of net operating loss deduction. A loss from operating a farm, or a casualty or theft loss in excess of income for the year, will result in a net operating loss. A net operating loss, may be carried back for three years and forward for five years. Section 806 of the 1976 Tax Reform Act extended the carryover period to 7 years. On top of that, under the new rules all taxpayers can elect not to carryback their losses and carry them forward only. However, a loss carryback may result in a refund of part or all of the income tax paid in the past three tax years. In figuring the net operating loss, all business income and expenses must be considered. Also, non-business deductions may not exceed non-business income for the tax year. In figuring the net operating loss, the following items should be reported as business expenses or deductions, thus increasing the amount of the net operating loss deduction:

1. Any state income taxes, for example on salaries and wages earned during the year.
2. Qualifying moving expenses paid or incurred during the year in connection with work at a new place of business.

3. Net loss from rental property.
4. Any loss on sale of real or depreciable property used in business or trade.
5. Loss on the sale of accounts receivable, if the taxpayer adopts the accrual method of accounting.
6. Casualty and theft losses related to property used in business as well as property used for personal purposes. If casualty and theft are related to a business asset, the holding period is important (more than 6 months, or 6 months or less).
   Also, the net casualty and theft gain or loss must be figured first from all business assets with a holding period in excess of 6 months, before treating the loss as an ordinary loss or a capital loss. For property used for personal purposes, the first $100 of loss from each casualty or theft is not deductible.
7. Losses on stock in small business corporations or Section 1244 stock that qualify as ordinary losses are allowable in determining the net operating loss.
8. A pro rata share of a Subchapter S Corporation's net operating loss. However, the pro rata share of the taxable income of a Subchapter S Corporation is considered a non-business income in figuring the net operating loss (Rev. Rul. 66-327, 1966-2 CB 357).

4.17. Using a Loss from a Disaster

A special tax rule can be used to refund an income tax paid in a prior year if a loss from a disaster is sustained. If the disaster occurs in an area, later determined by the President of the United States to warrant assistance by the Federal Government under the Disaster Relief Act of 1970, the taxpayer may deduct the loss from the income of the year immediately preceding the year of loss or wait and deduct it in the year in which the loss actually took place. For example, a disaster loss in 1977 may be deducted on the 1976 income tax return, or reported and claimed on the 1977 income tax return (Sec. 165 (h)).

If the taxpayer receives a Federal loan to replace property lost, damaged or destroyed as a result of a Presidentially-declared disaster, the amount of the loan cancellable under the Disaster Relief Act of 1970 should be reported as income and this will reduce the amount of deductible loss. If the disaster loss is claimed in one tax year and the disaster relief loan is canceled in another year, the loss will be deducted in one year and the Federal loan canceled is added to the income of a different year. (Under Section 2103 of the 1976 Tax Reform Act a special rule is used for deducting 1972 disaster losses.)

Under Section 2102 of the 1976 Tax Reform Act, any payments received under the Agricultural Act of 1949, as amended, as a result of (1) destruction or damage to crops caused by drought, flood, or any other natural disaster, or (2) the inability to plant crops because of such a natural disaster shall be treated as insurance proceeds received as a result of destruction or damage to crops.

This means a farmer can include payments from insurance as well as payments from the Department of Agriculture in his income in the tax year following the year of receipt if the income from the failed crops would normally have been included in the later year. Also, the new rules of Section 2141 allow a cash basis farmer, who has been forced to sell off livestock on account of a drought, to include any gain in income in the year following the year of the sale or exchange if he establishes that, under his usual business practices, the sale or exchange would not have occurred in the taxable year in which it occurred if it were not for drought conditions, and that these drought conditions had resulted in the area being designated as eligible for assistance by the Federal Government. The new rules of Section 2141 apply to taxable years beginning after December 31, 1975.

4.18. Electing the Income Averaging Method

It is usual for a farmer to show a relatively large income and good return on capital investment in one year, and low income or no profit in another year. Acts of nature play a substantial role in determining the final income of a farmer. The income averaging rules supply a needed relief. A farmer can elect the income averaging method for any tax year with an averageable income in excess of $3,000 if the taxable income for the year is more than one-fifth higher than his average income for a base period of the four preceding years. Notice that a farmer electing the income averaging method cannot use the following (Sec. 1304 (b); 1.1304-2 (a)):

1. The optional tax tables,
2. The averaging of the ordinary income distributions from self-employed retirement plans,
3. The exclusion of foreign source earned income,
4. The exclusion of income from sources within U.S. possessions,
5. The alternative tax on net long-term capital gains, and,
6. The maximum 50 percent tax rate on earned income

4.19. Contributing to a Self-Employed Retirement Plan

A farmer is considered as a self-employed taxpayer and qualifies for the retirement plans available for postponing the tax on current income to some later date. For more details about the self-employed retirement plans, see **1.12** of Chapter 1.

4.20. Tax Credits Available to a Farmer

An owner, tenant, or operator of a farm may be entitled to one of more of the following credits against his income tax:

1. Tax credit for the Federal Excise Tax paid on gasoline bought for use on a farm, on lubricating oil in other than a highway vehicle, and on fuels used on a farm for farming purposes (including diesel, special motor fuels, and aviation fuels). However, a farmer may purchase diesel, special motor, and aviation fuels free of Federal Excise Tax if the dealer delivers them into his storage tank.
2. If the taxpayer is 65 years of age or over, he may be entitled to a tax credit for the elderly. Persons under 65 may be entitled to a retirement income credit only if they receive a pension or annuity under a public retirement system.
3. The investment credit as explained under **4.10** of this chapter.
4. A work incentive program credit of up to 20 percent of wages paid to certain employees hired under the U.S. Department of Labor's Work Incentive (WIN) Program. Qualifying wages include cash wages, and must be paid or incurred for services performed by the employee during the first 12 months of employment (whether or not those 12 months are consecutive). Wages paid to certain related persons do not qualify for the credit.
5. A special credit for earned income is allowed under the Tax Reduction Act of 1975. The maximum earned income credit is equal to 10 percent of the first $4,000 of earned income. Above the first $4,000 of earned income, the credit is reduced by an amount equal to 10 percent of adjusted gross income over $4,000. Therefore, at the $8,000 adjusted gross income level, the entire credit is eliminated.
6. A credit for purchasing a new home constructed or under construction before March 26, 1975. The tax credit is equal to 5 percent of the purchase price not to exceed a maximum of $2,000.
7. A tax credit for 50 percent of political campaign contributions, not to exceed the maximum of $50 for joint returns ($25 for single returns and married taxpayers filing separately).

Chapter 5

TAX SAVING OPPORTUNITIES FOR PARTNERS AND PARTNERSHIPS

5.1. Admitting a Family Member to a Partnership

Admitting a family member to a partnership will result in income splitting. Both the taxable income and taxable estate of each partner will be less. Before admitting a family member (husband, wife, children, grandchildren) observe the following:

1. If capital investment is a major income-producing factor, arrange a reasonable compensation for the sale of part of the partnership. If the partnership is in a trade or manufacturing industry, then the new partner should "purchase" his share. He can do this through gifts (or other means) which will enable him to contribute to the needed purchase price (because the gift tax can be avoided through serial gifts or some other ways).
2. If the partnership is in a service industry, a major element is the personal skill of the newly-admitted partner. If his service can contribute to the profitability of the partnership, then admitting him as a partner is good for business.
3. If a family member is admitted to a partnership, there should be no limitation on his right to sell his interest and he should be treated publicly as a partner.
4. The transfer of part of ownership should be in writing, indicating the terms of the transfer.

5. Admitting a spouse to a partnership will not lower taxable income if husband and wife file jointly. However, if a spouse becomes a partner of a partnership in the field of trade, manufacturing or service industry, her share of earnings will be subject to the self-employment tax. This will lead to an extra tax liability (i.e., the self-employment tax) and to more Social Security benefits for the spouse since her Social Security coverage increases.
6. Splitting income by admitting a minor child is accomplished by transferring the rights of the child to a trust or guardianship. The child's mother can be the trustee or guardian. Admitting the child as a partner will not cancel the right of the parents to claim him as an exemption if they continue providing more than 50 percent of his support.

5.2. Accumulating Profits and Incorporating the Business

The net profit of a partnership is distributed annually between the partners and each one of them pays income tax on his distributive share without regard to whether the profit was actually paid to the partners or not. To avoid this unfair treatment of undistributed profit, and for other tax and legal reasons, sometimes it is advisable to incorporate the partnership. The change of form of business from a partnership to a corporation will be considered tax free if the following two rules are satisfied:

1. Property of the partnership is exchanged solely for stock and long-term obligations of the corporation.
2. Immediately after the exchange, the partners who incorporated own 80 percent or more of the corporation's outstanding capital stock.

The tax advisor may suggest the partnership form if profits are distributed concurrently between the partners. However, if accumulation of profit is desirable (for example to provide the business with needed working capital), then the corporate form of business should be examined.

5.3. Sale of Shares in a Partnership and Payments to a Retiring or Deceased Partner

The sale of shares in a partnership is treated like the sale of capital stock in a corporation (Sec. 741; 1.741-1(a)). It leads to a long-term or short-term capital gain depending on the ownership period. However, if part of the sale price is related to sale of accounts receivable or appreciated inventories, then that part of the sale price will be taxed as ordinary income. Observe the following:

Payments by the partnership (not remaining partners or outsiders) to a retiring or deceased partner for his entire share in the partnership are subject to Section 736 and, consequently, a clear distinction should be made between payments for interest in partnership assets and other payments. If the other payments are based on the future income of the partnership (say for five or ten years), then they are taxed as ordinary income of the retiring partner and are excluded from the income of the remaining partners (Sec. 1.736-1(a)(4), (6)). However, if the other payments are not based on future income of the partnership (i.e., a fixed amount for five or ten years), then they will be taxed as ordinary income of the retiring partner and deducted by the partnership as a business expense (Sec. 1.1736-1(a)(4)). The tax advisor should represent either the interest of the retiring (or deceased) partner, or protect the interest of the remaining partners.

5.4. Claiming the Deduction for First Year Additional Depreciation

In a partnership, each partner used to be able to deduct separately his share of the first year additional depreciation. The total cost of a newly acquired qualifying depreciable property was divided among the various partners. Each partner deducted 20 percent of his share of costs up to $10,000 ($20,000 for a married filing jointly) as a first year additional depreciation bonus (i.e., up to $4,000 for each partner filing jointly, or $2,000 for each partner filing a separate return). In this area a partnership used to have a tax advantage over a corporation or a sole proprietorship. However, for partnership taxable years beginning after December 31, 1975, the 1976 Tax Reform Act makes the $2,000 maximum first year additional depreciation applicable at both the partnership and the partner level. As a result, the partnership will only be able to claim through its partners their allocable shares of the maximum $2,000 (or 20 percent of cost up to $10,000) limit.

5.5. Maximizing the Effect of the Investment Credit

When a partnership acquires depreciable tangible personal property, the investment tax credit is allocated between the partners according to their share of partnership profit, unless the partnership agreement adopts a different method of allocation. To maximize his share of the investment credit, a partner should consider the following:

1. The partner's share of the investment credit should be stated in the partnership agreement. If the partnership agreement does not allocate different items in different proportions, the investment credit

will be shared in the general profit and loss ratio. When a partnership agreement is made or changed, a partner may require a special ratio to allocate the investment credit.

2. If qualified depreciable tangible personal property is disposed of, ceases to be qualified, or becomes public utility property before its useful life ends, part or all of the investment credit may be recaptured. The partnership agreement may include a special provision that allows a partner to avoid recapture when he retires (Sec. 1.46-3(F)).
3. The admission of a new partner may reduce the interest of an old partner in the partnership. If the interest in partnership is reduced by more than one-third of what it was when the property was acquired, part of the investment credit claimed in a prior year may be recaptured in the year of sale of part of the interest. Therefore, before selling a substantial share of ownership in a partnership, it is better to check if the investment credit recapture rules apply (Sec. 1.47-6). For example, Partner B sells half of his 50 percent interest in the Partnership of ABC. His sale of part of the interest took place three years after he claimed an investment tax credit of $1,400 on his share of qualified investment made by the partnership. The sale of half of his interest in this partnership would result in the recapture of $700 (one-half of the $1,400) of the original credit. The investment credit recapture is reported in the year of sale.
4. Coordination between the business activities of the partnership and those of the partners will save taxes. When a partner expects a high taxable income and a high income tax bill, the partnership can help by carrying on any needed replacements and acquisitions of depreciable personal properties. On the other hand, the partnership should not acquire property in a year when the partners expect low or no taxable income. Through proper timing, acquisitions of qualifying property can be delayed or made prematurely.

5.6. Allocating Capital Gains and Losses Between the Partners

The partnership agreement may allocate capital gains and losses between the partners. If the agreement is silent, the gain or loss is shared in the general profit and loss ratio. The following observations may assist in reducing the effects of the tax on capital gains:

1. A partner who acquired his interest by purchase or upon the death of a partner is called a transferee partner. If the transferee partner paid more for his interest in appreciated assets than the partnership's basis for the assets, he may find it advantageous to request the partnership to adjust the basis of its assets. The partnership's electing to adjust the basis of the property will not affect any old partners and the effect of the election

is limited only to the transferee partner. The election to adjust the basis of partnership property will benefit the transferee partner since it will produce a higher basis in appreciated assets. Upon the partnership's sale of the appreciated assets, the transferee partner will report a lower capital gain since he will use the higher basis due to the elective adjustment to basis of partnership property (Sec. 1.743-1(b)).

2. Each partner will pick up his share of partnership capital gains and losses and include them in his individual tax return, whether distributed to him or not. The short-term or long-term tax treatment depends on the partnership's holding period, not the length of time a partner held his partnership interest. The partnership does not take a long-term capital gain deduction. Each partner takes the deduction on his individual return. The partnership does not take a capital loss deduction. Each partner takes his share of capital loss and claims it on his individual return, if it does not exceed his adjusted basis in the partnership (before reduction by the current year's losses). Therefore, to take advantage of the special tax treatment of capital gains and losses, coordination is needed between the partnership and the activities of the partners. The principle of "timing" should be used to serve the partners since there is no income tax imposed on the partnership. A schedule for disposing of partnership assets can be adopted in advance rather than taking a partner by surprise.

3. When property subject to the recapture of depreciation under Section 1245 and Section 1250 is sold at a gain, only the excess of total gain over depreciation recapture is reported as Section 1231 gain. Each partner (not the partnership) will pick up his share of Section 1231 gain and report it on his individual return with his other Section 1231 gains and losses. If his net from all Section 1231 transactions is a gain, then each gain or loss is a long-term gain or loss. However, if his net from all Section 1231 transactions is a loss, then each gain or loss is an ordinary income or loss item. Therefore, the partnership should realize a gain from Section 1231 property only when the partner (especially a major partner) has a loss sufficient enough to offset it from the disposition of his other Section 1231 transactions. The partnership through proper "timing" may also line up the disposition of its Section 1231 assets in order to show a net loss from all of them in one specific tax year.

4. The partnership may elect the installment method to report the gain from sale of real property and certain personal property. When the gain from sale is reported under the installment method, the partners will generally benefit from the deferment of tax on the unrecognized gain. However, if the partner expects a net capital loss from his other activities, or a low taxable income for the year, it could be advantageous for him not to elect the installment method by the partnership.

5. When a partner receives money other than his distributive share of earnings, gain is recognized only to the extent that the money received exceeds his basis for interest in the partnership. If a partner receives property other than his distributive share of earnings, then the gain or loss is generally not recognized until the partner disposes of the property. Special rules apply to distribution of unrealized receivables or inventories, and distributions in complete liquidation of partner's interest (Sec. 735(a)(1); 735(a)(2)). Generally the distribution of property will create problems for both the partnership and the recipient partner since the distribution reduces the partner's basis for his partnership interest. It is better to make money distributions and use the property (or other than money) distribution only upon the complete liquidation of the partner's interest.

5.7. Partnership Elections That Influence Each Partner's Share of the Net Operating Loss Deduction

A partner is allowed to claim his distributive share of the partnership's net operating loss for the year. He should, also, take into account his distributive share of allowable non-business deductions in order to combine it with his individual non-business deductions (e.g., charitable contributions, tax return preparation fees, expenses of property not currently productive, political contributions, etc.). Since the net operating loss deduction is not available to partnership, each partner should try to maximize the benefit from his share of net operating loss by offsetting his income from other sources against it, or using it as a loss carryback or carry over on his individual return.

Notice that although the partnership cannot use its own net operating loss and does not pay tax on its taxable income, it can affect the amount of net income or loss reported by each partner through a choice of selecting different methods of reporting income. Elections available to a partnership cover the following main areas:

1. Cash or accrual method of accounting.
2. Installment method of reporting gain from sale of stock in trade, real property and certain personal property.
3. The completed contract or percentage of completion method.
4. Election of depreciation method.
5. In certain cases the choice of deducting or capitalizing certain expenditures.
6. Election of a method for pricing merchandise inventory.

In these situations, each partner cannot make his own election. Therefore, the partnership must make the election after a careful consideration of the effects on each partner.

5.8. Allocating Different Income and Expense Items in Varying Proportions Between the Partners

The partnership agreement may allocate different income and expense items in varying proportions among the partners. If an item is not subject to a special agreement, it should be shared in the general profit and loss ratio. This general rule is very important and should be well remembered since it affects more than one area of partnership taxation. For example, upon the sale of a Section 1245 or Section 1250 property, depreciation recapture will be allocated to the partners in the general profit and loss ratio, unless the partnership agreement adopts a different method. The partnership agreement may allocate all of the depreciation recapture to the original contributor of the property, to present partners only, or to present, as well as, ex-partners. Thus, the agreement may provide a tax saving or an extra burden to the partner. The tax advisor should pay attention to this area especially if the basis of an asset contributed by a partner is other than the fair market value of the property when it was exchanged for a capital interest in the partnership.

For example, Mr. Smith owns a depreciable personal property that cost him $10,000 and he claimed on it $4,000 of depreciation. He and Mr. Brown formed a partnership. The partnership accepted this personal property assigning to it a current fair market value of $9,000. If the partnership sells this property in a future year, Mr. Brown may end up with a share of depreciation recapture when the property was owned by Mr. Smith. The only way to protect the interest of Mr. Brown is to adopt a partnership agreement allocating depreciation or/and depreciation recapture in varying proportions.

5.9. Maximizing the Benefits Under the Pension Reform Act of 1974

An active partner who receives income from self-employment can participate in pension and profit sharing plans. Since the partner is considered an "owner-employee," he cannot get coverage for himself unless he provides coverage for all full-time employees with three or more years of service. If a partner owns more than 10 percent capital or profit interest in more than one business, he must cover all the qualifying employees in all the businesses he controls. A partner who owns more than 10 percent of either the capital or profit interest in a partnership is considered an owner-employee and may contribute annually to his retirement plan up to 15 percent of his earned income or $7,500, whichever is the lesser. His annual minimum deduction is the lesser of $750 or 100 percent of earned income. If the partner is not considered an owner-employee, he will still qualify for retirement contributions as a self-employed individual, and may deduct the lesser of 15 percent of his earned income or $7,500. For maximizing the benefits under the Pension Reform Act of 1974, a partner may consider the following:

1. If the partner owns 10 percent or more interest in a partnership, he is considered an owner-employee and the partnership may contribute on his behalf more than $7,500 per year to a qualified retirement plan. The excess of contributions over the deductible amount are subject to a cumulative 6 percent excise tax only. In addition, an owner-employee can make nondeductible voluntary contributions up to $2,500 or 10 percent of his earned income, whichever is the lesser, without incurring the 6 percent excise tax on the excess contributions, if the other employees are permitted to make similar voluntary contributions.

2. It may be desirable to form a husband-wife partnership or admit the wife as a partner, which would qualify the wife for retirement benefits. This may double the deductible contribution to a retirement plan. The tax advisor must check first the validity of such a family partnership from an income tax point of view.

5.10. Fringe Benefits Available to a Partner

The owners of a corporation usually resort to one or more of the following methods in order to minimize their tax liability:

1. "Thin capitalization" or making a small capital investment in the corporation in order to advance the corporation interest bearing loans.
2. Payment of salaries to shareholder-employees, deducting the salaries from the gross income of the corporation.
3. Having shareholders lease property to the corporation.

In case of a partnership there is no need to resort to these methods. Double taxation is eliminated under the partnership form of ownership since there is no federal income tax imposed on the partnership. Hence, for tax saving purposes the partnership may use, instead, the route of providing one or more of the following fringe benefits for its partners:

1. Under IRC Sec. 101, amounts received by reason of death are excluded from gross income. In order to enjoy this exclusion the following two conditions must be met:

(a) The proceeds are paid under a life insurance contract, and,

(b) The proceeds are paid by reason of the death of the insured.

A partner has an insurable interest in the life of another partner and may carry a life insurance contract on him. Any proceeds he receives upon the death of the insured are tax-free. Notice that under the "transfer-for-value" rule a limitation is placed on proceeds from a policy transferred for valuable consideration, prior to the insured's death. Under the limitation of the transfer-for-value rule the amount excluded by the transferee may not exceed an amount equal to the sum of (1) the actual value of the consideration, and (2) the premiums subsequently paid by the transferee. However, the transfer-for-value limitation does not apply to the following transfers:

(a) If the partnership transfers a policy directly to the insured and he in turn "gives" the policy to his wife or beneficiary.

(b) If the insured transfers a policy directly to his partner or to the partnership (in which the insured is a partner).

2. Amounts received for personal injuries or sickness are excluded from gross income. For example, if a partner in the course of his work suffers from an injury and collects under both the Workmen's Compensation Act as well as in settlement of his claims for personal injuries, such amounts are excluded from gross income under Section 104.

3. A partner-employee can exclude from his income all or part of three benefits related to the employer's contributions to accident and health plans. These are: (1) sick pay, (2) reimbursement for medical expenses, and (3) benefits paid for bodily harm or injury by the partner-employee or a member of his family. The partnership should adopt a qualified accident or health plan and establish a wage continuation plan. It does not matter whether benefit payments are made directly by the partnership or through an insurance company. The partnership contributions, whether under insured or self-insured plans and whether made for one or many employees, are excluded from the employee's gross income. The amounts paid by the partnership are deductible as a business expense. However, such plans must benefit both partner-employees as well as other qualifying employees. Notice that, the 1976 Tax Reform Act tightened up the exclusion for sick pay. The new rules apply for years beginning after 1975 and limit the sick pay exclusion to taxpayers under 65 who retire on disability.

4. Under IRC Sec. 109, no amount is to be included in gross income of a landlord because of improvements made by the lessee. Also, the value of any improvements made will not be added to the basis of the real property of the lessor even if the real property and improvements will return to the lessor upon termination of the lease. Therefore, a partnership can lease a real property (land or land and buildings) from a partner, and erect a building or do other improvements. If improvements are not made

in lieu of rent, the owner (partner) will not add the value of the improvements to his gross income. The lessee (partnership) will write off the cost of the improvements over the shorter of the remaining period of the lease or the estimated useful life of the improvements. When the owner (partner) sells the real property, the difference between the sale price and the adjusted basis of the real estate will be taxed as a capital gain (and not as ordinary income).

5. IRC Sec. 119 states that the value of meals and lodging furnished to an employee for the convenience of the employer is not to be included in the employee's gross income. A partner-employee may enjoy the exclusion if the meals are furnished at the employer's (or partnership) business premises; and he may exclude the value of lodging only if he is required to accept it as a condition of his employment.

6. Group-term life insurance can be purchased for employees as well as a partner-employee. For more details about group-term life insurance see **5.11** of this chapter.

7. Moving expenses are deductible either by the partner as a self-employed or by the partnership as an employer if the partnership reimburses the partner for his moving expenses. Notice that for tax years beginning after 1976 the rules for deducting moving expenses are eased to qualify shorter moves (35 miles down from 50 miles), and to increase the maximum deduction for moving expenses (premoving expenses up to $1,500 and total qualified moving expenses increased from $2,500 to $3,000).

8. A partner-employee may participate as an "employee" in a qualified Section 401 plan. An inactive partner who gets income entirely from his investment cannot participate in a formal pension or profit-sharing plan. A partner can take tax deductions for contributions he makes to formal pension or profit-sharing plans, and the partnership may deduct its contributions for partners under such plans. The following requirements should be met in order to qualify for the plan:

(a) Coverage is provided for all full-time employees with three or more years of service.

(b) The plan provides for immediate vested benefits for all covered employees.

(c) The benefits to an employee start not later than age 70 1/2 or the year he retires, or to a partner-employee, not later than age 70 1/2.

(d) Benefits cannot be paid to a partner-employee before he reaches age 59 1/2 unless he becomes disabled. If it is a profit-sharing plan, a definite formula for determining contributions to be made for employees must be used (does not apply to a partner-employee).

9. For taxable years beginning after December 31, 1976, and ending before January 1, 1982, any amounts contributed by an employer on behalf of an employee, his spouse, or his dependents under a qualified group legal services plan are not included in the gross income of the employee. To qualify for this new exclusion under Section 2134 of the 1976 Tax Reform Act, observe the following:

(a) An employee can exclude the value of personal (or non-business related) legal services provided under a qualified group legal services plan or exclude instead of that any amounts paid by the employer for legal services to the employee, his or her spouse, or his or her dependents. The exclusion does not apply to direct reimbursements made by the employer to the employee.

(b) The group legal services plan should not discriminate in favor of individuals who are partners or highly compensated employees.

(c) Not more than 25 percent of the amounts contributed under the plan during the year may be provided for employees who are partners, each of whom owns more than 5 percent of the capital or profits interest in the partnership.

(d) The plan should be written and must specify the benefits that will be provided through prepayment of, or provision in advance for, legal fees in whole or in part.

5.11. Using Group-Term Life Insurance Plans

Group-term life insurance represents a major fringe benefit which may be provided by an employer. It will lead to the following tax savings:

1. The employer may take a tax deduction for the full premium he pays since it is considered a necessary business expense.
2. Premiums paid by an employer to provide coverage of up to $50,000 are not added to the income of the employee.
3. If the employee is a "substandard" insurance risk, (e.g., substantially overweight), the term life insurance will cost more. There is no provision disallowing the employer a deduction for this added cost of insurance.

Under the IRS Reg. 1.79-1(b)(1) distinction is made between a group-term life insurance plan covering less than ten employees, and a plan covering ten employees or more. If less than ten employees are covered by the plan, the following three requirements must be met:

1. All full-time employees with more than six months of service are covered unless they do not qualify for coverage on the basis of a medical questionnaire (not the same as a medical examination).
2. The amount of coverage is computed as a uniform percentage of salary.

3. The eligibility and the amount of insurance cannot be made contingent on a medical examination.

If the group-term life insurance plan covers ten employees or more, the employer may provide coverage for all employees or only a specified part of them. If the owners (or partners) are the only ones covered, however, this section will not be applicable.

5.12. Adoption and Change of a Tax Year

Under IRC Sec. 706 a newly-formed partnership should adopt either (1) a tax year which is the same as the tax year of all its principal partners (a principal partner for this purpose is one having a 5-percent or greater interest in the partnership capital or profit), or, the same as the tax year to which all its principal partners with different tax years are concurrently changing, or (2) a calendar year if all its principal partners are not on the same taxable year. A prior Revenue Service approval is needed for adoption of a fiscal year different from that of all its principal partners. This general rule prevents a new partnership from adopting a fiscal year and the partners reporting on a calendar year basis. Therefore, if a partnership is formed, say, February 1, 1977, and adopts a taxable year ending January 31, 1978, the tax on the first 11 months of income cannot be postponed for a full year under the rules of IRC Sec. 706.

If the newly formed partnership adopts a tax year different from that of one or more of the partners, then the partners will have a sufficient "business reason" to request a change in their tax year to the partnership tax year (the application is made on Form 1128). For example, Mr. Brown and Mr. Smith are calendar year taxpayers. On August 1, 1977, they formed a partnership with a fiscal year ending July 31, 1978. They may request from the Revenue Service a change in their tax year to that of the partnership. On approval of the change, Mr. Brown and Mr. Smith must file returns for the short period from January 1, to July 31, 1977. In this way the partners will benefit from filing a return for the short period of January 1, to July 31, 1977. Therefore, in the year of establishing a new partnership, a tax saving can be achieved by adopting a different fiscal tax year to which all its principal partners are concurrently changing. Notice that the changing partners must file their request for a change in tax year by the 15th of the second month after the end of the short period for which a return is required because of the change.

5.13. Partners Receiving Money or Property in Excess of Their Distributive Share of Earnings

A partnership may distribute to its partners money or property in excess of their distributive share of earnings. The effect of the excess distribution could result in either a gain or loss to the partners or no recognized gain or loss. If the distribution is in cash, a gain is recognized only to the extent that the cash received exceeds the basis for the partner's interest in the partnership. If the excess distribution is in property other than money, however, gain or loss is generally not recognized until the partner disposes of the property.

Therefore, if the partners wish to receive distributions in excess of their distributive share of earnings, observe the following:

1. Do not make the excess distribution in money, instead distribute property.
2. Do not include in the distributed property any inventory items or unrealized receivables. Any gain from sale of such items will be taxed as ordinary income (if the inventory item is disposed of within five years from the date of distribution to the partner).
3. If the partnership distributes property, assigning to it a value different from the partnership's basis for such property, an optional adjustment is allowed: (a) the partnership can elect to maintain the same basis for the property it retained not affected by the distribution, or (b) the partnership may elect under Section 754 to adjust the basis of the retained property to reflect (1) any gain or loss recognized to the distributee partner on the distribution, and (2) any excess of the adjusted basis of the distributed property in the hands of the partnership over its basis in the hands of the partner. This optional adjustment may lead to an increase or decrease in the basis of property retained by the partnership. The adjustment method is recommended in case of distributions for liquidation of the partner's interest. For example, partner (A) owns one third interest in a partnership with a basis of $20,000. The partnership has assets consisting of cash, $22,000, and property with a basis of $38,000 and a value of $45,000. Partner (a) realizes a gain of $2,000 when he receives, in a liquidating distribution, a cash payment of $22,000. If the partnership elects to adjust the basis of the property it retained, the partnership basis for the property becomes $40,000 ($38,000 plus $2,000).
4. No gain or loss is recognized (or taxed) to the partnership making the distribution, whether the distribution is of money or of other property.
5. Gain is recognized to the partner receiving the distribution only to the extent that any money distributed exceeds his basis for his partnership interest.
6. Loss is recognized to the partner receiving the distribution if the distribution is in liquidation of his interest in the partnership, the distribution consists only of money, unrealized receivables and inventory, and the money plus the basis to the partner for such other property is less than his basis for his partnership interest.

5.14. Minimizing the Tax Liability of a Withdrawing Partner

Payments to a withdrawing (or retiring or deceased) partner may result in a capital gain or loss, or ordinary income to the withdrawing partner. Generally, payments for the interest in partnership assets (other than unrealized receivables, substantially appreciated inventory, good will, or payments measured by partnership income) are treated as distributions resulting in a capital gain or loss. But other payments are taxed as ordinary income. To minimize the tax liability of the withdrawing partner, notice the following:

1. Payments for interest in partnership assets can be reported under the installment method. If mixed payments are made in installments, each annual amount must be allocated between payments for the interest in assets and other payments.
2. Payments based on partnership income will be taxed as ordinary income to the withdrawing partner without regard to the period over which they are paid. They are considered as distributive shares of the partnership's ordinary income.
3. Payments should be defined as payments for interest in assets or other payments. In case of an expected loss to the withdrawing partner, a larger amount should be specified as other payments. On the other hand, in case of an expected gain to the withdrawing partner, a larger amount should be allocated to payments for assets.
4. The agreement with the partnership should make it clear whether such payments represent amounts paid by the surviving partners in purchase of the deceased partner's interest or represent the estate's share of the income of the partnership of which the estate is, in effect, a partner. The tax treatment these payments receive affects not only the tax liability of the withdrawing partner (or his estate) but also the tax liability of the remaining partners. The terms of the partnership agreement and the nature of the partnership will determine the tax effect of such payments.

5.15. Tax Saving Ideas While Negotiating the Sale of a Partnership

Under IRC Sec. 751 any amount received from selling a partnership, or an interest in a partnership, which is attributable to unrealized receivables or to inventory items that have appreciated substantially in value, is to be treated as received on the sale or exchange of a noncapital asset, and therefore. taxable as ordinary income. Unrealized receivables include the right to payment for goods delivered or to be delivered, or for services, to the extent that those rights are not currently included in income under the partnership's method of accounting. Also, unrealized receivables include mining property, real and personal property subject to depreciation recapture under Sections 1245, 1250, and 1251, to the extent that the sale of such property by the partnership at its fair market value would have given rise to ordinary income rather than to capital gain.

Appreciated inventory includes not only stock in trade (or merchandise inventory), but also any property which is not a capital asset, e.g., a literary property. Inventory is considered to have appreciated substantially in value if its fair market value is more than 120 percent of its adjusted basis and more than 10 percent of the value of all the partnership assets other than money. While negotiating the sale of a partnership, the following factors should be considered:

1. The sale price should be allocated between the various assets sold. Also, allocation is made between the various items within one type of assets. The idea is to reduce the difference between the value and basis of the assets within the class (or type). Thus, a gain or excess of value over basis will be offset against a loss or a decrease in value below basis of another item.
2. If real property and personal property are sold, special care should be exercised in the assignment of values since the recognized capital gain (loss) or/and ordinary income (loss) will depend on this assignment of values.
3. If the components of real property were depreciated separately, the sale price assigned to the real estate should be broken down to cover the various parts included in the sale.
4. The gain from sale can be reported under the installment method if the seller elects this method of reporting and satisfies all the requirements of installment reporting.
5. Since the sale price will not, usually, be paid entirely upon the consummation of the agreement, the seller may charge interest on the unpaid balance. The seller may offer a lower interest rate in exchange for a relatively higher total sale price, with a larger portion of this sale price assigned to the capital assets of the partnership.

5.16. Minimizing the Self-Employment Tax While Enjoying the Rules of Maximum Tax on Personal Service Income

A partner in a partnership engaged in a trade, business or services, is considered a self-employed. This creates a liability for the self-employment tax, and may generate a tax saving under the provisions of the maximum tax on earned income.

1. If a partner has more than one business, his self-employment income is his net share from all businesses. The self-employment tax on a partner is computed on his total self-employment income including his distributive share of the partnership net income, without regard to whether or not it was actually received. Notice the following special situations and suggestions:

(a) Although a Subchapter S Corporation is treated like a partnership for income tax purposes, the share of a stockholder of the Subchapter S Corporation's net income is not subject to the self-employment tax. Only the compensation for services received by the stockholder-employee of a Subchapter S Corporation is subject to the Social Security tax. This adds another tax advantage to Subchapter S Corporations advantage over "partnerships" to Subchapter S Corporations.

(b) If the partnership deals with farming activities, such income is subject to special rules. Income from farming may be taxed under an optional method for the computation of the self-employment tax.

(c) The nature of the activities of the partnership (e.g., trade, manufacturing, service, etc.) determines the liability for the self-employment tax, and not the services contributed by the individual partner.

(d) It may be desirable to form a husband-wife partnership, instead of operating as a sole-proprietorship, in order to pay a self-employment tax on the distributive share of the wife. This will maximize the combined retirement benefits of the husband and wife.

2. Section 302 of the 1976 Tax Reform Act establishes a maximum marginal tax rate of 50 percent on personal services taxable income. Therefore, Section 302 provides a tax relief since income from personal services cannot be taxed at a rate higher than 50 percent. If the partnership is in a service industry, all the distributive share of the partner is considered as personal service income (even if a substantial capital investment is needed). However, if both personal services and capital are material income-producing factors, personal service income may not exceed 30 percent of net profit (from trade or business). Notice that the maximum rate on personal service taxable income cannot be used if the tax liability for the year is figured under the income-averaging method, or if a husband and wife file separate returns. The tax advisor should try, whenever the partner is in a high tax bracket, to combine the special rules of the maximum tax on earned income with the alternative tax on capital gains.

Chapter 6

TAX SAVING OPPORTUNITIES FOR OWNERS OF CLOSELY HELD CORPORATIONS

6.1. Special Tax Saving Idea in the Year of Incorporation

A new corporation can end its tax year at any date within 12 months from the date of incorporation or active conduct of regular business activities. If the corporation is profitable, the 26 percent corporate surtax on profit in excess of $50,000 can be avoided by selecting a first short tax year. Therefore, in the year of incorporation, special care should be exercised before electing to use a first short tax year, or to use a regular 12-months accounting period. For example, a corporation was created on September 10, 1975. As an end to its tax period, either December 31, 1975, can be selected or September 10, 1976, or any other date. The tax advisor should realize the tax break offered for the year of incorporation since a proper selection of tax year can lead to avoidance of the corporate surtax for at least part of the first tax year.

6.2. Purchasing Life Insurance on the Life of Controlling Stockholders with One or More of the Employees as Beneficiaries

Section 264 provides that a taxpayer may not deduct premiums paid on life insurance covering the life of (1) an officer, (2) employee, or (3) any person with a financial interest in the business, if the taxpayer is directly or indirectly a beneficiary under the policy. Therefore, if the company carries insurance on the life of one of its executives, with the company as a beneficiary, the premiums paid by the company are not deductible. If, however, the company carries insurance on the life of an executive with the executive's estate or his own beneficiaries as the recipient of the insurance proceeds upon his death, then any premiums paid by the company are deductible business expenses since they represent an additional compensation for services paid to the executive. The premiums in this case are deductible by the company and added to the taxable income of the executive.

The rules of Section 264 can be employed to serve economic as well as tax objectives. For example, a controlling stockholder may not have anyone in his family to take over the corporation after his death. At the same time, this controlling stockholder may have special interest in seeing the corporation continue after his death (e.g., to continue paying dividends to his estate, to protect the value of his shares of capital, or to continue a business venture he started and developed into a successful corporation, etc.). This key stockholder may favor an executive in his organization although this executive lacks the capital needed to own stock in the company. The solution here could be to use the rules of Section 264 as follows:

> The company will purchase life insurance on the life of the controlling stockholder with one or more of the employees as beneficiaries. The employee-beneficiary will use the proceeds upon the death of the controlling stockholder to pay for stock purchased under a pre-arranged purchase agreement.

The tax and economic effects of this plan can be summarized as follows:

1. The corporation will deduct as an expense the annual life insurance premiums since the company is not named as the beneficiary from the life insurance policy.
2. The selected employee (or employees) will add the premiums to his (or their) periodic taxable income.
3. Upon the death of the controlling stockholder the beneficiary-employee will use part or all of the insurance proceeds to acquire shares of capital from the estate of the deceased stockholder.
4. The estate of the deceased stockholder will receive extra cash for part of its holding (or all of its holding) and the corporation will be controlled by the new management which was preselected by the deceased stockholder.

6.3. Splitting the Capital Investment in a Corporation Between Capital Stock and Loans

Any dividend paid by a corporation is not a deductible expense by the corporation and is taxable to the stockholder. A dividend paid to stockholders is considered as distribution of income and not an ordinary business expense. However, through "thin incorporation" the stockholder can split his capital investment between capital stock and loans. In this case, any interest paid on the loans is deductible as an expense from the taxable income of the corporation. The repayment of the loan itself is a tax-free return of debt (neither deductible by the corporation nor taxable to the lending stockholder). If "thin incorporation" is used observe the following (*Northern Fire Apparatus Co.*, 11 BTA 355; *Comm. v. Hood,* 141 F 2d 467, 32 AFTR 423; Rev. Rul. 68-54, 1968-1 CB 69):

1. The debt instrument should be in writing and a specific reasonable rate of interest should be stated. The debt should be due at a specific date or upon demand. Repayment of the debt and interest is not related to earnings and profit.
2. In general the ratio between the investment in capital stock and the amount of debt should not exceed three-and-one-half dollars of debt to one dollar of stock investment.
3. The debt and interest are recorded and reported separately in the accounting books and financial statements.
4. If the corporation is owned by more than one stockholder, the percentage of stock ownership should differ from the percentage of debt-ownership.

6.4. Avoiding the Penalty on Excessive Accumulation of Retained Profit

A corporation may become subject to a penalty on accumulated earnings. The accumulated earnings penalty is 27 1/2% of accumulated taxable income up to $100,000 and 38 1/2% of the amount of accumulated taxable income over $100,000. To avoid this penalty on excessive accumulation of retained profit, adopt one or more of the following:

1. Establish the business need for the accumulation of net profit. Draw in writing specific plans for business expansion. Proper business needs cover the areas of increasing working capital, replacement and expansion of plant and equipment, retirement of debts, setting up a reserve to insure against contingent liabilities, adding a new product, acquisition of a new business, etc. Do not use as a reason for the accumulation of earnings any of the following:

(a) Payments of loans to stockholders, their friends or relatives.

(b) Purchase of life insurance covering the lives of stockholder-employees.

(c) Investment in certificates of deposit, marketable securities, and saving accounts.

(d) Payment of fringe benefits to stockholder-employees.

(e) Investment in activities unrelated to the business activities of the corporation.

2. Elect to be taxed as a Subchapter S Corporation.

3. Pay dividends during the tax year or/and within two-and-one-half months after the end of the tax year. This is the least desirable solution since it leads to double taxation. If dividends are paid, the stockholder receiving the dividend will pay income tax on them, while at the same time, the distributing corporation will not claim the dividend distribution as a deductible item.

6.5. Using Stock Redemption Plans

If a closely held corporation is profitable and is expected to continue generating profits, a stock redemption plan can be used to absorb any accumulated earnings and subsequently avoid the penalty on excessive accumulation of earnings. For example, if a father owns a corporation, he can transfer part of his stock ownership to his son. Assume that the value at the date of transfer is $5 per share and the son holds the stock for at least ten years; then he offers the stock to the corporation for redemption at $20 per share. The first $5 paid to the son is a return of his capital investment and it has no tax effect. The remaining $15 per share is a long-term capital gain and enjoys the special treatment granted to long-term gains. The corporation will use its accumulated earnings to redeem the stock and therefore escape the penalty on excessive accumulation of retained profit.

Under a stock redemption plan watch for the following:

1. Before a stockholder redeems any stock he should hold it for at least ten years (Sec. 302 (c) (2) (B)).
2. After redeeming the stock, the same stockholder cannot reacquire shares in the same corporation for at least ten years unless acquisition is through bequest or inheritance.
3. Redemption of stock of a shareholder should cover all (not part) of his stock ownership.
4. For at least ten years after stock redemption, the stockholder cannot act as an officer of the corporation, a director, or employee.
5. In the year of redemption, the stockholder must file a statement notifying the IRS.

6.6. Getting Cash Out of Your Own Corporation Without the Declaration of Dividend

If a stockholder receives cash from his corporation and such payment is called a dividend, he should pay income tax on it. If the cash received is in exchange for the cash surrender value of a life insurance policy transferred to the corporation, then he will not pay any income tax on the amount received. If the stockholder transfers an insurance policy with a cash surrender value to his corporation charging the corporation with an amount not in excess of the value of the policy, he will not realize any gain. This is a good way for a stockholder to get cash out of his corporation without the declaration of dividend. Eventually if he dies, the corporation will receive money from the insurance policy in a tax-free transaction.

Before selling your insurance policy to your corporation, be sure to establish that the corporation has an insurable interest in you (which is easy to establish). Also, avoid receiving from the transfer an amount in excess of the value of the life insurance policy. Any payment in excess of policy value is completely taxable to the stockholder as ordinary income.

6.7. Transferring Investments in Capital Stock of Various Corporations to Your Own Corporation

An individual taxpayer can exclude each year up to $100 or $200 from dividend income received from domestic corporations. On the other hand, a corporation can deduct 85 percent of dividend income received from other non-affiliated domestic corporations. Therefore, an individual stockholder will realize a tax saving from transferring his investment in capital stock of various corporations to his own corporation. When the stocks in the various corporations pay dividends, the dividend exclusion will not be limited to $100 or $200 per year. Since the stock is owned by a corporation, 85 percent of the dividend received will not be taxed. For tax saving purposes just remember not to run into the penalty on the personal holding company. This penalty is imposed on closely-held corporations with income mainly from investments such as rent, dividend, interest, royalties, etc. Suggestions for avoiding the penalty on the personal holding company are covered in 7.3 and 7.19 of Chapter 7.

6.8. Electing the Treatment of a Subchapter S Corporation

If you fear a penalty from unreasonable accumulation of earnings, you can, at the end of the year, try to elect the treatment as a Subchapter S

Corporation and within two-and-a-half months declare a dividend. The dividend declared within two-and-a-half months after the end of the year can be considered a dividend made in the year before. This method of avoiding the penalty on unreasonable accumulation of earnings is allowed, although the dividend declared by the Subchapter S Corporation is related to retained earnings, accumulated when the corporation was taxed as a regular corporation. For more details about Subchapter S Corporations, see Chapter 7 of this book.

6.9. Deducting Payments for Salary, Interest, Bonus or Other Expenses Owed to a "Relative"

If a corporation is using the accrual method of accounting, it should actually pay in the year the expense is incurred, or within two-and-a-half months after the end of its accounting period, any expense connected with salary, interest, bonus, or any other expense owed to a "relative." The term "relative" includes for the purpose of this rule: a spouse, child, brother, sister, grandparent, grandchild, or a more than 50 percent stockholder of the corporation (Sec. 267 (b) (2)). If the corporation is on accrual basis, the "relative" is on cash basis, and if the payment for salary, interest or bonus is not made within two-and-a-half months from the end of the accounting period of the corporation, the IRS will disregard such a deduction as a business expense claimed by the corporation and tax it to the stockholder as dividend. This same rule applies to partners and proprietors. Late payment to a "relative" of theirs who is on cash basis may result in the same loss of a business deduction. The solution is to remember this rule and if cash is not available for the payment, borrow and use the proceeds to make payment within two-and-a-half months from the end of the accounting period. Another solution is to give a note for the payment. Payment in notes meets the payment condition (*Musselman-Hub-Brake Co. v. Comm.*, 139 F. 2d 65, 31 AFTR 1001; *Miller, Inc. v. Comm.*, 164 F. 2d 268, 26 AFTR 250; Rev. Rul. 55-608, 1955-2 CB 546).

6.10. Maximizing the Benefit from the Investment Credit

If your individual tax bracket is higher than your closely-owned corporation tax rate, you can maximize the benefit from the investment credit by acquiring any needed machines and equipment under your own name. In this way, you will claim the investment credit on your personal tax return. After that, incorporate and transfer the machines and equipment to the newly-created corporation. Such a transfer is not subject to the investment credit recapture rules. Another way is to purchase the machines and equipment and claim the investment credit on your personal tax return and after some business-related use, transfer the machines and equipment to an already existing corporation you own. This second method can be used if the newly-acquired machines and equipment can be put to use in another business venture of your own while "waiting" for a transfer to the already existing closely-owned corporation.

6.11. Avoiding Unfair Taxation of Excessive Compensation for Services Paid to a Stockholder-Employee

If the compensation for services paid to a stockholder-employee is deemed excessive, the IRS will consider the excess compensation as a dividend income and tax it to the recipient stockholder (Sec. 1.162-7; 1.162-8). At the same time the corporation cannot claim such payment as a deductible business expense. To avoid a case like this, state in writing in the corporate minutes that any payment as compensation for services made to a stockholder-employee and considered by the IRS as excessive should be repaid back to the corporation. If the stockholder-employee has a pre-existing obligation to return such payments, they cannot be taxed to him as dividend income.

6.12. Using a Deferred Compensation Plan

A stockholder-employee may earn a large income and pay tax at a relatively high rate before the years of his retirement. Normally, he may also pay tax at a lower rate after his retirement. To minimize the total tax liability, a deferred compensation plan can be adopted. Under the plan, the stockholder-employee will be paid for previous services. The corporation can still deduct the payments as compensation for services, and the stockholder-employee will pay tax on such compensation at lower tax rates. To pass the examination of the IRS, such deferred compensation plans need to meet the following requirements (Rev. Rul. 60-31, 1960-1 CB 174; Rev. Proc. 71-19, 1971-1 CB 698):

1. The plan is in writing and is established before the compensation actually earned.
2. The deferred compensation is not set aside or deposited in a special escrow or fund account.
3. Income from the plan is not currently available to the employee. The right of the employee to receive the compensation will start at a certain predetermined future date or when the employee reaches a specific age.
4. It is better to state in the deferred compensation plan that the employee agrees not to engage in a competing business activity. Also, that the employee will make himself available for consultation after

his retirement. This will support the conversion of the employee status from full-time to part-time employee.

6.13 Taking Advantage of the Lower Tax Rate on Long-Term Capital Gains Taxed Under the Regular Method

The long-term capital gain of a corporation is taxed under the regular method or the alternative method. Under the regular method, the capital gain is added to the ordinary income of the corporation and taxed at the ordinary corporate tax rates (starting at 20 percent). Under the alternative method, the capital gain is not added at all to ordinary income, rather it is taxed at a special capital gain tax rate of 30 percent. Of course, the regular method with its 20 percent tax rate (assuming no surtax payment) is better than the alternative method with its 30 percent tax rate. To take advantage of the lower rate under the regular method you may consider one or more of the following ideas:

1. To use the installment method in order to defer part of the gain to future years.
2. To sell part of the property in one year and to sell the remaining in another year or future years.
3. To sell a property with a loss in the same year of selling a property with a gain.
4. To switch from the regular method of taxing the capital gain to the alternative method and vice versa, depending on whether or not the corporation is paying tax on its ordinary income at 20 percent, 22 percent or 48 percent.

6.14. Tax-Free Withdrawal of Corporate Surplus Under Section 303

Many closed or family corporation owners desire to carry life insurance. The proceeds from such insurance will be used to pay any estate tax which will accrue upon death with any remaining cash left for their families. If an individual acquires life insurance coverage on his own life, the premiums paid are not deductible for income tax purposes since any proceeds received upon death are not taxable. It is not desirable for many individuals to pay a premium of $2,000 or $3,000 each year on a life insurance policy without being able to deduct it on their income tax returns. The solution is simple if you are an owner of a closely-held corporation.

Sell any life insurance policy you own with a market value (usually equal to cash surrender value) to your corporation. Require the corporation to acquire any desired additional life insurance. If the corporation is made beneficiary from the life insurance policy, the premiums paid by the corporation are deductible for income tax purposes. Upon the death of the owner of the closely-held corporation, his company receives the proceeds from the life insurance policy without paying tax on it. Afterwards, his family will redeem enough shares of capital stock under Section 303 in order to receive any cash needed to settle the estate and pay the estate tax. Any funds withdrawn from the corporation under Section 303 to pay death taxes (including interest), and funeral and administration expenses, qualify for a tax-free withdrawal of corporate surplus (and not as a dividend distribution). Redemption under Section 303 should meet the following three conditions (Sec. 303; 1.303-1—1.303-3):

1. The stock to be redeemed was included in the gross estate of the deceased stockholder, and
2. The value placed on all of the stock of the deceased stockholder, in the redeeming corporation, is either (a) more than 35 percent of the value of the decedent's gross estate, or (b) more than 50 percent of the value of the decedent's taxable estate, and
3. The redemption takes place after death and within three years and 90 days after the date the federal estate tax return is due to be filed or, if there is a Tax Court proceeding, within 60 days after the Tax Court's decision becomes final.

When the closely held corporation owns a life insurance policy on the life of a stockholder, be sure that the corporation has "full" ownership of the policy. The corporation should be the beneficiary and the stockholder should have no right to change the beneficiary or exercise any power related to ownership.

The 1976 Tax Reform Act changed the redemption requirements under Section 303. To qualify for capital-gain treatment under Code Sec. 303, the value of the decedent's stock in the corporation whose stock is being redeemed will have to be more than 50 percent of the value of the adjusted gross estate (i.e., gross estate less the deductions for administration expenses, debts, taxes and losses). Also, the new law extends the time for redemptions in cases where deferred payment of estate taxes is elected. The new rules apply to estates of decedents dying after December 31, 1976. Furthermore, under the new rules the decedent's basis is carried over and as a result a redemption under Section 303 will mean a capital-gain tax on the excess of the stock's value over the carryover basis. Therefore, the tax advisor should consider carefully whether an estate prefers to distribute the stock rather than to redeem it.

6.15. Deducting Contributions to a Retirement Plan

Qualified pension, profit-sharing or annuity plans are given favorable tax treatment. Qualified plans can be established by a corporation, partnership, or a sole proprietorship. All earnings of a qualified plan, including capital gains, are tax-exempt. This will allow the accumulation of investment income and capital gains without payment of an income tax. The contributions of the employer to the qualified plan are deductible by the employer in the year in which they are made. The employee participating in the qualified plan is not taxed until the year or years in which he actually receives the distributions. All of the following requirements should be met to qualify a plan under Sec. 401 (a)(d):

1. The plan is for exclusive benefit of the employees, or their beneficiaries.
2. The sole purpose of the plan is to offer the employees or their beneficiaries either (a) a share of the profits of the business, or (b) an income after retirement.
3. Contributions or benefits provided under the plan will not discriminate in favor of employees who are officers, shareholders, supervisory employees, or highly paid employees.
4. The employer intends the plan to be permanent.
5. The plan is in writing and is communicated to the employees.
6. The plan provides non-forfeiture of benefits when it ends.
7. Benefits cannot be paid to an owner-employee before he reaches age 59 1/2 unless he becomes disabled. A premature payout to him does not adversely affect the qualification of a plan in regard to his employees covered under the plan.
8. The benefits to an owner-employee begin not later than age 70 1/2, and to his employees not later than age 70 1/2 or the year of retirement.

It is advisable to request, on Form 4574, a Revenue Service determination letter regarding the approval of the initial qualification or amendment of a plan.

6.16. Avoiding the Creation of Unwanted Dividends to the Stockholders

Payment of dividends is disadvantageous from a tax point of view since dividends are taxable to the stockholders but not deductible by the corporation. Shareholders of a closely-held corporation may create unwanted dividend income as a result of one or more of these activities:

1. Regular withdrawal of "loans" from the corporation, without actual repayment by the shareholder (Sec. 163 (a); 1.163-1(a)).
2. Unreasonable compensation for services paid to the stockholder-employee (Sec. 1.162-7, 1.162-8).
3. Improper reimbursement for out-of-pocket expenses incurred by the shareholder and charged to the corporation, such as travel expenses, meals and lodging, medical expenses, entertainment, etc.

4. Sale of corporate property to the shareholder for a price below the fair market value of the property.
5. Payment of interest on loans from the shareholders, if the investment in the corporation is deemed as "thin capitalization" (Sec. 385).
6. Use or enjoyment of corporate assets (e.g., cars, yachts...) by the shareholders and for personal purposes without proper payment of rent.
7. Excessive payment by the corporation to the shareholder for consulting fees, rent, interest, or royalties.
8. Payment by the corporation of personal expenses of the shareholder.
9. Payment by the corporation for the purchase of a property from a shareholder, if the price is in excess of the property's fair market value.

Chapter 7

TAX SAVING OPPORTUNITIES FOR OWNERS OF SUBCHAPTER S CORPORATIONS

7.1. Preventing the Loss of Election to be Treated as a Subchapter S Corporation

The election to be treated as a Subchapter S Corporation will be lost if a new shareholder fails to file a consent within 30 days after becoming a shareholder (Sec. 1372 (e); 1.1372-4). To prevent such failure, amend the corporation bylaws to show either one of the following provisions:

(A) "No one can transfer stock without first offering it to the corporation" or,

(B) "If an existing stockholder wants to revoke his consent, he must first offer his shares of capital stock to the corporation."

Amendment (A) of the bylaws will prevent a sudden transfer of stock to a new stockholder without knowledge of the other shareholders. Amendment (B) of the bylaws will prevent "revenge" by a dissatisfied stockholder.

Section 902 of the 1976 Tax Reform Act changed the rule of terminating a Subchapter S election when the corporation adds a new shareholder. Effective for taxable years beginning after December 31, 1976, the election as a Subchapter S Corporation continues unless the new shareholder affirmatively acts to terminate it. Most new shareholders must elect to terminate a Subchapter S election within 60 days after acquiring stock in the corporation. Therefore, under the new rules, a new stockholder does not need to consent to the election. He needs to act only if he wishes to terminate it. To prevent a new stockholder from electing to terminate the election, add to the bylaws of the corporation either one of the above-mentioned provisions. Such provisions should positively act as an added precaution protecting majority shareholders.

7.2. Paying Salaries to Stockholders

Income of a Subchapter S Corporation is taxed to the shareholders. For tax purposes it makes no difference whether the payment to the shareholder is labeled as salary or dividend. Both salaries and dividends are reported by the shareholders as ordinary taxable income. However, since the maximum tax on earned (or personal services) income provides an optional limit of 50 percent on the rate of tax on earned (or personal services) income in excess of $52,000 for a married filing jointly ($38,000 for a single or head of household), it could be advantageous to make the payment to the stockholder as salary. Notice that the compensation for the stockholder-employee's services should be reasonable and not excessive.

7.3. Saving Taxes Through the Election as a Subchapter S Corporation

Election to be treated as a Subchapter S Corporation will lead to the following tax advantages:

1. Eliminate double taxation which usually results from incorporation since there is no tax on the Subchapter S Corporation.
2. Avoid the penalties on personal holding companies or the unreasonable accumulation of earnings.
3. The net operating loss suffered by the Subchapter S Corporation is distributed among the stockholders and each can deduct his share (on his personal tax return) as an ordinary loss.
4. The gain from sale of stock in the Subchapter S Corporation is treated as a capital gain and taxed as long-term or short-term gain, depending on the stock holding (or ownership) period.

7.4. Timing the End of the First Accounting Period

A one-shot, large tax saving can be achieved by incorporating a profitable sole proprietorship or partnership and immediately electing the treatment as a Subchapter S Corporation. The reason for this tax saving is that if the tax rate of the business owner is high, then his total tax for the year will be less if he can split his annual income between two tax periods. The first period is up to the date of incorporation and the second period depends on the end of the tax year of the corporation. For example, if you incorporate on July 1, 1977, then elect the treatment as a Subchapter S Corporation with a first short year from July 1, 1977 to February 28, 1978, the income from six months before incorporation is taxed in 1977 and since it belongs to a half year only, the top tax bracket will be relatively lower. When the newly created corporation ends its first short tax year on February 28, 1978, file a tax return reporting net income from eight months (July 1, 1977, through February 28, 1978). Beginning with March 1, 1978, use a 12-months tax year. If the stockholders report on a calendar year basis, the Subchapter S Corporation should adopt an accounting period ending on the last day of January or a subsequent month (instead of the preceding December 31). This way, the income of the corporation will not be taxed to the stockholders until the following year.

It may also be desirable to time the end of the first fiscal year so that it will immediately precede the high income season. This would enable the new corporation to defer reporting the tax for the longest possible period. The new corporation may also change its adopted annual accounting period, with the approval of the Commissioner (Sec. 1.442-1(c)). A return for a corporation from the date of incorporation to the end of its first accounting period is not considered a fractional year return and the income for the short tax year does not need to be annualized (Sec. 443). Returns for periods of less than 12 months due to change of accounting period must, however, be placed on an annual basis (Sec. 443 (b)).

7.5. Using an Operating Loss from a Corporation

If you expect an operating loss from your corporation while you show profit from other sources of income, you can elect the treatment as a Subchapter S Corporation and write off your share of loss against your other income. In the following year, if you expect a profit from the corporation, you can terminate the election and be taxed again as a regular corporation. A point to remember is that once an election has been terminated (or revoked), a new election (to be treated as a Subchapter S Corporation) cannot be made for five years, unless the IRS consents to an earlier election (Sec. 1372 (f); 1.1372-5).

7.6. Offsetting Losses and Gains from Various Business Enterprises

If you own two regular corporations and you expect a gain from one corporation and a loss from the other, you can elect to treat both of them as

Subchapter S Corporations. This way, on your personal income tax return you can offset the loss from one corporation against the gain from the other.

7.7. Eliminating Double Taxation Before Selling a Greatly Appreciated Corporate Asset

If you own a regular corporation and this corporation owns a greatly appreciated asset, when the corporation sells the asset it will realize a large capital gain and pay tax on it. Eventually, you will take the money from the corporation and again pay a tax on it, since it constitutes a dividend income to you. To eliminate this double taxation, before selling the corporate asset, convert the corporation to a Subchapter S Corporation, and then sell the appreciated asset. The capital gain will be taxed as your personal gain. In the year after the sale, you can terminate the election and the corporation again will be a regular corporation. Since after revoking or terminating the election as a Subchapter S Corporation, you need to remain as a regular corporation for at least five years; it will be a good planning device to line up all the greatly appreciated corporate assets and to sell them while the election as a Subchapter S Corporation is still in effect. Notice the special limit imposed upon the capital gains of a Subchapter S Corporation if its net long-term capital gain exceeds $25,000 (Sec. 1378 (a); 1.1378-2). Any net long-term capital gain in excess of $25,000 is taxed to the Subchapter S Corporation. This capital-gains tax provision can be avoided if the Subchapter S Corporation was treated as such for the three years immediately preceding the taxable year in which a net gain exceeding the $25,000 limit occurred. The capital-gains tax provision does not apply if the Subchapter S Corporation is new and has been in business for less than four years operating under a continuing election for each of its tax years.

Generally, a Subchapter S Corporation will not pay any tax on its ordinary income or capital gains. Both ordinary income as well as capital gain pass through to the shareholders and are taxed to them. Existing corporations that make the election to be taxed as a partnership (or Subchapter S Corporation) may, however, have to pay a capital-gains tax during the first three years they operate under the election. An electing corporation is liable for tax only if its taxable income for the year is more than $25,000 and the excess of net long-term capital gain over net short-term capital loss is both more than $25,000 and more than 50 percent of taxable income. The tax on capital gain is not imposed on the electing corporation after three years of operating under the same election.

7.8. Distributing Retained Earnings upon Termination of the Election as a Subchapter S Corporation

Upon termination of the election to be taxed as a Subchapter S Corporation be sure to distribute any retained earnings which have been taxed to the stockholders. The distribution can be made within two-and-a-half months after the end of the tax year of the Subchapter S Corporation. In this way, you avoid double taxation on such earnings when the regular corporation will later declare dividends from earnings accumulated while the corporation was treated as a Subchapter S Corporation.

Since a delay in making distributions may result in double taxation, it is suggested that a Subchapter S Corporation make an actual distribution each year equal to the amount of the shareholders' "constructive dividend" as defined under Section 1373 (b). This will lead to complete distribution of earnings without retention of profits in the corporation. Such a proposal is possible if the corporation can finance its operations without retaining part or all of its earnings. Notice that if the corporation distributes earnings, and the shareholders, by prearrangement, advance the money as loans to the corporation, the IRS may not consider the distribution as cash dividend and it may also consider the "obligations" as a second class of stock, thus, resulting in a termination of the election as a Subchapter S Corporation.

7.9. Maximizing the Benefit from Passing Through a Net Operating Loss to the Stockholder

Net operating losses of a Subchapter S Corporation are passed on to its shareholders. If the current income of a shareholder is not large enough to absorb his share of the loss, the loss will be carried back for three years and over for five years, like an operating loss. The 1976 Tax Reform Act increased the carry forward period to seven years. The amount claimed by a stockholder as his share of operating loss cannot exceed the adjusted basis of his stock plus the adjusted basis of any indebtedness owed him by the corporation. If the shareholder wishes to claim his share of operating loss without losing any part of it and to receive some tax refund from carrying backward or forward part or all of the loss, the shareholder and his tax advisor should observe the following special rules:

1. The corporation or its shareholders may not apply a loss carryback or carryover from a non-electing year against the income of an

electing year (Sec. 172 (h); 1.1374-1 (a)). Therefore, if a non-electing corporation has a loss, carry the loss backward to its non-electing years, or wait until the loss is written off completely against taxable income of future years, before making an election to be taxed as a Subchapter S Corporation.

2. The corporation cannot carryback or forward a net operating loss arising during an electing year. Only the shareholders (on pro-rata basis) can claim the deduction for such a loss (*Byrne v. Comm.*, 17 AFTR 2d 1272, 361 F. 2d 939).

7.10. Paying Fringe Benefits to the Shareholder-Employee

Shareholder-employees in a Subchapter S Corporation should channel as much of their income as possible into fringe benefits paid by the corporation. The tax advantage to the shareholder-employee is to receive benefits without any increase in taxable income. The Subchapter S Corporation paying for the fringe benefits will deduct the payments, and as a result, lower the net earnings and profit available for distribution as a taxable income to the shareholders. Certain types of fringe benefits will also defer income of the shareholder-employee to future years when the taxpayer is in a lower tax bracket. In addition, the use of fringe benefits in lieu of other compensation or direct distributions of profit is also advantageous to Subchapter S shareholder-employees because the fringe benefits would be purchased at special group rate prices and with before tax dollars. Without the fringe benefits, the undistributed income of the Subchapter S Corporation would be higher, resulting in higher taxes for the shareholder-employee, and also higher rates (or cost) for the individual fringe policies. The following types of fringe benefits should be considered carefully:

1. The cost of meals and lodging is not taxed to the shareholder-employee if paid for the convenience of the employer.
2. The first $5,000 of payments to beneficiaries of a deceased employee are deductible by the employer and not taxable income to either the employee or his beneficiaries.
3. The employer may furnish an auto for business use or reimburse the shareholder-employee for the use of personal auto for business purposes.
4. If the employer adopts a wage continuation plan (also called a sick pay plan), both the employer and employee will benefit, since any payment under such a plan is also exempted from the Social Security tax. The employee may qualify for the sick pay exclusion.
5. The corporation may reimburse part or all of moving expenses.

6. The corporation may pay part or all of the medical expenses and medical insurance of the employee and his family.
7. The employer may provide $50,000 of tax-free group life insurance for shareholder-employees as well as for other employees.
8. The shareholder-employee may enjoy the use of entertainment facilities financed by the corporation such as boats, hunting lodges, memberships in clubs, etc.

7.11. Adopting a Retirement Plan, Stock Option Plan, or a Profit-Sharing Plan

A Subchapter S Corporation, like a regular corporation, may offer part or all of the following benefits to its own employees including any shareholder-employee:

1. Retirement plan,
2. Stock option plan,
3. Profit sharing plan.

If the electing corporation adopts a retirement, stock option or profit sharing plan, any shareholder-employee owning more than 5 percent of the outstanding stock (ownership by related persons is added under the constructive ownership of stock rules) must include in his gross income, and pay tax each year on the amount which the corporation contributes on his behalf in excess of (1) 15 percent of his compensation, or (2) $7,500, whichever is less. However, this excess contribution is still completely deductible by the corporation.

The 15 percent or $7,500 limitation applies only to "defined contribution" (or profit sharing and stock option plans) and does not apply to "defined benefit" (or pension) plans. However a Subchapter S Corporation's stock option or profit-sharing plan is not "qualified" unless it provides that forfeitures of contributions or benefits by employees on account of termination of employment, etc. cannot benefit an employee who is also a more-than-5 percent shareholder.

Of course any individual who is not an active participant in a tax qualified retirement plan should check into the possibility of setting up his own individual retirement plan.

7.12. Using the Income Averaging Method

The income of a Subchapter S Corporation is distributed among its shareholders and is taxed to them. A shareholder may experience a significant increase in his income and may find income averaging a worthwhile tool in tax saving. An individual taxpayer may elect the income averaging method for any tax year with an averageable income of $3,000 if the taxable income for the year is more than one-fifth higher than his average income for a base period of the four preceding years. Notice that by electing the income averaging method, the taxpayer cannot use the following (Sec. 1304(b); 1.1304-2(a)):

1. The optional tax tables,
2. The averaging of the ordinary income distributions from self-employed retirement plans,
3. The exclusion of foreign source earned income,
4. The exclusion of income from sources within U.S. possessions,
5. The alternative tax on net long-term capital gains, and
6. The maximum 50 percent tax rate on earned (or personal service) income.

7.13. Saving the Self-Employment Tax

A sole-proprietor or a partner in a partnership must pay a self-employment tax on taxable self-employment income from a non-exempt trade or business. However, income from a corporation that has elected to be taxed as a partnership (or a Subchapter S Corporation) is not income from self-employment (Rev. Rul. 59-221, 1959-1 CB 225). Therefore, by incorporating a trade or business and electing the treatment of a Subchapter S Corporation, the self-employment tax can be eliminated.

If a shareholder in a Subchapter S Corporation desires to be covered by Social Security under the Federal Insurance Contributions Act, he may render services to the corporation as an employee. A shareholder-employee is subject to the F.I.C.A. tax and the employing corporation is entitled to a deduction for both compensation paid and the F.I.C.A. tax on the employer.

7.14. Dealing with Tax-Exempt Income

Certain items or transactions qualify under the non-taxable income rules. However, when a non-taxable income item is received by a Subchapter S Corporation, it will increase its accumulated (retained or undistributed) profits. While the recipient corporation enjoys the item without any payment of tax, the shareholders will not be as fortunate when the dividend distribution is made to them. A tax-exempt item retains its status between the hands of the receiving corporation but loses its special tax treatment the moment it enters into the retained earnings account of the corporation (Rev. Rul. 68-128, 1968-1 CB 381). Therefore, any tax-exempt income should be realized among the hands of the shareholders and not the corporation itself. The area of tax-exempt income affects mainly the following two types of income:

1. Tax-exempt interest from state and municipal bonds should be reported by the shareholders, and, the corporation should not own any tax-exempt securities.

2. A more important area of tax-free income is life insurance proceeds. The proceeds of life insurance policies, if paid by reason of death of the insured, are excluded from gross income of the recipient. The exclusion applies to a corporation taking out the policy with an insurable interest in the life of the insured. The shareholders will be taxed on dividend when the corporation uses it proceeds from life insurance to pay the dividends.

7.15. Paying Fringe Benefits vs. Thin Capitalization

One of the widely used methods of reducing the taxable income of a corporation is to resort to "thin capitalization" and payment of interest on loans from shareholders. A Subchapter S Corporation affords a "cleaner" method of avoiding double taxation. Offering loans to the corporation and charging interest, and offering personal services to the corporation and charging unreasonable compensation, is less desirable under a Subchapter S Corporation. Instead, the availability of fringe benefits for shareholder-employees becomes more significant since the election as a Subchapter S Corporation would automatically neutralize the problem of double taxation.

Notice that if thin capitalization is used, the IRS may consider the prearranged "obligations" of the corporation as a second class of stock, and as a result, the corporation may lose the election as a Subchapter S Corporation (Rev. Reg. 1.1371-1 (g); See also *Henderson v. U.S.,* 245 F. Supp. 782, 16 AFTR 2d 5512). If the debt obligations are owned in substantially the same proportion as the creditors' stock holdings, they would be treated as contributions to capital (or equity investment) rather than true debt.

7.16. Using a Subchapter S Corporation for Farming Activities

A cash basis taxpayer in the business of farming must keep an excess deductions account if he sustains a farm net loss. Any farming net loss should be added to the EDA if the individual taxpayer has over $50,000 in non-farm adjusted gross income for the year and the addition to the EDA is only to the extent his farming loss exceeds $25,000. Special rules apply to corporations (other than Subchapter S Corporations) and trusts. A regular corporation or trust must add all of its net farming losses to its EDA, without regard to the two limits applicable to individual taxpayers. Therefore, an individual taxpayer has a tax advantage over regular corporations in the area of net farming losses since his addition to an EDA is required only if both his non-farming adjusted gross income is over $50,000 and his net farming loss for the years is over $25,000. Notice that if a cash basis taxpayer has a balance in his EDA, part or all of the gains realized upon his sale of the following property will be recaptured as ordinary income:

1. Depreciable personal property held for more than six months,
2. Cattle or horses held for two years or more, and other livestock held for one year or more for draft, breeding, dairy or sporting purposes, and
3. Unharvested crops growing on land held for more than six months.

A Subchapter S Corporation has a mixed treatment in the area of recapture of farm losses and the EDA. If the shareholders of a Subchapter S Corporation carry all their farming activities (i.e., transfer all their farms) through the Subchapter S Corporation, then the corporation applies the rules related to an individual taxpayer regarding the addition to an EDA. However, if a stockholder in a Subchapter S Corporation has his own farming loss, or owns stock in another tax-option corporation with farming loss, the corporation adds to its EDA in accordance with the rules applicable to regular corporations.

To reduce the possibility of having any gain from selling farming depreciable personal property, livestock or unharvested crops taxed as ordinary income from recapture of farming losses, the shareholders of a Subchapter S Corporation should transfer all their farming activities to one Subchapter S Corporation. For tax years ending after December 10, 1971, if the corporation has a shareholder who owns stock in another tax-option corporation reporting a farm net loss, the rules related to a regular corporation should be used (Sec. 1251 (b)(2)(B)).

Section 206 of the 1976 Tax Reform Act added a special rule terminating the addition to excess deduction (EDA) accounts. For any taxable year beginning after December 31, 1975 there will be no further additions to excess deduction accounts of farmers. However, the old rules for EDA accounts still apply to existing accounts.

7.17. Maximizing the Benefit from the Investment Credit

The investment tax credit is available to qualified investment in either new or used property. However, only $100,000 ($50,000 for years beginning before 1975 and after 1980) of the cost of used property is eligible for the credit. Also, the investment credit cannot be more than the first $25,000 of the tax liability, plus half of the excess. If the credit is not completely used in one year, it may be carried back to the three preceding years and forward for seven years. Section 802 of the 1976 Tax Reform Act provides for a first-in, first-out use of the investment credits. Under the new law, carryover credits are used first, then credits earned in the current year, and finally carryback credits. To maximize the benefit from the investment tax credit, spread the purchases of used qualifying property over more than one accounting period since there is a limit on the amount of cost of used qualifying property. For more details about the tax benefits of the investment credit, see Chapter 12 of this book.

7.18. Liquidating a Subchapter S Corporation

Under Code Section 337 (a), if a corporation adopts a plan of complete liquidation, and distributes all of its assets (less assets retained to meet liabilities) within a 12-month period beginning on the date of the adoption of the plan, the corporation will not recognize any gain or loss from the sale or exchange of property. Only the shareholders of the corporation will recognize a gain or loss upon the redemption of their stock holdings at the end of the complete liquidation. The IRS (Rev. Rul. 65-235, 1965-2 C.B. 88) has ruled that an informal agreement by shareholders owning 75 percent of the stock of a closely-held corporation, which states that the corporation should sell its assets and distribute the proceeds in complete liquidation, would be considered an adoption of a liquidation plan, even though the formal shareholders' meeting and decision to adopt a liquidation plan followed the sale of assets. Liquidating a corporation under Section 337 (a) will lead to avoiding the possibility of a double tax. However, Section 337 does not apply to the sale of the following assets:

1. For the purposes of the nonrecognition treatment, "property" does not include stock in trade, inventory and installment obligations. Section 337(b) provides that installment obligations do not constitute "property" subject to Sec. 337(a), unless they arose from the sale of non-inventory property after adoption of the plan of liquidation, or from a qualified "bulk sale" of inventory under Section 337(b)(2). Notice that when a corporation is arranging for a sale of its assets under Section 337, its shareholders have nothing to gain from a sale on installment basis since the fair market value of the obligations must be taken into account in computing the shareholders' gain or loss on the liquidating distribution.

2. Recapture of excess depreciation under Sections 1245 and 1250 (Sections 1251 and 1252 related to certain farming properties), as well as recapture of investment credit on an early disposition of the property on which the credit was based (Section 47(a)), will be imposed without regard to the non-recognition rules of Section 337.

In addition, the rules of Section 337 will not apply in the following situations:

a. Liquidation of "collapsible" corporations.
b. Gain of a qualified electing shareholder under the rules of Section 333.
c. Liquidations of subsidiary corporations under Section 332.

Liquidation of a Subchapter S Corporation may produce better results than liquidation under Section 337, for the following reasons:

1. In Rev. Rul. 65-292, 1965-2 C.B. 319, the Service ruled that if the corporation elected to report capital gain on the installment method (under Section 453), the deferred capital gain can be passed through ratably to the shareholders under Section 1375 (a). Passing the gain from an installment sale to the shareholders only when collection is made from the sale, can be applied by the Subchapter S Corporation only, and is not available under Section 337.

2. The rules of Section 337 cannot be used by a "collapsible" corporation. However, the rules of Section 341 regarding collapsible corporations do not apply to sale of assets by a Subchapter S Corporation. Even if a Subchapter S Corporation is a "temporary" corporation, it is not subject to the rules applicable to collapsible corporations.

3. A complete liquidation under Section 337, requires a rigid statutory timetable regarding the adoption of a complete liquidation plan, sale of assets, and distribution of proceeds within 12 months of the "plan" date. Sale of assets by a Subchapter S Corporation is not subject to the restrictive rules of Section 337. Therefore, in general, the use of Subchapter S by liquidating corporations may yield superior results to the nonrecognition rule of Section 337. However, if the corporate assets would produce ordinary gain when sold (and not a capital gain), then Section 337 is superior to Subchapter S in that corporate non-recognition can be obtained with respect to sales of such assets under Section 337 (while the use of Subchapter S would result in a pass-through of ordinary income to the shareholders).

7.19. Avoiding the Loss of Election Because of Passive Investment Income

Under Section 1372 (e)(5), the election to be treated as a Subchapter S Corporation will be lost if in any taxable year more than 20 percent of the corporation's gross receipts constitute "passive investment income," such as rents, dividends, interest, royalties, annuities, and gains from the sale or exchange of stock or securities. However, under an amendment enacted in 1966, this restriction is not applied to an electing corporation for the first or second taxable year of active conduct of trade or business if its passive investment income is less than $3,000. To avoid losing the election as a Subchapter S Corporation because of Section 1372(e)(5) restrictions, the following items should be considered carefully:

1. Section 1372 (e)(5) covers "gross receipts" and not "gross income." Therefore, gross receipts include the total amount received or accrued, depending on the method of accounting, from services, sales and investments. Gross receipts are not reduced by items of cost, returns, or allowances. Not included in gross receipts are collections from nontaxable sales or exchanges, loans, or contributions to capital.

2. Although the term "passive investment income" is similar to "personal holding company income," there are important differences. Rents and royalties are included in full in "passive investment income" without any limit. Also, tax-exempt interest is "passive investment income" although it is not "personal holding company income."

3. Rental income is "passive investment income" unless "significant services" are rendered to the lessee. Therefore, amounts received from operating a parking lot, a hotel, or a warehouse, are not considered "passive investment income."

4. Under the rules of constructive receipt a taxpayer may be required to add to his income amounts under an option to receive or within the control and disposition of the taxpayer (Sec. 1.451-2). The rules of "constructive" receipt apply and may cause an unexpected loss of Subchapter S election.

5. To eliminate the chance of losing the election (as a Subchapter S Corporation) because of Section 1372(e)(5) rules, the corporation should diversify its gross receipts to include more income from service, trade or manufacturing.

7.20. Avoiding the Recapture of Investment Credit

If an item of Section 38 property is disposed of before the end of the useful life used in determining the investment tax credit, part or all of the credit is recaptured. If the Subchapter S Corporation prematurely disposes of property on which an investment credit was previously taken and a recapture must be made, each shareholder must pay his share of such recapture. The term "disposition" of qualifying property is broadly defined to affect a Subchapter S Corporation in at least two situations.

First: Sale by a shareholder of stock in a Subchapter S Corporation constitutes an early disposition of Section 38 property if his stock is sold before expiration of the minimum period used in computing the credit. However, if the shareholder sells less than one-third of his interest in the Subchapter S Corporation, the investment credit recapture will be waived.

Second: Recapture applies when a regular corporation makes an effective election to be treated as a Subchapter S Corporation. However, the way to avoid such a recapture is to request all shareholders to accept (in writing) the liability for any possible recapture on subsequent early disposition of Section 38 property, and the shareholders must consent to notify the IRS of any such dispositions.

Notice that the sale of stock by a Subchapter S Corporation shareholder is considered a disposition for recapture purposes. However, the termination of election to be treated as a Subchapter S Corporation will not result in credit recapture. Therefore, before selling any stock by a shareholder you may consider first terminating the election as a Subchapter S Corporation.

Chapter 8

TAX SAVING OPPORTUNITIES FOR THE STOCKHOLDER-EMPLOYEE

8.1. Adopting an Employer Medical Reimbursement Plan

Your corporation can pay all your personal medical and drug expenses under a medical reimbursement plan. Such expenses are completely deductible by the corporation (Sec. 162; 1.162-1; 212). The basic tax features of an employer medical reimbursement plan are the following:

1. Unlike qualified retirement plans, medical reimbursement plans are allowed to discriminate in favor of certain employees. Therefore, a plan for medical reimbursement can be limited to employees within certain wage brackets. If the employee is also a stockholder, the corporation should set up the plan in such a way that it covers any other employee performing the same type of work and earning a compensation within his wage bracket.

2. The contribution of the employer to the medical reimbursement plan is not considered as a taxable income to the employee (Sec. 105(b); 1.105-2).

3. The corporation may adopt different medical reimbursement plans for different employees or classes of employees.

If an employee is not covered by a medical reimbursement plan, he cannot deduct 100 percent of his medical expenses as itemized deductions.

Medical expenses paid directly by an employee are subject to various limitations. For example, Mr. Robert Brown is an executive of the XY Corporation and has an adjusted gross income of $30,000 in the year 1975. During the year he incurred the following medical expenses:

Medical insurance	$ 480.00
Drugs and medicine	350.00
Doctors and hospitals	1,220.00
Total	$2,050.00

Only $850.00 is deductible as medical expenses and the remaining $1,200.00 cannot be claimed as an itemized deduction by Mr. Robert Brown. His deductible medical expenses are figured as follows:

First 1/2 of medical insurance up to $150.00		$150.00
Drugs and medicine	$ 350.00	
Less: 1% of adjusted gross income	300.00	
Balance of drugs and medicine	50.00	
Doctors and hospitals	1,220.00	
Balance of medical insurance	330.00	
Total	1,600.00	
Less: 3% of adjusted gross income	900.00	700.00
Total deductible medical expense		$850.00

As an alternative, the XY Corporation may adopt a medical reimbursement plan and pay all (or part) of Mr. Brown's medical expenses. In this case, Mr. Brown's employer would claim all the $2,050.00 as a deductible expense and Mr. Brown would not pay any income tax on the $2,050.00 assumed by the employer. This way, a limited deduction expense (i.e. medical cost) is changed to a completely deductible item. In order to protect a medical reimbursement plan against any attack from the Internal Revenue Service (Rev. Rul. 69-141, 1969-1 CB 48), observe the following:

1. The medical reimbursement plan should be a bona fide plan and its existence must be reasonably known to the employees.
2. The plan covers stockholder-employees and not "stockholders" who are not in the employment of the corporation.
3. Benefits under the plan are related to amounts of compensation for services and not to the number of shares owned by the shareholders.
4. Benefits under the plan are reasonable and not overly exorbitant. The plan should set limits as to the maximum annual reimbursement for medical expenses. Any unused annual limit may be accumulated for the duration of the employment of each participant.

5. The employer's contributions, whether under insured or self-insured plans, and whether covering the employee or the employee and his family, are excluded from the employee's gross income. Also, the same exclusion can be enjoyed by active as well as retired employees. The plan may be contributory or noncontributory.

8.2. Using Group Health Insurance Plans

An employer can deduct any payments made for the medical insurance of one employee or a group of employees. Therefore, the insurance could be a group health insurance plan or an individual insurance policy covering only one employee. Neither premiums paid by the employer for health insurance nor direct payments by the employer under a health plan to compensate employees for medical expenses are taxed to the employees. Notice that the exclusion does not apply if the employee is eligible to receive payments under the plan regardless of whether or not he had incurred medical expenses (Rev. Rul. 69-141, 1969-ICB 48).

The employer can deduct, as a business expense, his payments for a group health insurance plan adopted under any one of the following four arrangements:

1. Direct payment of insurance premiums by the employer under medical insurance policies.
2. Reimbursement for all medical expenses paid by employees.
3. Reimbursements to the employees for the employer's share of insurance premiums.
4. Reimbursements to the employees for the employer's share of medical expenses.

In the area of group health insurance, the corporate form of ownership has a tax advantage over sole-proprietorship and partnerships. The stockholder-employee can be covered under a group health insurance plan and the plan can even be written with discriminating terms, giving him a preferential treatment. Such insurance can cover medical expenses, payments for injury or loss of bodily functions, and payments in lieu of wages during a period of absence from work as a result of injury or illness.

8.3. Acquiring Group-Term and Split-Dollar Life Insurance

Ordinary life insurance premiums paid by an employer on the life of an employee represent a taxable income to the employee if the proceeds are payable to the employee's beneficiaries (Sec. 1.61-2(d)). However, to avoid adding such life insurance premiums to the taxed income of the stockholder-employee, either one of the following two devices may be used:

1. The corporation pays the insurance premiums on the life of the stockholder-employee (or any stockholder), with the corporation as an owner and beneficiary of the policy. Premiums paid by the corporation in this case are not income to the insured.

2. The corporation pays all or part of the insurance premiums under a group-term life insurance for coverage up to $50,000. The cost of coverage up to $50,000 is not taxed to the employee. Cost of coverage over $50,000 is taxed as income to the employee if the proceeds are payable to the employee's beneficiaries.

Notice that premiums paid by the corporation on group-permanent life insurance, providing paid-up continued insurance, are taxable to the employee, unless his rights are forfeited when he ceases to work for the corporation. Before adopting a group life insurance plan, Code Sec. 79, and Reg. 1.79-1—1.79-3 should be reviewed carefully since insurance coverage can vary from one type of policy to another type. Insurance protection is not standardized and the terms of coverage may lead to tax consequences affecting both the employer and employee.

A special type of insurance is called split-dollar insurance. Under it the employer pays the part of the premium equal to the increase in the cash surrender value of the policy, and, the employee pays the remainder. When the proceeds of the policy are collected after the employee's death, the employer is reimbursed for the sum that he expended. The rest of the proceeds goes to the employer's beneficiaries. Under a split-dollar insurance policy the employer is not allowed a deduction for his share of the annual premiums paid. Also, the employee is taxed on the value of the economic benefit of the insurance protection received each year but not paid by him. The advantage of this type of insurance is that the employee can acquire more insurance protection at an extremely low cost. Meanwhile, the employer is protected at all times, since he will eventually recover all the amounts disbursed by him.

8.4. Receiving Income Under a Wage Continuation Plan

An employer can deduct any contributions made to a wage continuation plan. The plan can be either formal or informal. Also, it does not matter whether or not benefit payments under the plan are provided by the employer, an insurance company, or any other party. On the other hand, the employee can exclude from his income all or part of the benefits received under a wage continuation plan due to absence from work because of illness or injury. The extent of exclusion enjoyed by the employee depends on whether or not his period of absence from work extends beyond the waiting period applicable in the particular case (i.e., it depends upon whether or not he was hospitalized and the period of absence).

Payments made directly by an employer under a wage continuation plan are subject to withholding taxes, just as a regular compensation for services. However, the employer may keep the following records, and, as a result, the withholding requirement will be waived (Sec. 31. 6001-5(a)(12)):

1. Record of the beginning and ending dates of each period of absence from work due to illness or injury.
2. Sufficient information regarding the weekly rate and actual amount of each payment under the wage continuation plan.

Regarding sick-pay under a wage continuation plan, observe the following:

1. The amount of exclusion enjoyed by the employee will depend on three factors:
   a. the amount of sick-pay as a percentage of the employee's regular weekly pay,
   b. whether the employee was hospitalized at least one day during his absence, and
   c. the number of absent days.
2. The employee cannot enjoy a sick pay exclusion in excess of $100 per week.
3. Employees covered by the wage continuation plan should be aware of its coverage.

Notice that, for years beginning after 1975 the sick pay exclusion by an employee is limited to taxpayers under 65 who retire on disability and are totally and permanently disabled when they retire. Under Section 505 of the 1976 Tax Reform Act, qualifying taxpayers can exclude up to $5,200 of sick pay each year (or $100 per week). However, the maximum exclusion is reduced on a dollar-for-dollar basis by any amount of adjusted gross income (including disability income) in excess of $15,000. Therefore, when adjusted gross income (including disability income) reaches $20,200, the exclusion for sick pay would be eliminated.

8.5. Participating in a Pension or a Profit-Sharing Plan

A corporation can claim as a deduction contributions made to pension, stock bonus and profit-sharing plans. The deduction is limited to

15 percent of the compensation paid or accrued during the tax year to the employee covered by the plan (Sec. 404(a)(3)(A)). Pension plans are also called defined benefit plans. Funds are set aside under a pension plan in order to pay retirement benefits to covered employees. Payments to the funds are not related to the employer's profits. Newly adopted pension plans can take into account present as well as past services of the covered employees. Profit-sharing plans are also called defined contribution plans. Under a profit-sharing plan, the employer pays to covered employees certain amounts which are based on the profit of the corporation, as well as, the salary or performance of the employees. Therefore, the employer's contribution to a profit-sharing plan represents an addition to the regular pay of the covered employees. Profit-sharing plans are related to present, and not past, services of employees.

A stockholder-employee should observe the following requirements regarding his participation in a pension or a profit-sharing plan:

1. If the employee is under 25 years of age, he does not have to be covered. However, if the employee is 25 years of age or over, he must be allowed to participate after one year of service.
2. To qualify as an employee at least 1,000 hours of service must be accounted for in any 12-month period, beginning the day an employee starts work for an employer.

A popular method of setting up a pension or a profit-sharing plan is to create an employees' trust (Sec. 401(a), 501(a); 1.401-1). Contributions of the employer to the trust are deductible by the employer as part of payments for compensation paid to employees. Income of the trust is exempted from tax, except for tax on unrelated business income. The tax advisor or employer may request a determination letter from the Internal Revenue Service. The request is usually on Form 5301. A determination letter will prove the trust's (or plan's) exemption from tax.

8.6. Paying Death Benefits to a Deceased Stockholder-Employee's Beneficiaries

The corporation may pay up to $5,000 to a deceased stockholder-employee's beneficiaries. Employee death benefits are deductible by the corporation and not taxed as income to the deceased employee or his estate. It makes no difference whether or not the employer is legally obligated to make the payments (Sec. 101(b)(1); 1.101-2). If the employee had more than one employer, the total exclusion cannot exceed $5,000. Death benefits are not subject to the Social Security tax since they are not considered as wages.

The employer may make a lump sum payment to the widow, children, or estate of the deceased employee. In some cases, the amount paid is determined according to a formula which has been adopted by the company (e.g., one month's, three months', or six months' salary). The corporate form has a tax advantage over sole proprietorships and partnerships in the area of death benefits. The reason is that to exclude death benefits, they must be paid to an employee. A stockholder can qualify as an employee by performing regular employment-related services to the corporation. However, sole proprietors or partners are not considered as employees and their beneficiaries do not receive the $5,000 exclusion. The corporation may even finance the death benefits. This is done by borrowing the money which is to be paid to the employee's beneficiaries. Another method of acquiring money needed for paying death benefits is to purchase insurance on the life of the employee. The employer owns the policy and deducts any premiums paid. Upon death of the employee, the employer is the recipient of the proceeds. Those proceeds are received income-tax-free by the employer and paid to the employee's beneficiaries.

The tax advisor should examine the relationship between the corporation and the stockholder-employee. If the stockholder-employee is a controlling shareholder, the payment of death benefits may be considered by the Internal Revenue Service as a constructive dividend. In a case like this, the tax strategy should be to adopt in writing the death benefits plan and to show the payment of the corporation as being made under a legal obligation, (i.e., not a voluntary payment). Also, the payment should be shown to be reasonable and to have been, more preferably, made according to a predetermined formula (e.g., equal to three or six months' salary).

8.7. Furnishing Free Meals and Lodging

Under Code Section 119 an employer may furnish free meals and lodging to his employees. The cost of meals and lodging furnished for the convenience of the employer is deductible by the employer as a business expense and is not taxed as income to the benefiting employee. In order to enjoy this special treatment under Section 119, the tax advisor should observe the following:

1. Meals offered to the employees must be furnished at the employer's business premises. The main issue is that the meals should be consumed on the business premises of the employer.
2. The value of lodging is not taxed to the employee, if he is required to accept the lodging as a condition of his employment. It does not matter whether or not the value of lodging is figured as part of the compensation of the employee. The main criterion is that the em-

ployee is not given a choice between selecting his own lodging or the lodging furnished by the employer.

3. The exclusion applies only to meals and lodging furnished in kind. The employee is not given a cash allowance for meals and lodging.
4. Lodging includes the cost of utilities acquired by the employer. It does not include utilities purchased directly by the employee from the utility suppliers.

8.8. Reimbursing Part or All of Moving Expenses

The corporation may reimburse the stockholder-employee for part or all of the expenses of moving from the old to the new place of work. In order to safeguard this fringe-benefit, observe the following:

1. Moving expenses include the cost of moving household goods, travel, including meals and lodging, cost of a house-hunting trip, meals and lodging while occupying temporary quarters, and qualified residence sale, purchase or lease expenses. For more details about moving expenses, see **2.18** of Chapter 2.
2. The new place of work should be at least 50 miles further from the employee's residence than was his former place of work (or his old residence if he had no former principal place of work). For taxable years beginning after 1976, the mileage limitation is reduced to 35 miles.
3. During the 12-month period following the moving, the employee must be a full-time employee in the new location for at least 39 weeks. The 39-week requirement is waived in case of death, disability, or involuntary separation of the employee (military personnel are subject to special rules).
4. The reimbursement of the employer is added to the gross income of the employee. However, the reimbursement for moving expenses is not subject to withholding taxes, unless the reimbursement exceeds actual moving expenses. The reimbursement of the employer is not subject to the Social Security tax. The employer reports the reimbursement as an added amount to the gross income of the employee. The employee, in turn, claims the moving expense as a deduction for his adjusted gross income.

8.9. Adopting a Stock Option Plan

Employee stock option plans provide a supplement to the regular compensation of an employee. This supplement, if used well, receives a favorable income tax treatment. Generally, the employee is not taxed when he receives the stock option or when he exercises it. If he sells the stock within three years (in the case of qualified option plans) from the date of exercise, he realizes an ordinary income equal to the difference between the proceeds from sale and the option price. However, if the employee sells the stock after three years (in the case of qualified plans) from the date of exercise, he realizes a long-term capital gain equal to the difference between his option price and the proceeds from sale. Before setting up a stock option plan, observe that there are three types of stock options:

A. Qualified stock options.

B. Options under an employee stock purchase plan.

C. Restricted stock options granted before January 1, 1964.

(A) A qualified stock option plan has neither specified limits as to the number of shares that may be acquired under the plan nor any requirement of non-discrimination. The options would receive favored tax treatment if they meet the following requirements (Sec. 422(b); 1.422-1(b)):

1. The plan is approved by the stockholders within 12 months before or after the date of adopting the plan.
2. The plan must state the employees or classes of employees entitled to receive options, the total number of shares to be optioned, and, the plan must not run for more than ten years.
3. The plan is granted by an employer corporation, its parent, or subsidiary to purchase stock of any of these corporations.
4. The option provisions must provide the following: (i) it is exercisable only during the five-year period from the date the option was granted; (ii) it is exercisable during the employee's lifetime only; (iii) it is not exercisable while the employee has a prior outstanding qualified or restricted stock option. Under Section 603 of the 1976 Tax Reform Act, all qualified and restricted stock options must be exercised by May 21, 1981. If the option is not exercised by that date, it will be given the same tax treatment as that accorded to nonqualified stock options. Also, the new rules of Section 603 (amending Code Section 422(b) and (c) add new restrictions on qualified stock options granted after May 20, 1976.
5. The option price must be at least equal to the fair market value of the stock at the time the option was granted.
6. At the time the option is granted, the employee cannot own more than 5 percent of the total combined voting power of all classes of stock of the employer or its parent or subsidiary corporations.

(B) An employee stock purchase plan includes all employees except officers, highly compensated personnel, certain part-time workers, and those employed less than two years. An employee stock purchase plan should meet the following requirements (Sec. 423(b); 1.423-2):

1. The employee receiving the option must be an employee of the granting corporation from the date of the grant to three months before the option is exercised.
2. Only employees owning less than 5 percent of the stock (of the employer) can participate.
3. The option price must be at least 85 percent of the value of the stock at the time of grant or exercise.
4. No more than $25,000 of stock, valued at date of grant, may accrue for purchase in any one year. Under an employee stock purchase plan, no income is realized when an option is granted or exercised. If an option is exercised and the stock is held for at least six months after it was acquired, and at least two years after the option is granted, gain on sale or exchange of such stock is treated as a long-term capital gain. If the holding requirements (the six months and the two years) are not met, the employee must report an ordinary income when he sells the stock.

(C) Restricted stock options are individual options granted before 1964 (Sec. 424(c)).

Notice that if stock is acquired by an employee or a stockholder-employee without a qualified stock option plan, and, if the purchase price is below the fair market value of the stock, the general rules of property transfers for less than market value would apply. At the time of granting the stock option, no income is recognized by the employee. When the option is exercised or sold, the employee realizes an ordinary income equal to the difference between the purchase price and the fair market value of the stock. Therefore, the tax treatment is not favorable under a non-qualified stock option plan. For tax saving purposes, only a qualified plan or an employee purchase plan should be used. A qualified stock option plan serves highly-paid executives, while an employee stock purchase plan can serve all other employees. Qualified and restricted stock options exercised after May 20, 1981 will be treated in the same manner as non-qualified options.

8.10. Receiving Payments Under a Deferred Compensation Arrangement

Various arrangements for payments to employees after their retirement can be made. A deferred compensation arrangement serves to postpone income from the employee's high-earning years to those years following retirement when his earnings and tax bracket are expected to be lower. The corporation cannot claim a deduction until the deferred compensation is paid. As for the employee, he is not taxed until he receives the compensation. The following tax-related issues should be considered in order to use a deferred compensation arrangement for the benefit of both the corporation and the employee:

1. The deferred compensation plan should provide restrictions and limitations on payments so that the employee cannot receive the compensation until some date in the future. For example, the plan should consider the effects of termination of employment, conversion from full-time to part-time employee status, or partial or total disability.
2. If the employee's rights under the plan are non-forfeitable, the employer can deduct the payments to the plan in the year in which they are made. In turn, the employee must report in the year of receipt the payments as a compensation for service or ordinary income.
3. If the employee's rights are forfeitable, the employer cannot deduct the contributions until the year of payment to the employee. If the rights of the employee are forfeitable, the obligation of the corporation is unsecured and the employee must depend upon the willingness and ability of the corporation to fulfill the obligation at some future date.
4. If the employee's rights are non-forfeitable, the corporation may invest the amount of deferred compensation, in order to afford a degree of protection to the employee. In this case, and as long as the deferred payments are not placed in escrow, or trust, or otherwise physically segregated for the employee's benefit, no tax on their present value to the employee is imposed.
5. If the corporation contributes to a fund that cannot be reached by the creditors of the corporation, the payments would be currently taxed to the employee

8.11. Enjoying Fringe Benefits Under Code Section 162

A corporation may pay or incur a wide variety of expenses with a double feature. On the one hand, these expenses are deductible by the corporation as ordinary and necessary business expenses. On the other hand, they are enjoyed by the stockholder-employee without being taxed as income to him. These types of expenses mainly include the following items:

1. Cost of recreational facilities such as boats, lodges, or swimming pools.
2. Educational courses and seminars provided for by the employer.
3. Bargain or discount purchase of company products.
4. Use of company dining rooms, automobiles, typewriters, etc.
5. Company-assisted home purchasing, e.g., through low interest loans.
6. Paying the cost of medical checkups, legal, and tax consultations offered to the employees.

Basic requirements for the deduction of these expenses under Section 162 are the following:

1. The expenses should be considered as ordinary and necessary. In case of an expense enjoyed by a shareholder-employee, the reasonableness test is used. Under this test only a reasonable amount paid as compensation for services actually rendered can be deducted. In determining whether the compensation for services is reasonable, the following factors are taken into account: (a) the nature of the services performed, (b) the compensation paid in prior years for the same type of work, (c) whether or not the compensation is on a contingent basis (if the compensation is contingent, a larger amount is considered as reasonable), and (d) the amount of compensation the employee could have earned from another (or unrelated) employer for the same work performed.

2. The expense is paid or incurred during the taxable year. This requirement is related to the accounting method used by the corporation (i.e., cash or accrual method), and the adopted taxable year (i.e., fiscal or calendar year).

3. The expense is related to a trade or business and not to a personal purpose of use.

8.12. Distributing or Selling Stock and Other Property to a Stockholder-Employee

If a stockholder-employee buys property from the corporation for less than its fair market value, the difference between the purchase price and the fair market value is included in the gross income of the employee (Sec. 1.61-2(d)(2)). However, if the bargain or discount price is offered as "courtesy" to the employee, the discount is not taxed as ordinary income to him (Treasury Department booklet "Your Federal Income Tax," 1976 Ed., p. 34). Employees' discounts should meet the following requirements in order to enjoy the exemption from tax:

1. The discounts are offered to promote employee welfare or efficiency.
2. The discounts are of relatively small value.

These two requirements for exempting employees' purchase discounts are fairly easy to meet. However, for tax saving purposes, the area of distributing stock and property in connection with performance of services is far more important. Property sold or distributed by the corporation may take the form of either restricted or unrestricted stock and other property.

A corporation may give or distribute stock or other property to an employee and restrict the employee's right to sell the property and/or vote the stock. Therefore, the stock or property rights are "held hostage" by the corporation until certain specified services are performed by the employee. This type of distribution or sale constitutes an excellent tax saving vehicle. The value of restricted stock or property is not added to the gross income of the employee until he receives full ownership without any limitation. Through the timing principle, of course, the full ownership should be given when the taxable income of the employee is low and the taxable income of the employer is high. When restrictions are lifted, whatever is taxable to the employee as ordinary income will be deductible by the employer as a compensation for services (Sec. 83(h)).

If a corporation gives an employee stock or property without any restrictions, the entire value of the given property should be considered as a compensation for services. Therefore, this type of distribution is not recommended for tax saving purposes since the employee will be taxed on the full value of property received in the year in which he receives it.

Before using a restricted stock or restricted property distribution as a tax saving device, observe the following two provisions under Code Section 83:

1. The rights of the employee to the distributed stock or property are subject to a risk of forfeiture by the employer, and,
2. If the employee sells or transfers the restricted property, the recipient will also be under the same risk of forfeiture by the employer.

An example of a restricted distribution under Section 83 is to give or sell stock or other property to an employee without giving him full ownership until he has worked a specified number of years (e.g., three years) for the corporation, or, until the corporation's sales or gross profits have reached a certain level. If the employee fails to meet the stipulated requirements, the corporation could forfeit the stock or property. Try to relate the restriction to stock or property to a substantial performance of future services by the employee. This would rule out relating the restriction to an occasional or part-time performance of consulting services by an employee.

The employee is given a "gambler's choice" in the case of receiving restricted stock or property. He can, within 30 days of receiving the restricted stock or property, elect to be taxed in the year of receiving the property even though the property remains subject to a substantial risk of forfeiture or remains non-transferable (Sec. 83(b)). If this election is exercised, the result could be either a substantial saving or a large tax loss to the electing employee.

To illustrate, let us assume that Mr. Robert Brown is given a bonus of 1,000 shares of restricted stock worth $50 per share. He is a gambler at heart and feels the stock will be worth $200 per share in eight years when the restriction will lapse. Therefore, he elects to be taxed on $50,000 in the year of receiving the restricted stock. If his guess is correct, the stock will be worth $200,000 after eight years. If he sells it at that time for $200,000, only $150,000 will be taxed as a long-term capital gain and will receive the long-term capital gain favorable tax treatment. Of course, if he did not exercise the election, the entire amount of $200,000 will be added to his gross income as a compensation for services when the property restrictions lapse.

Chapter 9

TAX SAVING OPPORTUNITIES FOR INVESTORS IN STOCKS AND BONDS

9.1. Claiming the Deduction for the Stamp or Securities Transfer Tax

The stamp tax or securities transfer tax should be claimed as a deduction from adjusted gross income (i.e., a personal deduction) if the taxpayer is itemizing deductions on Schedule A. This leads to claiming the entire amount of tax paid as an itemized deduction rather than deducting the stamp tax from the gross proceeds from sale of stock. For example, if a taxpayer sells stock for $10,000 and pays a securities transfer tax of $50, he may elect to deduct the $50 from the gross proceeds from the sale of stock, or, claim it as an itemized deduction. If the holding period of stock is over six months, the gain (or loss) from sale is a long-term capital gain (or loss) and only 50 percent of it is taxable (or deductible). Instead of using the $50 payment for stamp tax as a reduction (or addition) from the long-term capital gain (or loss), it should be claimed as an itemized deduction, reducing gross income on a dollar for dollar basis.

9.2. Investing in Tax-Exempt Bonds

Interest earned on bonds issued by a state or local government (e.g., county, city, or town) and bonds issued by the District of Columbia is exempt from the federal income tax (Sec. 103). This allows a high-bracket taxpayer to enjoy a relatively acceptable after tax rate of return on his investment. For example, a married taxpayer filing a joint return with a taxable income of $45,000 is subject to $14,060 income tax on the first $44,000 of taxable income. The remaining $1,000 of taxable income is taxed at the rate of 50 percent. If this taxpayer invests in a tax-exempt bond paying an interest rate of 6 percent, his equivalent (or before tax) rate of return, is 12 percent per year. This same situation can be analyzed from a different point of view. If the taxpayer invests in corporate (or taxable) bonds, or opens a savings account, he should earn at least 12 percent per year. The reason is that every dollar of his taxable income in excess of $44,000 is taxed at a 50 percent rate. Therefore, from the 12 percent interest earned from a corporate bond, or a savings account, he retains only an interest income of 6 percent per year.

To protect a taxpayer investing in tax-exempt bonds, observe the following:

1. Not all interest on government obligations is tax-free. Interest on U.S. obligations is, generally, taxable. There are two types of tax-exempt bonds which are called general obligations and revenue bonds. A general obligation bond is backed by the general credit of the city or state issuing it. If cash is needed to pay the interest, the city or state can levy a tax to raise the needed cash. Therefore, this type of bond is considered a better risk. Revenue bonds are related to a specific project such as an airport or a housing project. The cash needed to pay the interest due on this type of bond can come only from the specific project in question. Consequently, revenue bonds pay a higher interest rate than general obligation bonds.

2. Interest on arbitrage bonds (or bonds issued to service other outstanding obligations) issued after October 9, 1969, are usually not tax-exempt. Therefore, before investing in an arbitrage or a state or local government bond, first be sure of the exemption status of the bond.

3. If a corporation invests in a tax-exempt bond, the corporation will enjoy the exemption. However, when income from a tax-exempt source enters the retained earnings account of a corporation, it will lose its nature or identity. As a result, when the corporation pays dividends to its stockholders, they must pay federal income tax on the dividend income without regard to whether or not the money for the dividend originally came from a tax-exempt or a taxable source. Therefore, to maximize the benefit from a tax-exempt bond, regular corporations should shy away from this type of investment. An individual investor in a high tax bracket is served best by tax-exempt bonds.

4. The exemption applies to interest income only. It does not apply to capital gain (or loss) from the sale or exchange of state and municipal

bonds. Therefore, if the taxpayer acquires a tax-exempt bond at a premium, the premium paid must be amortized even though the interest from the bond is not subject to tax and the amortization is not deductible. The amortization of the premium paid is needed only to figure the basis of investment in the bond (Sec. 171, 1016(a)). After figuring the basis, the difference between it and the net proceeds from the sale or exchange constitutes a taxable, or deductible, capital gain or loss. However, when such bonds are held by an original buyer until maturity, generally neither gain nor loss on their redemption will be realized.

5. Since the income from state and municipal bonds is tax-exempt, neither interest incurred in borrowing money needed to purchase tax-exempt bonds nor expenses allocable to tax-exempt income are deductible. Any proceeds from borrowing should not be used for acquiring tax-exempt bonds.

6. Under Section 2105 of the 1976 Tax Reform Act, interest earned from municipal bonds issued for financing student loan programs is exempt from the federal income tax. The bonds must be issued by a state-sponsored, nonprofit organization established and operated exclusively for the purpose of acquiring student loan notes incurred under the Higher Education Act of 1965.

9.3. Borrowing Against the Cash Surrender Value of a Life Insurance Policy

A taxpayer may borrow from an insurance company or another source against the cash surrender value of a life insurance policy and reinvest the proceeds at a rate of return in excess of interest paid to the creditor. For example, if a taxpayer borrows against the cash surrender value of a life insurance policy paying an interest rate of 5 percent per year, and reinvests the proceeds at a rate of 11 percent per year, his net profit before tax will be 6 percent per year. This income and tax savings can be achieved if the investor is careful in dealing with the following two situations:

1. Generally, interest incurred to purchase or carry life insurance is not deductible, if the policy is acquired under a plan of purchase which contemplates the systematic borrowing of part of all of the increases in the cash surrender value of the policy (Code Section 264(a)(3)). However, this rule has the following five exceptions:

(a) It does not apply to policies purchased on or before August 7, 1963, if the taxpayer is the original policyholder.

(b) Regardless of whether or not there is a systematic plan of borrowing, the interest deduction is allowed if it does not exceed $100 per year. Notice that if the annual interest charge exceeds $100 a year, the entire amount of interest (and not the excess over $100) becomes non-deductible.

(c) If the policyholder meets an unforeseen substantial loss of income, or unforeseen substantial increase in financial obligations, the interest for a loan against the insurance policy is completely deductible.

(d) If the taxpayer borrows against the insurance policy and invests the proceeds in his trade or business, the interest on the loan is deductible.

(e) Interest will be allowed when at least four of the annual premiums remitted during the first seven-year period are paid by means other than borrowing. Also, once the seven-year period is completed, there seems to be no limit on the amount of interest expense that can be deducted because of loans to pay premiums on the policy. Therefore, the taxpayer should pay any four annual premiums (not necessarily in sequence) out of his own funds, and then, pay the premiums for the other three years (i.e., out of the first seven years) from borrowed funds. After the first seven-year period requirement is met, he could borrow each of the annual premiums and still deduct the interest for income tax purposes.

2. The proceeds from borrowing against the cash surrender value of an insurance policy should not be used to acquire tax-exempt securities. Expenses connected with tax-exempt income are not deductible.

9.4. Maximizing the Dividends Received Deduction

Not all dividends received from a U.S corporation are subject to the federal income tax. The effect of dividends' exclusion depends on whether or not the taxpayer acquires the stock on his own, through his corporation, or through a small business investment company:

1. A husband and wife may each exclude up to $100 of dividends received from a U.S. corporation. When stock is held by the husband, wife, and children, the $100 annual exclusion will be related to each stock owner. Therefore, try to transfer stock to each family member in order to claim the $100 exemption per owner, per year.

2. A corporation, receiving dividend income from another U.S. corporation, receives an 85 percent dividends received deduction. However, the remaining 15 percent will be subject to double taxation. For example, corporation (A) paid $10,000 as dividend to corporation (B). Company (B) will claim a dividend received deduction of $8,500 and pay a corporate income tax on the remaining $1,500. Company (A) originally paid federal

income tax on the entire amount of $10,000 (as net earnings). Company (B) will pay an income tax on the $1,500 as dividend income, and, eventually company (B) will distribute part or all of what is left to its own shareholders who in turn will report a taxable dividend income (after claiming the exemption of $100 per year). This sequence of paying more than one tax on the same sum of money seems to suggest the owning of the stock by the individual taxpayer himself. However, when other than tax factors (e.g., desire to control another corporation) interfere, the corporation may find it necessary to acquire capital stock of another corporation without regard to the effect of double taxation.

3. Under Code Section 242, a small business investment company gets a 100 percent dividends received deduction. However, to qualify for this deduction the stock must be acquired by the small business investment company. Also, the company claiming the deduction must file a statement with its tax return showing that it is entitled to the special treatment.

9.5. Investing in Stock Issued Under Section 1244

If you make a loan to a friend or a family member and the loan is not collected, you used to be able to claim it as a non-business bad debt. Non-business bad debts used to be treated as short-term capital losses and as such they were written off against capital gains or against ordinary income in an amount not in excess of $1,000 per year for taxable years beginning before 1977; $2,000 per year for taxable years beginning in 1977; and $3,000 maximum per year for taxable years beginning after 1977. Under the new rules of Section 605 of the 1976 Tax Reform Act, if a loan or guaranty was not a transaction entered into either for profit, or as part of the guarantor's trade or business, no deduction is to be available in the event of a payment under the guaranty. To avoid the treatment as a non-deductible loss, ask the borrower to incorporate and then exchange the loan for stock issued under Section 1244. A loss from investing in Section 1244 stock is a business loss and can be deducted from ordinary income as an ordinary business expense.

In general, when an investment in a corporation becomes worthless, or sold for less than cost, the investor's loss is treated as a capital loss. In contrast to this capital-loss treatment of most corporate investments, two important devices allow an individual investor, who participates in a losing business venture, to deduct his losses as ordinary items. The first device is the Subchapter S Corporation. The net operations loss of a Subchapter S Corporation is passed through to the shareholders and claimed as a deduction on their individual tax returns.

The second device is the issuance of stock under Section 1244. The loss from Section 1244 stock is deductible by the shareholder as an ordinary item. However, the deductible amount of loss in one tax year cannot exceed $25,000, or, in the case of husband and wife filing a joint return, $50,000. The $50,000 limit applies to a joint return even though the loss from stock may have been sustained by only one of the spouses (Reg. 1.1244(b)-1). If the loss (up to $25,000 or $50,000) cannot be used in the tax year, it becomes part of the taxpayer's net operating loss. Like all net operating losses, it can be carried back for three years and forward for five years (increased to seven years for years ending after 1975). Carrying the loss backward may result in a needed tax refund. Notice that any loss from Section 1244 stock in excess of $25,000 and $50,000 is treated as a capital loss. Therefore, if Section 1244 stock is sold at a loss, try not to sell in one tax year stock generating more than $25,000 or $50,000 of loss.

9.6. Matching Short-Term and Long-Term Capital Gains and Losses

Before the end of each tax year remap your investment strategy. Here are a few tips:

1. If you have no capital gains or losses for the year, you can sell a stock that will give you a short-term capital loss of up to $1,000 ($2,000 for taxable years beginning in 1977; $3,000 for taxable years beginning after 1977), which is the maximum amount deductible against ordinary income.
2. If you have a net short-term capital gain, take a long-term capital loss to eat it up; otherwise, the short-term gain will be taxed as ordinary income.
3. If you have a long-term gain, do not realize a long-term loss. Save the long-term loss for a year with a short-term gain.
4. If you have both long-term and short-term gains, try to realize a short-term loss to cancel the short-term gain. Then, enjoy the special tax treatment available for long-term gains.
5. If you have both long-term and short-term losses, try to realize short-term gain up to the amount of both losses.
6. If you have long-term gains and short-term losses, try to realize short-term gain up to the amount of short-term losses only.

9.7. Selling Stock After the Declaration of a Cash Dividend

When the board of directors of a corporation declares a cash dividend, its resolution must specify the following points:

1. Date of declaration.
2. Date of record.
3. Date of payment.
4. Rate or amount of dividend per share.

On the date of declaring a cash dividend, the market price of related stock will usually increase by the amount of dividend declared. If the taxpayer waits until he receives the dividend, he will realize ordinary income from the dividend received. However, this ordinary income can be converted to a capital gain by selling the stock after the date of declaration and before the date of dividend payment. The appreciation or increase in the market value of the stock, due to the declaration of dividend, will be taxed as a long-term capital gain, if the holding period of the stockholder exceeds six months. Notice that both cash and accrual basis taxpayers can benefit from this tax saving device. The reason is that dividends are subject to tax only when they are made available for the demand of the shareholder without any qualification. Therefore, if the dividend is declared on September 10, and is payable on October 10, both cash and accrual basis taxpayers would not report any dividend income, if they sell their stock before the date of dividend payment on October 10.

9.8. Giving Stock or Bonds as a Gift to a Family Member or Friend

If you plan to give stock or bonds as a gift to a family member or friend, the following two items will have special significance for you and for the donee:

1. When you make the gift, state in writing the date you acquired the gifted stock or bonds, its basis or cost, any gift tax paid, and the fair market value at the date of the gift. The donee will need this information when ultimate sale of the securities takes place.

2. When the donee sells the gifted stock or bonds at a gain, his basis is the same as the donor's basis plus any gift tax paid. However, if the donee sells the securities at a loss, his basis is the lower of the donor's basis plus any gift tax paid, or, the fair market value at the time of the gift (Sec. 1015(a); 1.1015-1). If your stock appreciated in value, (or is worth more than its original cost) keep it since it is better to pass it on to your family upon death. If your stock depreciated (or is worth less than its original cost) in value, sell it and report the loss on your personal tax return. For the purpose of giving a gift, select the securities that have a market value close to the original cost to you.

9.9. Maximizing the Deduction for Short-Term Capital Losses and Avoiding the Wash Sale Rules

A short-term capital gain is taxed as ordinary income. A short-term capital loss is also deductible in full against short-term gains, long-term gains, as well as ordinary income (the deduction from ordinary income cannot exceed $1,000 per year for taxable years beginning before 1977; $2,000 for taxable years beginning in 1977; $3,000 maximum for taxable years beginning after 1977). Therefore, to maximize the use of short-term capital losses, each investment in stock and bonds should be checked at least once after five months (in 1976; eight months in 1977; 11 months after 1977) from the date of acquisition. The holding period starts one day after the day of the property purchase. This policy of checking each investment before the end of five months (for taxable years beginning before 1977) from the date of acquisition is important not only to determine whether or not a loss should be realized, but, it also is needed to avoid the rules of "wash sale." A "wash sale" means the sale of securities and the purchase of identical securities within 30 days before or after the date of sale. A loss sustained from a "wash sale" is not allowed. The disallowed loss is added to the basis of the newly-acquired stock or security.

Checking an investment in stock or securities may lead to the decision to sell and realize a loss. It may also lead to the purchase of similar stock or securities, if the taxpayer believes in the future potential of such securities. The "wash sale" rules do not apply to a sale that results in a profit. Therefore, if you expect a loss from selling your stock or securities, do not acquire the same type of stock or securities within 30 days before or after the sale.

If you own stock and the fair market value of the stock is below the original cost of purchasing it, and at the same time, you are confident that this stock will stage a comeback, you can realize the paper loss while avoiding the restrictions of the "wash sale" rule by adopting the following steps:

1. Sell your stock and claim a capital loss from the sale.
2. Invest the proceeds from the sale in stock with a similar potential (e.g., stock issued by another corporation in the same industry).
3. After 31 days sell the new stock and acquire again stock similar to that which you originally sold at a loss.

9.10. Receiving Property Dividends

Although most dividends are in cash, a corporation may choose to pay a dividend in the form of merchandise, securities of another company, or any other asset. In the case of property dividends, it is usual to find a difference between the book value of the assets being distributed (i.e., their value in the books of the distributing corporation) and their fair market value. Also, the tax effect of a cash dividend is different from the effect of the distribution of property. While a cash dividend is subject to tax when the dividend is made available for the unqualifying demand of the stockholder, the effect of a property dividend depends upon the identity of the recipient. Stockholders receiving property dividends are classified into the following two groups:

1. Individual stockholders receiving property dividends are taxed on the fair market value of property received on the distribution date (Sec. 301(d)(1); 1.301-1(h)). For tax saving purposes, a property dividend is recommended if the stockholder assumes liability against the received property. Any liability assumed by the shareholder or to which the property remains subject will reduce (but not below zero) the amount of distribution taxed to the shareholder.

2. Corporate stockholders are taxed in a more favorable way in the area of property dividends. A corporate stockholder receiving a distribution in property is taxed on the lesser of (1) the fair market value of the property, or, (2) the adjusted basis of the property in the hands of the distributing corporation (Sec. 301(b)(1)(B)). Therefore, it is advisable to distribute an appreciated property to another corporation you own, instead of receiving the property directly as a dividend made to an individual shareholder.

9.11. Receiving Stock Dividends

In recent years an increasing number of corporations have chosen to pay stock dividends. The most popular type of stock dividend is the distribution of additional shares of common stock to the stockholders in proportion to their existing holdings. Stock dividends are non-taxable, unless, they come within a specific exception. A non-taxable stock distribution has no effect on the shareholder's income in the year of receiving it. The receipt of a non-taxable stock dividend will affect only the basis of old and new stock and the holding period of new stock. Under the 1969 Tax Reform Act (Sec. 305; 1.305-1), the following types of stock dividends do not qualify for nontaxability:

1. Where a stockholder had a choice between receiving a stock dividend, or cash, or other property.
2. Where the result of the distribution is disproportionate. For example, some stockholders receive cash or other property, while the others receive stock, which results in an increase in their proportionate interests.
3. Where some common stockholders receive common stock, and other common stockholders receive preferred stock.
4. Where there is a distribution of convertible preferred stock (except where its effect is not disproportionate).

Receiving stock dividends is not taxable, but the above-mentioned exceptions should be examined carefully. The exceptions are broad enough that shareholders may fall into the trap and end up with a taxable distribution. Therefore, any distribution, other than a proportionate common stock dividend, should be examined for its tax status before adopting it.

9.12. Receiving Stock and Bond Rights

A corporation may distribute stock warrants or certificates conveying to the holders rights to purchase shares of its stock at a specified price. This privilege of purchasing a fractional share or a specified number of shares of capital stock is not considered as taxable to the recipient. Stock rights are subject to the same rules applicable to stock dividends. However, an investor receiving stock rights will enjoy a tax break, if the market value of the rights when distributed is less than 15 percent of the stock's value at that time (Sec. 307(b)(1), (2); 1.307-1). In this case the stockholder has the right not to allocate any value to the newly received rights and may use this privilege in order to minimize his tax liability.

For example, on February 1, 1975, Mr. Robert Brown bought 1,000 shares of XY Corporation at $10 per share. On April 1, 1975, he received 500 rights entitling him to subscribe to an additional 500 shares at $9 per share. On the day the rights were issued, the fair market value of the stock was $12 per share and that of the rights at $3 each. Mr. Robert Brown may allocate a zero basis to the rights since their market value when distributed (i.e., 500 @ $3) is less than 15 percent of the stock's value (i.e., 1,000 @ $12) on April 1, 1975. If Mr. Brown does not allocate any basis to his stock rights, his old stock will remain at $10 per share. He will not pay tax on the stock rights unless he sells them. In this case, his other capital transactions for the year resulting in capital gains and losses, as well as his intention to sell the rights or keep them, would determine whether or not he should exercise the election to allocate a zero basis to the rights received. If his other capital transactions for the year result in a net capital loss, he may consider allocating a zero basis to the rights, if he sells them in 1975. The sale of rights at a gain will offset his net capital loss from the other capital transactions.

Bond rights are treated like non-taxable stock rights, if (1) the bonds are convertible into stock, and (2) the value of the rights result from the conversion privilege. Notice that if the bonds are not convertible into stock, the bond rights are subject to tax as property dividends.

9.13. Selling Appreciated Stock to a Third Party

A dividend received by an individual shareholder is taxed as ordinary income at relatively high income-tax rates. However, this ordinary income can be converted into a long-term capital gain through the following method:

> Instead of declaring distributions of corporate earnings, the corporation will accumulate its profits. As a result, the stock appreciates or increases in value. The stockholder sells his stock to a third party. The appreciation in stock value will be taxed at a more favorable long-term capital-gain rate if the holding period is over six months for taxable years beginning before 1977, "more than nine months" for taxable years beginning in 1977, and "more than one year" for taxable years beginning after 1977. Furthermore, if the stockholder dies while still owning the stock, the appreciation in value prior to death is never taxed as income. Therefore, if the stockholder does not need immediate dividend income, he is in a better tax position if he allows the corporate earnings to accumulate, resulting in an increase in the value of his stock.

Notice that this tax saving technique encounters tax complications in the following two situations:

1. The accumulated earnings tax is imposed as a penalty on the excessive accumulation of corporate earnings. To avoid this tax, the corporation should show that the accumulation is for the reasonable needs of business (Sec. 1.537-2).

2. The stockholder's gain from sale of stock in a collapsible corporation is taxed as ordinary income (Sec. 341(d); 1.341-4). A corporation is not collapsible, if the unrealized appreciation in its assets held primarily for sale (or Section 341 assets) does not exceed 15 percent of the corporation's net worth. For example, if the unrealized appreciation in inventory is 15 percent or less of the corporation's net worth, and, if inventory is the only asset with unrealized appreciation, the sale of stock will be taxed as a capital gain.

To avoid the rules applicable to collapsible corporations, at least five avenues of escape are available:

1. Sale or exchange of stock under Section 341(e)(1). This exemption is granted on a shareholder-by-shareholder basis.
2. Gain on the complete liquidation of an otherwise collapsible corporation is, in certain circumstances, taxed as a capital gain because of Section 341(e)(2). This exemption is also granted on a shareholder-by-shareholder basis.
3. Certain collapsible corporations are made eligible for the benefits of Section 303 (i.e., distributions in redemption of stock to pay death taxes). This exemption is granted to the corporation itself.

4. Certain corporate gains or losses on sales within a 12-month period following adoption of plan of complete liqudiation under Section 337. This exemption is also granted to the corporation itself.
5. Under Section 341(f) (enacted in 1964), if the corporation consents to recognize gain on disposition of its "subsection (f) assets", the shareholder can sell his stock using the capital gain rules. Subsection (f) assets mainly include real estate and non-capital assets. Therefore, the collapsible corporation consents to recognize the gain on its Subsection (f) assets when it ultimately disposes of them. Whether or not the corporate gain will be taxed at the time of disposition as capital gain or as ordinary income depends upon the asset sold and the applicable rules at date of sale. Filing a consent under Section 341(f) is effective for six months. During this period, any shareholder may sell stock of the consenting corporation under the capital-gain rules. When the consent period expires, another six month period can be started by filing a new corporate consent. The process of filing consents may be continued indefinitely.

9.14. Redeeming Stock to Pay Death Taxes

Special relief is offered under Section 303. Stock redeemed in a closely-held business to pay death taxes qualifies for the capital-gain treatment. Under Section 2004(e) of the 1976 Tax Reform Act, the decedent's basis in stock of closely-held business is carried over. Therefore, a redemption of such stock will mean a capital-gains tax on the excess of the stock's value over the carryover basis. Redeeming stock to pay death taxes qualifies for the capital gain treatment if the following conditions are met:

1. The value of the stock is included in the decedent's gross estate.
2. The stock is redeemed after death. The amount of qualifying redemptions that are made more than four years after the decedent's death is limited to either the amount of taxes and funeral and administration expenses remaining unpaid at such a redemption date, or those that are paid within a one-year period beginning at the redemption distributions, whichever is less. In cases where deferred payment of estate taxes is elected, the time for stock redemptions extends to the time permitted for the payment of the estate tax installments.
3. The stock is redeemed for an amount not in excess of the sum of the estate, inheritance, legacy and succession taxes (including interest) and funeral and administration expenses deductible by the estate.
4. The value of all the stock of the corporation, which is included in determining the gross estate, is more than 50 percent of the value of the decedent's adjusted gross estate (i.e., gross estate less the deductions for administration expenses, debts, taxes and losses).

If the above mentioned conditions are met, cash and other assets can be withdrawn from the decedent's corporation without being taxed as dividend or ordinary income. Notice that there is no requirement that the redemption price paid for the stock by the corporation actually be used to pay estate taxes or funeral and administrative expenses. The redemption money in cash, as well as other assets, can be used in any way the administrator of the estate desires. Section 303 applies whether an estate is liquid or not. Also, the relief under Section 303 can be enjoyed together with the deferment of time for payment of the federal estate tax (Code Sec. 6166). A finding of "reasonable cause" (previously undue hardship) permits the I.R.S. to defer the time for payments of estate taxes for reasonable periods of up to ten-years.

9.15. Selling Securities Acquired at Different Dates

When an investor acquires stock on different dates and at different prices, and the identity of the lots sold cannot be determined, the stock sold must be charged first against the earliest purchases on a First-In, First-Out basis (or F.I.F.O.). However, with a good record of stock sold, the taxpayer is allowed to use a specific identification method where stock sold is identified with a specific date and cost of acquisition. For tax saving purposes, observe the following steps:

1. Keep an accurate written record of the various dates of acquisition, quantities, and cost of the stock lots.
2. After qualifying for the specific identification method, figure the amount of capital gain or loss for the tax year and from all the security transactions under both the F.I.F.O. and the specific identification methods.
3. The method which shows the lowest amount of net gain, or the highest amount of capital loss, should be used for the tax year. The holding period is also affected by the method used.
4. The same process should be continued each year. However, if in any year no accurate written record of purchases and sales is kept by the taxpayer, the Internal Revenue Service will require the use of the F.I.F.O. method.

9.16. Purchasing Estate Tax Bonds

An investor may purchase certain United States Treasury Bonds at a discount and use them in payment of estate taxes at their face or par value. For more details regarding the purchase of estate tax bonds, see 16.26 in Chapter 16.

9.17. Investing in Federal Obligations

Interest on U.S. obligations is taxed as ordinary income. There are two main types of U.S. Saving Bonds:

1. Series E Bonds issued at a discount and not paying any periodic interest income. The longer this type of bond is held, the more they increase in value. The entire increase in value is taxable. However, if the taxpayer is on a cash basis, he may elect to report the annual increment for each year as taxable income for that year, or he may elect to be taxed on the entire amount of increment in value in the year of redemption or maturity. Notice that such election is binding for all bonds owned by the same taxpayer and applies to present, as well as all future years.

Through the timing principle, an investment in Series E Bonds can produce a tax saving. If the taxpayer is on a cash basis and elects not to recognize any increase in the value of his bonds until maturity, and if the bonds' maturity date falls in a low income-tax period, the effective tax rate on the investment could be lowered. Therefore, buy Series E Bonds and elect to postpone the increase in their value to a year when your income is low. If the owner of Series E Bonds dies, the increment in their value is reported as either income in respect of a decedent or included in his final income tax return. Furthermore, if the investor is on the accrual basis, he must report the annual increment in value each year as income for that year.

2. Series H Bonds are issued at par value with interest paid semi-annually. If the taxpayer is on a cash basis, he reports the interest when he receives it. If the investor is on an accrual basis, he accrues at the end of each tax period the interest income earned for the period.

The tax advisor should consider Series E Bonds carefully, since interest may accumulate for a long period of time without being taxed. Also, it is possible to exchange these bonds for Series H Bonds without paying tax on this interest. Under Code Section 1037, U.S. obligations may be exchanged tax free for other such obligations, except to the extent that money (or boot) is received in the exchange (for more details see **10.11** in Chapter 10.

Chapter 10

TAX BENEFITS UNDER THE NON-TAXABLE EXCHANGE RULES

10.1. Arranging an Exchange of Like Property

Knowledge of the area of tax-free exchanges is very rewarding. Rather than selling an appreciated property (i.e., with market value in excess of cost) and paying part of the sale price as tax on the capital gain, a tax-free exchange can be arranged. Also, with a modest degree of care, more future exchanges can be arranged to acquire other property or properties through tax-free exchanges. If a taxpayer keeps exchanging appreciated properties for other like properties, the result could be an indefinite postponement of any liability for a capital-gain tax.

Exchange of property held for productive use in a trade or business, or for investment, for similar property is not considered to be a sale and it will not necessarily lead to recognition of gain from the exchange. An exchange of like property with no money received will qualify as a tax-free exchange. One suggestion is to keep the newly-acquired property until the taxpayer's retirement, and then to sell it and recognize the postponed capital gain when taxable income and the tax bracket are low. Another suggestion is to keep the newly-acquired property until the owner's death. Upon his death, no gain is recognized on the property and it will pass on to the beneficiaries or new owners without any income tax on the postponed capital gain. To enjoy the tax-free status of an exchange, however, observe the following factors:

1. To qualify as a non-taxable exchange, both the property received and the property given should be "like" property (Sec. 1031 (a)). Be sure that real property is exchanged for real property and that a personal property is exchanged for a personal property of a like type, e.g., a farm for a farm, an apartment building for an office building, etc. Check whether an exchange qualifies as tax free or not before closing the deal.

2. If money is received in a non-taxable exchange, capital gain can be recognized up to the amount of money received. However, if money is given in order to complete the exchange, still no gain may be recognized. Therefore, an upward exchange (i.e., for a more valuable property) is better than a downward exchange (i.e., an exchange for a less valuable property) (Sec. 351(b), 1031(b); 1.351-2, 1.1031(b)-1).

3. If a mortgaged real property is exchanged for another mortgaged real property, the amount of mortgage relief (or net decrease in liability) is considered as money (or boot) received. Again, the tax rule is that even though the exchange is non-taxable, capital gain can be recognized (or taxed) up to the amount of decrease in liability.

10.2. Using Two-Way and Three-Way Exchanges

To avoid the tax on a capital gain, a non-taxable exchange should be arranged. An exchange may take one of the following forms:

1. A two-way exchange where (A) owns property on which he has received an offer from (B). At the same time (B) owns property which (A) would like to acquire. Therefore, (A) and (B) exchange the two properties with each other, with or without money given or received.

2. A three-way exchange by making an arrangement with the prospective buyer of your property wherein he purchases the property you wish to acquire, then he exchanges this property for the property you already own. For example, (A) owns property on which he has received an offer from (B). If the sale was made, (A) would like to use the proceeds from the sale to buy property owned by (C). Therefore, (A) may ask (B) to acquire the property from (C) and trade with (B) in a tax-free exchange.

10.3. Applying Cash from the Exchange Against Outstanding Debts on the Received Property

A tax-free exchange is a successful way of postponing tax on capital gain. However, when boot is received in a tax-free exchange, gain is recognized (or taxed) up to the amount of boot received. Boot means money and other "unlike" property. Also, when a taxpayer exchanges mortgaged property in a tax-free transaction, any relief from (or decrease in) his mortgage is considered as boot received. Therefore, in a well planned tax-free exchange, little or no boot is received. To minimize the amount of boot received, apply any expected cash from the exchange against an outstanding debt against the newly acquired property.

For example, Mr. Richard Smith owns a ranch with an adjusted basis of $100,000 which has no mortgage. He exchanges it for a farm worth $130,000, subject to $30,000 mortgage, and the transferee offers to pay Mr. Richard Smith $50,000 in cash. If Mr. Smith receives the $50,000 in cash, and assumes the debt, he realizes a gain of $50,000, figured as follows:

Value of property received			$130,000
Cash received			50,000
	Total consideration received		$180,000
Less:	Adjusted basis of property transferred	$100,000	
	Assumed mortgage on property received	30,000	130,000
	Gain realized		$ 50,000
Gain recognized: Up to the amount of boot received			$ 50,000

In this example, Mr. Richard Smith can reduce his recognized (or taxable) gain to $20,000 if he requests to apply part of the expected cash against the outstanding debt on the new farm before making the trade. Thus, assuming no debt in this case, receiving $20,000 in cash will lead to the following:

Value of property received		$130,000
Cash received		20,000
	Total Consideration received	$150,000
Less:	Adjusted basis of property transferred	100,000
	Gain realized	$ 50,000
Gain recognized:-		
	Up to the amount of boot received	$ 20,000

10.4. Setting Up the Values of Exchanged Properties

When you acquire business or investment property in a tax-free exchange, the effect of both the capital-gain tax, as well as the deduction for future depreciation charges, should be taken into consideration. Assigning values to the exchanged properties is needed for the following two main reasons:

1. To determine the difference between the total amount received and the total amount given, or what is called the realized gain (or loss).

2. To assign "basis" to the newly-acquired property. This new "basis" will be used in determining future depreciation charges. In many practical instances, money or its equivalent in liabilities is used to influence the "basis" of newly-received property. To show how money (or its equivalent in liabilities) can influence the computation of basis, and, consequently future depreciation charges, we can use the following three examples. In the first example, we will assume that no boot is given or received in the exchange. In the second example, we will assume the receipt of boot. In the third example, we will assume that boot is given.

Example 1: A taxpayer traded a machine having an adjusted basis of $4,000 for another machine having a fair market value of $5,000. The exchange is made with no money given or received. Since the exchange is tax free, no gain is recognized. However, the "basis" of the newly acquired machine is $4,000, as the adjusted basis of the old machine.

Example 2: A taxpayer had a truck with a basis of $6,000. He exchanged it for another truck with a fair market value of $7,500. In addition, he received $200 in cash.

Amount given:	
Old truck, basis	$6,000
Total	$6,000
Amounts received:	
New truck, fair market value	$7,500
Cash	200
Total	$7,700
Gain realized	$1,700
Gain recognized:	
Up to the amount of boot received	$ 200
Basis of new truck:	
Fair market value of new truck	$7,500
Less: Unrecognized gain (i.e. $1,700-$200)	1,500
Basis of new truck	$6,000

Example 3: A taxpayer had a building with an adjusted basis of $50,000. He traded it for another building having a fair market value of $70,000. In the exchange he paid $10,000 in cash.

Amounts given:	
Old building, basis	$50,000
Cash	10,000
Total	$60,000
Amount received:	
New building, fair market value	$70,000
Total	$70,000
Gain realized:	$10,000
Gain recognized (or taxable):	0
Basis of new building:	
Fair market value of new building	$70,000
Less: Unrecognized gain	10,000
Basis of new building	$60,000

From these examples the following recommendations can be made:

1. In order to increase the "basis" of newly received property, give money or its equivalent in assumed liabilities. The additional investment will increase the basis available for future depreciation and at the same time will postpone all of the realized gain from the exchange.

2. The basis of the newly-acquired property is equal to its fair market value reduced by any unrecognized gain. Therefore, if deducting higher future depreciation charges is important to the taxpayer, increase the amount of recognized gain from the exchange. If all of the realized gain is taxed, the basis of the newly-received property will equal its estimated fair market value. Paying a tax on the realized capital gain may not be a bad idea if the gain is treated as a long-term gain, while the increase in basis will result in higher depreciation charges claimed in future years against ordinary income. Of course, to recognize more gain in the year of exchange, receive (and do not give) more boot. Although immediate tax savings may result from postponement of all the gain from an exchange of property, the taxpayer must look beyond the immediate tax savings. If a taxpayer is in the high income brackets, it may be to his advantage to have a higher annual depreciation deduction, rather than to escape taxation of the capital gain.

10.5. Combining Installment Reporting with Nontaxable Exchanges

A combination of benefits of the non-taxable exchange rule and the installment method of reporting gains can reduce the amount of capital gain subject to tax in the year of exchange. The taxpayer has the right to elect the installment method, or to recognize all the gain from exchange in the year of reporting the exchange of properties. If the exchange involves large sums of money, the installment method should be considered seriously.

Example: A taxpayer had a shopping center with an adjusted basis of $600,000. He traded it for another shopping center having a fair market value of $650,000. In addition, he received $20,000 in cash and a mortgage for $80,000, payable by the other party to the exchange in semi-annual installments of $10,000 with the first installment to be paid on January 10th of the year following the year of exchange.

Amounts received:	
New shopping center, fair market value	$650,000
Cash	20,000
Mortgage	80,000
Total	$750,000
Amount given:	
Old shopping center, basis	$600,000
Total	$600,000
Gain realized:	$150,000
Gain recognized:	
1. If the taxpayer does not elect the installment method; the taxable gain is up to the amount of cash received or	$ 20,000
Basis of new shopping center:	
Fair market value	$650,000
<u>Less:</u> Unrecognized gain	130,000
Basis of new property	$520,000
2. If the taxpayer elects the installment method:—Profit to be reported in year of exchange ($20,000 x $\frac{\$150,000}{\$750,000}$	$ 4,000
Profit to be reported in years of mortgage collection: $80,000 x $\frac{\$150,000}{\$750,000}$ =	16,000
Total taxable gain	$ 20,000

Basis of new shopping center:	
Fair market value	$650,000
Less: Unrecognized gain ($150,000-$4,000-$16,000)	130,000
Basis of new property	$520,000

From this example we can draw the following tax consequences: (1) The taxable gain reported in the year of exchange is reduced by electing the installment method. As a result, the tax on capital gain in the year of exchange would be less too. (2) The basis of the newly-received property is not affected by the election to use the installment method. The deduction for depreciation in the year of exchange, as well as later years, will not increase or decrease because of electing the installment method.

10.6. Assigning Values to the Components of Exchanged Properties

Assigning values to the components of exchanged properties is essential for the following tax related areas:

1. After computing the basis of property received in the exchange, the total basis should be broken down between the various components of the property. For example, after figuring the total basis of a building received in a tax-free exchange, allocate it between land, building, leases, landscaping, driveways, plumbing, air-conditioning, electric signs, furniture, heating system, hot water system, lighting fixtures, electrical wiring, paneling, etc. Each one of these components may have a different useful life. As a result, assigning shorter estimated lives to some of the components would result in a higher depreciation deduction in the early years following the exchange of properties.

2. The investment credit applies to both used and new qualified property. However, only $100,000 (or $50,000 for a married person filing separately) of the cost of used property is eligible for the credit. In case of a non-taxable exchange, another limit is imposed on the cost of qualified used property. The cost of used property received in a non-taxable exchange is limited to boot given. Since most exchanges involve used properties, the tax advisor should consider carefully this limitation imposed on received used property which is eligible for the investment credit. An upward exchange (i.e., receiving a more valuable property) coupled with payment of money would enhance the chances of claiming the investment credit whenever Section 38 property is involved.

10.7. Selling vs. Exchanging Properties

An owner of property held for productive use or investment has the choice of either selling his property or exchanging it for property of a like kind. Selecting the sale route and recognizing the capital gain, or postponing the recognition of gain under the nontaxable exchange rules, is not an easy matter and depends upon the following six main factors:

1. The sale of property held for productive or investment purposes may lead to a capital gain or loss. The gain is taxable and the loss is deductible. However, if such property is exchanged for a like property, the capital gain may be postponed in full, or in part, while any capital loss is usually not recognized. For example, a taxpayer exchanged a machine with an adjusted basis of $10,000 for a new one. He also gave $1,000 cash and a $2,000 note. The fair market value of the new machine is $10,500. His realized loss is $2,500, but, he cannot claim it as deductible in the year of the exchange. The following computations illustrate the tax treatment:

Gave:		
Old machine, basis		$10,000
Cash		1,000
Note		2,000
	Total	$13,000
Received:		
New machine, fair market value		$10,500
	Total	$10,500
Realized loss		($2,500)
Recognized loss		None

The only situation in which a loss is recognized in a non-taxable exchange is when other property is given in the exchange. The loss in such a case is recognized to the extent of the difference between the basis and fair market value of the other property. For example, a taxpayer exchanged a truck with an adjusted basis of $6,000 for a similar truck. He also gave stock with an adjusted basis of $5,000 and a fair market value of $3,000. The fair market value of the truck received is $7,000. His realized loss is $4,000 and his recognized loss is only $2,000 and is determined as follows:

Gave:		
Old truck, basis		$ 6,000
Stock, basis		5,000
	Total	$11,000
Received:		
New truck, fair market value		$ 7,000
	Total	$ 7,000
Realized loss		($4,000)
Recognized loss:		
only to the extent of the difference between the basis and fair market value of the boot (i.e., $5,000-$3,000)		($2,000)
Basis of new truck:		
Basis of old truck		$ 6,000
Add: basis of stock transferred		5,000
	Total	$11,000
Less: loss recognized on stock transfer		2,000
Basis of new truck		$ 9,000

2. An individual's taxable capital gains are matched against his deductible capital losses and the net gain or loss is determined. Reporting a capital loss in a year with capital gains is desirable since the net taxable gain will decline. If a taxpayer has deductible capital loss in a certain tax period, he may sell a property held for productive use or investment and recognize the gain from sale, instead of arranging a non-taxable exchange. Therefore, the other capital-gain-and-loss activities of a taxpayer should be considered before making the decision to sell or to arrange a non-taxable exchange of a property.

3. Sale of Section 1245 property (depreciable personal property) or Section 1250 property (depreciable real property) may result in depreciation recapture. The recaptured depreciation is taxed as ordinary income. However, the recapture rules under Section 1245 and Section 1250 do not apply to disposition of property in a non-taxable exchange. Notice that this makes an exchange of depreciable property (real and personal) more advantageous than a sale. If Section 1245 or Section 1250 property is exchanged, observe the following:

a. Do not receive in the exchange boot or other than Section 1245 (or Section 1250) property. The recapture rules apply if boot or other property is received.

b. Any ordinary income from depreciation recapture will reduce the basis of the Section 1245 (or Section 1250) property received.

4. Sale of Section 38 property before the end of its estimated useful life may result in an investment credit recapture. The investment credit recapture rules apply to both sales and exchanges of Section 38 property. Any disposition of such property should be preceded by a study of the possibility of credit recapture.

5. When a taxpayer sells his property, there is no need to limit the amount of cash he can receive from the sale, unless he wants to elect the installment method for reporting the gain from sale. On the other hand, in case of a non-taxable exchange, the amount of cash and other property received should be considered carefully. The rule of recognizing gain in a non-taxable exchange transaction up to the amount of boot received places a limit on the amount of money that can be received and enjoyed from such an exchange. Generally, therefore, if the receipt of cash is desired, or needed, selecting a sale could be more advantageous than arranging an exchange.

6. The decision of selling vs. exchanging properties results in immediate tax impact affecting the year of sale or exchange. However, the tax advisor must look beyond the immediate tax effect to determine whether or not the present tax savings outweigh the expected future tax effects. The result of an exchange could be a lower basis for depreciation and for determining gain or loss on a subsequent sale. If a taxpayer is in the high income tax brackets, it may be to his advantage to have a higher annual depreciation allowance from a purchased property, rather than a property acquired from a non-taxable exchange. Also, the future plans of the taxpayer should be investigated. He may wish to keep on exchanging like properties and postponing the tax on capital gains. On the other hand, he may plan to sell the property and put the proceeds in a different type of investment. By combining the future plans of the taxpayer with his present tax situation, a better collection of data can be made available for making the decision of selling or exchanging a property.

10.8. Exchanging Depreciable Personal and Real Properties

Under Section 1245, gain from disposition of depreciable personal property, up to the amount of all depreciation deductions taken on it after 1961, is treated as ordinary income. The remainder of the gain from disposition, if any, is treated as Section 1231 gain. Also, under Section 1250, gain from disposition of depreciable real property, up to the amount of additional depreciation taken after 1963 (i.e., the excess of the depreciation deductions taken over the amount of deductions that would have been taken if the straight-line method of depreciation had been used), is recaptured in full or part. To minimize the effects of depreciation recapture under Section 1245 and 1250, observe the following:

1. The rules of Section 1245 and 1250 do not apply to non-taxable exchanges unless boot or other than Section 1245 (or Section 1250) property is received. Therefore, when exchanging depreciable property, check the possibility of depreciation recapture before accepting any boot or other property to complete the exchange.

2. If an exchange is made, and an ordinary income results from depreciation recapture, the basis of the Section 1245 (or Section 1250) property received will be decreased by the amount of any ordinary income from depreciation recapture. For example, a taxpayer purchased a truck in 1971 for $9,000 and claimed the following deductions for depreciation:

Year	Depreciation Expense
1971	$1,500
1972	1,500
1973	1,500
1974	1,500
1975	1,500

On January 1, 1976, he traded the truck for another in a tax-free exchange. The new truck had a fair market value of $3,000. He also received $1,000 cash in the exchange. His recognized gain of $1,000 is treated as ordinary income under Section 1245. In addition, the basis of the new truck is reduced by the amount of the ordinary income. The transaction is summarized as follows:

Gave:		
Old truck, basis ($9,000-$7,500)=		$1,500
	Total	$1,500
Received:		
New truck, fair market value		$3,000
Cash		1,000
	Total	$4,000

Realized gain:	$2,500
Recognized gain:	
Gain up to the amount of boot received is taxed as ordinary income under Section 1245	$1,000
Basis of new truck:	
Fair market value of new truck	$3,000
Less: Unrecognized ordinary income potential (total gain $2,500 less recognized gain $1,000)	$1,500
Basis of new truck	$1,500

Therefore, exchanging Section 1245 or Section 1250 property results in the same tax savings expected from a tax-free exchange unless boot or other than Section 1245 or Section 1250 property is received.

10.9. Using a Corporation to Complete a Wide Variety of Special Exchanges

Gain or loss may be recognized if an individual taxpayer receives money or other property in exchange for any stock or securities he owns. The reason is that the exchange does not involve like property. If this individual taxpayer creates a corporation, however, his ability to use tax-free exchanges will increase considerably to include the following additional four major types of exchanges:

1. No gain or loss is recognized on exchanging property solely for the corporation's own stock or securities. The term stock or securities does not include short-term notes. Also, if the corporation assumes liabilities in excess of the basis of the property transferred, the excess is taxable gain to the transferor. Therefore, to use the non-taxable exchange rules under Section 351, do not receive any boot from the exchange. If boot or short-term notes are received, part of the gain from the exchange will be recognized.

For example, a taxpayer transfers land with an adjusted basis of $20,000 and a fair market value of $100,000 to a controlled corporation in exchange for stock worth $60,000, cash of $30,000, and bonds with a fair market value of $10,000. His capital gain is $80,000, but only $40,000 of it is taxable. The computation is as follows:

Gave:		
Land, adjusted basis		$20,000
	Total	$20,000
Received:		
Stock, fair market value		$60,000
Cash		30,000
Bonds, fair market value		10,000
	Total	100,000
Realized gain		$80,000
Recognized gain:		
Up to the amount of boot and other property received ($30,000 + $10,000)		$40,000

Instead of receiving boot and other property from the exchange, this taxpayer could have eliminated the taxable gain by receiving stock and securities only. For tax saving purposes, use the route of Section 351 tax-free exchanges for appreciated property, while a separate sale of depreciated property for boot is arranged.

2. When a stockholder transfers stock to the issuing corporation in exchange for boot or other property, the exchange may be taxed as an ordinary sale of stock or as a dividend from the corporation. The relationship between the stockholder and the corporation and the circumstances surrounding the sale (e.g., through a broker or directly to the corporation) dictate the "sale" or "dividend" treatment. The tax advisor is given two escape routes from this problem. The first route is Section 333, or partial liquidations. The second route is stock redemption under Sections 302 and 303.

Under Section 333 a relief provision allows a corporation to be liquidated without the stockholders being taxed on the increase in value of the property they receive. The liquidation should be made pursuant to a plan, and the transfer of all the property under the liquidation should occur within one calendar month. This route is useful if a corporation has low profits, while its assets consist largely of property that appreciated in value. The second relief provision under Sections 302 and 303 allows the redemption of stock without being taxed on the proceeds as dividend income. When stock is redeemed, the transaction is treated as if the stockholder sold part or all of his stock to the corporation at a gain or loss. In practical life, what looks like a redemption could be a disguised dividend diverted from the ordinary income to the capital-gain route.

3. Exchanging common for common, preferred for preferred, or voting for nonvoting stock in the same corporation is not subject to tax under Section 1036. Such exchanges are often helpful for business or estate planning purposes since the exchange is non-taxable, whether it is between a stockholder and the corporation, or between two individual stockholders.

4. Under Section 368, reorganization exchanges are tax free. The easy ways to meet requirements for tax free reorganizations are:

a. The reorganization (unless a divisive reorganization) is pursuant to a plan.
b. The reorganization must have a business reason or purpose. An intention to avoid or reduce tax liability will not of itself make a reorganization ineffective.
c. There must be a continuity of interest in the corporation on the part of the stockholders (unless the reorganization is Type D or a transfer by a corporation of some or all of its assets to a second corporation).
d. The business must continue under a modified corporate form. Notice that the transferor corporation does not recognize any gain or loss on an exchange of property for stock or securities if a party to the reorganization. In addition, no gain or loss is recognized by stockholders if stock or securities are exchanged solely for stock or securities in the same corporation or in another corporation which is a party to the reorganization. If boot and other property are received in the exchange, gain can be recognized up to the amount of boot and other property received. For example, a taxpayer surrendered stock with a basis of $11,000 for stock with a fair market value of $15,000, securities worth $5,000, and $3,000 in cash. His realized gain is $12,000 and taxable gain $8,000, figured as follows:

Gave:		
stock surrendered, basis		$11,000
	Total	$11,000
Received:		
stock, fair market value		$15,000
securities, fair market value		5,000
cash		3,000
	Total	$23,000
Realized gain:		$12,000
Recognized gain:		$ 8,000
Basis of the new stock:		
Fair market value of new stock		$15,000

Less: unrecognized gain ($12,000-$8,000)	4,000
Basis of new stock	$11,000

10.10. Exchanging Insurance Policies

Section 1035 offers postponement of tax on the following exchanges of insurance policies:

1. An ordinary life insurance contract exchanged for another life insurance contract, or for an endowment or annuity contract.
2. An endowment contract exchanged for another endowment policy which provides for regular payments, beginning at a date not later than the date payments would have been made under the contract exchanged, or for an annuity contract.
3. An annuity contract exchanged for another annuity contract. This type of exchange applies also to exchanges between "fixed" and "variable" annuities.

Exchanging insurance policies may serve one or more of the following situations:

1. Changes in the insured's financial position.
2. Changes in the insured's family responsibilities.
3. Changes in the insured's business needs.

To avoid the tax on exchanges of insurance policies, the tax advisor should observe the following rules:

1. If cash is received in the exchange, gain will be recognized to the extent of cash. Also, no loss from the sale or surrender of life insurance, or endowment contracts is deductible.
2. The exchanged insurance and annuity contracts must be on the life of the same insured.
3. Gain or loss is recognized on the following taxable transactions:

a. Exchange of an endowment or annuity contract for a life insurance contract.

b. Exchange of an annuity contract for an endowment contract.

c. Exchange of an endowment contract for another endowment having a maturity date later than the original policy. Since the extended date increases the chances of the insured's dying before maturity, this results in the proceeds of the endowment policy escaping tax on the ground that they were paid as the proceeds of a life insurance contract.

10.11. Exchanging United States Obligations Issued Under the Second Liberty Bond Act

Obligations issued by the United States under the Second Liberty Bond Act may be exchanged tax free for other such obligations in taxable years ending after September 22, 1959. The postponment of tax is offered to encourage the exchange of bonds approaching maturity for new ones with a longer period to maturity. This tax saving feature becomes more important if the receipt of interest income from such bonds can also be deferred until later years when a taxpayer will be retired or will be receiving less annual taxable income. Notice that under the same principle, state or municipal bonds may be exchanged for substantially identical bonds issued by the same obligor with no gain or loss being recognized.

Under Code Section 1232, if the taxpayer sells, exchanges, or retires bonds issued at a discount and held more than six months, an amount equal to the "original issue discount" (or OID) is treated as ordinary income. If gain on the exchange of such bonds is not recognized (under Section 1037), then, when the bond received in exchange is disposed of or redeemed at a gain, ordinary income will be realized in an amount equal to what would have been ordinary income (or original issue discount) realized on the original bond. The tax advisor should proceed with extra care when bonds or other evidences of indebtedness are issued originally at a discount. Such discount may represent an interest income and could be taxed as ordinary income. To reduce the effect of tax on original issue discounts, the taxpayer may postpone the sale or exchange of such bonds until he retires or effects the sale or exchange in a year with low taxable income. Another method to reduce the effect of Section 1232 is to give such bonds as gifts to a friend or family member who is in a relatively lower income tax bracket.

10.12. Reinvesting Condemnation or Involuntary Conversion Proceeds in Other Like Property

The rules related to involuntary conversion provide a broad and important area of tax savings for individuals. Receiving proceeds from condemnation of property and reinvesting them in a similar property, produces the same effect of a tax-free exchange. In order to maximize the tax savings from the special treatment given to involuntary conversion, observe the following special situations:

1. If a business has use and occupancy (or business interruption) insurance, the proceeds qualify as proceeds of an involuntary conversion.

However, this special tax treatment will be lost if the proceeds from insurance are based on lost profits. Therefore, it is better to measure the insurance claim by a fixed periodic amount (*Miller V. Hocking Glass Co.*, 80 F. 2d 436, 16 AFTR 1448).

2. The sale or exchange of livestock because of disease or drought qualifies as an involuntary conversion. In this situation, you need to establish that the sale or exchange was solely due to the disease or drought (Sec. 1033(e); 1.1033(e)-1). Also, a farmer may sell or exchange a property in an irrigation project to conform to the acreage limitations of federal reclamation laws and treat the proceeds as amounts from an involuntary conversion (Sec. 1033(d)).

3. No gain is recognized from an involuntary conversion if the proceeds are invested in a similar property or in a property related in service or use. The replacement period starts at the earlier of date of destruction (or seizure), or the earliest date of the threat of condemnation. The end of the replacement period is two years (for personal property and for casualty and theft losses of all property) after the end of the tax year in which any part of the gain is realized (Sec. 1.1033(a)-2(c)(3)). Section 2140 of the 1976 Tax Reform Act extended the replacement period from two years to three years for condemned real property. Furthermore, the taxpayer may apply before the end of the two (or three) year period to the Internal Revenue Service for a special extension of replacement time.

4. Although the gain from condemnation may not be taxed under the replacement rules, the loss on an involuntary conversion is usually deductible. An involuntary conversion loss related to a business or investment property is fully deductible. However, a similar loss related to a personal use asset (e.g., personal residence) is deductible only after disallowing the first $100 of loss per event or casualty.

5. Replacement of property under the involuntary conversion rules is generally not subject to depreciation recapture rules under Section 1245 and 1250 if no gain is recognized from the conversion. To eliminate any depreciation recapture, invest all the conversion proceeds in another Section 1245 or Section 1250 property.

The recognized gain or deductible loss from the condemnation of business or capital assets held for more than six months (nine months in 1977 and one year after 1977) qualifies as Section 1231 gain or loss. Section 1231 provides a special tax break. If the net of all Section 1231 gains and losses is a gain, all the gains and losses are treated as long-term gains and losses. However, if the net of all Section 1231 gains and losses is a loss, all the gains and losses are treated as ordinary gains and losses.

7. It is not unusual to have only part of a property condemned or destroyed. This may leave the taxpayer with remaining property that he can no longer use for business or investment purposes. In this case, he may sell the balance of the property and reinvest the combined condemnation and sales proceeds in a new and similar property (Masser, 30 TC 741, Prentice-Hall "Federal Taxes" ¶31,712 (50)). This way, he will avoid the tax on any gain from both the condemnation and the sale.

Chapter 11

TAX BENEFITS FROM INSTALLMENT SALE REPORTING

11.1. Timing the Election to Use the Installment Method

Special provisions allow a taxpayer to spread his gain from installment sales over the years in which he receives payments. The installment method is available for dealers in personal property (Sec. 453(a)), sales of real property (Sec. 453(b)). If the taxpayer is not a dealer in personal property, the following two main conditions must be satisfied in order to qualify for the installment method:

1. Payments received in the year of sale do not exceed 30 percent of the selling price.
2. Payments are made in two or more tax periods.

Qualifying taxpayers are free to elect the installment method, thereby postponing part of the gain from a sale, or to recognize the entire gain in the year of sale. Non-dealers are also free to elect the installment method on one sale and not on another in the same year. Since the installment method is elective, care should be exercised to assure that the election is beneficial and fits the tax situation of the taxpayer. It is common to find a taxpayer reporting the gain on a sale on an installment basis in one year and forgoing the installment method in another year. Usually, the installment method is recommended in the following cases:

1. If the income of the taxpayer from other activities is high.
2. If the unpaid balance of the sale price can be scheduled to fall in years with lower expected income (e.g., after retirement).

3. When the sale produces capital gain and the taxpayer has a large net capital loss for the year from other sources.

In the following special cases it may be desirable not to use the installment method:

1. If the income in the year of sale is low and is expected to be higher in future years.
2. If the sale results in a capital gain and the taxpayer has a large net capital loss for the year from exchange or sale of other properties.

11.2. Reporting the Gain from Sale of Inventory or Stock in Trade

Dealers in personal property are subject to the following special rules:

1. The restriction of the installment method on sales where not more than 30 percent of the selling price was received in the year of sale, does not apply to them.
2. Dealers are allowed a great degree of flexibility. For example, they may use the installment method in one department and not in another. They may also report installment sales on an installment basis, while continuing to report their other sales on an accrual or cash basis.
3. If merchandise is sold on an installment basis and the notes received from the buyer are immediately discounted to a finance company, the entire amount of profit should be reported in the year of sale.
4. If a dealer repossesses merchandise he sold, he may report a gain or loss from repossession. If he does not repossess the goods, he is entitled to a bad-debt deduction (equal to the unrecovered cost of goods sold).

When the tax advisor is dealing with the sale of merchandise inventory (or stock in trade), he should observe carefully the following two special situations:

1. Installment sale of inventory covers any sale of stock in trade with payments made in two or more installments. The amount of down payment is immaterial. The profit from such an installment sale is ordinary income. Therefore, if a going business is sold, consider selling the merchandise inventory as a separate item. If a smaller portion of the total sale price is allocated to the value of inventory sold, the amount of reportable ordinary income from the sale of inventory will decrease too. Most of the cash received as a down payment from the sale of the entire business can also be allocated to the sale of inventory, since the amount of down payment related to its sale is immaterial.

2. A dealer in personal property may switch to the installment method without prior approval of the Internal Revenue Service (Sec. 453(c)(1); 1.453-8). However, any receipts from prior credit sales, received after adopting the installment method, are included in ordinary income when collected. This leads to double taxation since the income from such credit sales was already taxed when the sale was originally made. To eliminate this type of double taxation, the dealer in personal property should sell all his outstanding receivables from prior credit sales before switching to the installment method.

11.3. Raising Cash from the Buyer's Note

For income tax purposes, an installment sale requires payments in two different tax years of the seller. Therefore, at least two payments must be made by the buyer, each of which falls in a separate year. Also, total payments received in cash in the year of sale, by non-dealers in personal property, should not exceed 30 percent of the selling price. The seller usually feels the effect of these restrictions placed on the amount of cash he can receive in the year of sale. Meanwhile, he has the following two major alternatives for raising cash from any notes or installment obligations received from the buyer:

1. Pledging the installment obligations as collateral for a loan from a bank or any other creditor. Generally the position of the taxpayer is strengthened if the loan is limited to no more than 75 percent of the face value of the installment note pledged. However, to avoid problems with the IRS and to reduce the chances that such a pledging is, in fact, a disposition of the obligation, observe the following:

A. Treat the loan as a bona fide borrowing with all the formalities of a loan transaction, i.e., in writing, with due date, specific principal, and specific interest rate.

B. Avoid making the bank loan repayable at intervals which are identical with the payments to be made under the installment obligation. Such an arrangement may show the pledging as a disposition of the obligation.

C. The interest rates, due installments and due dates should not be the same as those of the installment obligation.

2. Selling the installment obligation or note and reporting a gain or loss equal to the difference between the basis (i.e., the excess of the face value of the obligation over an amount equal to the income that would be reportable if the obligation were fully satisfied) and (i) the amount realized when the obligation is sold or exchanged, or satisfied at other than face

value, or (ii) the fair market value when the obligation is disposed of other than by sale or exchange (Sec. 453(d); 1.453-9).

For example, a taxpayer sells a parcel of land with a basis of $4,000 for $10,000. The terms of the sale are $1,000 down and the balance payable in equal annual installments over the next nine years. The profit ratio is 3/5 or 60 percent ($6,000 ÷ $10,000). Therefore, his basis for the installment obligation is $3,600 ($9,000 face value less 60 percent or $5,400, the amount that would have had to be reported as income had the obligation been paid). If he sells the obligations in the next year for $5,000, he will have a gain of $1,400. Any gain on disposition of installment obligations is considered as the same type of gain reported at the original sale. Therefore, if the asset was a capital asset, the gain from the disposition of the installment obligations will also be a capital gain. A word of caution regarding the sale of installment obligations: do not dispose of them in the same year of the installment sale. The entire gain realized would not be eligible for the installment method since payments from the sale of property would not be received over more than one tax year.

11.4. Using a Wrap-Around Mortgage

A taxpayer may sell a property and receive a relatively low amount of cash payment in the year of sale, and yet find himself disqualified for the installment method. The reason is that under a special rule, any excess of an existing debt obligation over the adjusted basis of the property sold is considered as a payment received in the year of sale (Sec. 1.453-4(c)). The amount of excess of an existing debt obligation over the adjusted basis of the property sold may exceed 30 percent of the selling price and disqualify the seller for the installment method even without his receiving any cash down payment in the year of sale. Therefore, whenever the property sold is encumbered by a high debt, use, as a solution, a wrap-around mortgage. This means that the buyer agrees to pay the entire agreed-upon price directly to the seller and the seller agrees to continue to discharge (or pay) the existing indebtedness. In this way, the buyer does not assume the existing debt. The seller continues to make payments on the old debt, while the new debt from the installment sale "wraps around" the continuing old debt.

11.5. Assigning an Interest Rate on the Unpaid Balance of Sale Price

The seller may decide not to charge any interest on the unpaid balance of the sale price. By doing this he can ask for a higher sale price, and at the same time, avoid reporting the interest as ordinary income.

Under Code Section 483, however, if interest is not charged at all, or if the interest rate is reasonably low (i.e., less than 4 percent), the Internal Revenue Service would impute interest at a rate of 5 percent per year compounded semiannually, and a corresponding part of the selling price will be considered as interest. Any interest income imputed to the seller may be claimed as an interest expense deduction by the buyer of a capital asset reported under the installment method.

To avoid imputing interest by the Revenue Service and changing the selling price of the property, use one of the following routes:

1. Adopt in the installment sale contract an annual interest rate on the unpaid balance now below 4 percent.
2. The Revenue Service will allow an installment sales contract to be a "non-interest bearing" contract only in the following two cases:
   a. If the total sale price is $3,000 or less.
   b. If all installment payments are due within one year.

The tax advisor should observe the following two undesirable tax effects of unstated interest:

1. The rules for imputing interest apply when property is sold at a gain or a loss. The imputed interest is taxed as ordinary income, thus reducing the amount of taxable capital gain or deductible loss.

2. Deducting the unstated interest from the sale price has the effect of reducing the selling price and increasing the percentage of payments received in the year of sale. Of course, if the newly-computed percentage of amounts received in the year of sale exceeds 30 percent, the sale no longer qualifies as an installment sale. If this happens, then all of the gain from the sale must be reported in the year of sale.

11.6. Offering an Increase in the Sale Price in Exchange for a Lower Interest Rate on the Unpaid Balance

The seller will enjoy the following advantageous tax effects if he offers an increased sale price in exchange for lowering the interest rate on the unpaid balance:

1. Any interest income from an installment obligation is taxed as ordinary income. On the other hand, an increase in the property sale price would usually lead to a larger capital gain. If the gain qualifies as a long-term capital gain, only 50 percent of it is taxed as ordinary income. Therefore, reducing the interest rate for a higher sale price results in the exchange of ordinary income for a long-term capital gain.

2. With an increase in the sale price, the seller can receive a larger amount of cash in the year of sale without pushing the payments beyond 30 percent of the gross selling price.

Notice that the buyer may not object to the offer of increasing the sale price in exchange for a lower interest rate (or course, a rate not below 4 percent per year). This special arrangement would also produce the following tax advantages for the buyer:

1. With an increase in selling price, the basis of the property available for depreciation (and sometimes, the investment credit) would increase too. Higher future depreciation deductions would reduce his future income tax liability.

2. A lower interest rate on the unpaid balance of the purchase price means lower payments for interest charges and lesser cash drainage. In the long run, the buyer will be paying the same total sum of money. This special arrangement affects only the allocation of the total sum of money between interest charges and the price of property.

11.7. Selling Property on an Installment Basis and the Systematic Forgiveness of Due Payments

Whenever property is sold to a related party and the sale is reported under the installment method, observe the following tax saving opportunities:

1. A taxpayer may sell a greatly appreciated property to a trust or related party and report the gain from sale on an installment basis. The new owner of the property will resell it for cash with little or no gain to be reported. Then, the installments are paid out of the proceeds from the sale. This type of arrangement would allow the owner of the appreciated property to sell it indirectly for cash, and yet, adopt the installment method by splitting the sale into two separate transactions (i.e., the sale to a related party, and then, the sale to an outsider). This technique was accepted by the Fifth Circuit Court in *Rushing,* 441 F2d593 (CA-5, 1971). To restrict the popularity of this technique, the Internal Revenue Service issued Rev. Rul. 73-157, 1973-1 CB 213, and Rev. Rul. 73-536, 1973-2 CB 158. Despite the Revenue Rulings, the decision in *Rushing* is a good base for spreading out the gain from an installment sale to a related party.

2. If a taxpayer transfers depreciable or real property to a related party for less than its fair market value, the transfer is considered to be partly a gift and partly a sale or exchange. If the amount realized from the transaction exceeds the taxpayer's adjusted basis, he must report it as

ordinary income because of any depreciation recapture. Any depreciation which is not recovered or recaptured is carried over to the new owner or transferee to be reported by him in case of a later disposition.

For example, a taxpayer transfers depreciable personal property to his son for $32,000. At the time of the transfer the property has an adjusted basis of $30,000 and a fair market value of $60,000. His depreciation taken after 1961 was $25,000. He is considered to have made a gift of $28,000 ($60,000 fair market value less $32,000 sale price to the son). The taxable gain on the transfer is $2,000 ($32,000 sale price less $30,000 adjusted basis). The $2,000 gain must be reported as ordinary income from depreciation recapture. The remaining balance of depreciation is $23,000 ($25,000 total depreciation less $2,000 recognized gain) and must be carried over to the son to be recaptured between his hands in case of a later disposition. The holding period of the son in this case begins at the date of acquiring the property by the father. Therefore, the sale of depreciable property to a related party can be used to postpone the recapture of depreciation.

Also, a taxpayer may sell a property to a related party and report the sale on an installment basis. Later, the seller may cancel the buyer's installment notes without reporting any gain from the cancellation. (The taxpayer's cancellation of his son's installment notes was not a disposition of installment obligations in *Miller, Sr. v. Usry* (DC La, 1958), 1 AFTR 2d 1295, 160 F. Supp. 368.

11.8. Selling a Going Business and Reporting the Sale Under the Installment Method

The sale of a going business is considered as a sale of the various separate business assets. Gain or loss from the sale of each business asset is subject to its own tax rules. For example, any gain (or loss) from the sale of inventory is treated as an ordinary income (or loss) item. Fixed assets (such as land, buildings, equipment, and furniture), as well as intangible assets (such as goodwill) are treated as capital assets. The records maintained for the business, as well as the sale contract, provide the information needed to figure the gain or loss on the sale of the various individual business assets. Drawing a detailed sale contract with a specific sale price identified with each asset sold is very important for the following two main reasons:

1. While the gain from the sale of inventory is taxed as ordinary income, any gain from the sale of fixed assets is taxed as a capital gain, unless the depreciation recapture rules under Section 1245 and 1250 apply. Therefore, allocating a smaller portion of the total sale price to the sale of inventory would result in reducing the ordinary income reported from the sale of the business.

2. The sale of personal and real property may be reported under the installment method if the payments received in the year of sale do not exceed 30 percent of the selling price. When the sale price of the going business is allocated between the various assets sold, the cash received in the year of sale may be allocated to the sale of specific assets. Therefore, assets which appreciated (or increased in value) substantially may be assigned cash payments below the 30 percent limit and reported as an installment sale, while items with a loss or a low capital gain would be assigned larger amounts of cash received in the year of sale, and the gain or loss is reported in one year.

11.9. Repossessing a Property Sold on the Installment Basis

The repossession of property sold under the installment method may result in a gain or loss. The amount of gain (or loss) and the basis of the repossessed property depends upon the terms of the original sale contract, as well as the fair market value of the repossessed property. Repossessions and foreclosures usually take one of the following three forms:

1. The seller of real property may foreclose on a mortgage he holds against the property. The foreclosure of a mortgage by the seller is treated like a repurchase of the property. For example, a taxpayer sold a building for $60,000 and reported the sale under the installment method. The sale price is payable as follows: $10,000 down and $10,000 per year thereafter. The adjusted basis of the building was $45,000. The buyer made the first $10,000 annual payment and then defaulted. Upon foreclosure the taxpayer (i.e., the seller) reacquired the property using $20,000 of the unpaid notes for payment. The remainder of the notes were uncollectable. His gain on the foreclosure is $5,000, and the basis of the reacquired property is $20,000, figured as follows:

Selling price	$60,000
Adjusted basis	45,000
Total realized gain	$15,000
Total payments received	$20,000
Total profit reported:	
profit ratio = $15,000 / $60,000 =	25%
Collections $20,000 x 25% =	$ 5,000

	Face Amount	Unrecovered Cost, 75%
Total unpaid notes	$40,000	$30,000
Used on repurchase of property	20,000	15,000
Canceled as worthless	$20,000	$15,000

Fair market value of reacquired property-at bid price	$20,000
Basis of notes given	15,000
Gain on foreclosure	$ 5,000
Bad debt deduction (i.e. basis of canceled notes)	$15,000
Basis of reacquired property	20,000

2. If the seller retains the property's title until full payment has been made, the repossession of property is treated as if no sale had ever taken place. For example, a taxpayer sold a building for $60,000, retaining the title to himself. The sale price is payable as follows: $10,000 down and $10,000 per year thereafter. The adjusted basis of the building was $45,000. The buyer made the first $10,000 annual payment and then defaulted. The taxpayer took possession of the property. During the period that the buyer had the building, sustained depreciation (or depreciation the seller would have sustained had he not sold the property) amounted to $1,000. The taxpayer retained all the payments he previously cellected. His total gain from the entire transaction is $19,000, and the basis of the reacquired building is $44,000 ($45,000 less $1,000 depreciation), and the gain is figured as follows:

Selling price	$60,000
Adjusted basis	45,000
Total gain	$15,000
Payments received	$20,000
Amount reported as income	$ 0
Total gain on entire transaction: —	
Payments received and retained	$20,000
Less: Portion already reported as income	0
Gross amount of income to be reported	$20,000

Less: Depreciation	1,000
Net gain recognized	$19,000

3. When a dealer repossesses personal property he sold, the repossessed goods are added to his merchandise inventory at their fair market value. His gain or loss from repossession is equal to the difference between the fair market value of the goods and the unpaid amount of the outstanding obligations, less the amount that would be reportable as income if the notes were paid in full (Reg. 1.453-1(d)). For example, a dealer sold for $500 an article that had cost $250, receiving $50 down and the balance payable in 20 monthly installments of $22.50 each. After paying four of these installments, the buyer defaulted. Under the agreement, the dealer repossessed the article when it had an estimated market value of $200. Gain (Loss) on repossession is $20 figured as follows:

Value of property at time of repossession		$200
Basis of obligations surrendered (16 unpaid installments):		
Face value (16 x $22.50)	$360	
Less: Unrealized profit (50%)	180	
		180
Taxable gain on repossession		$ 20
Profit to be reported on 4 installments:		
50% of $90		45
Total income		$ 65
The repossessed article is added to inventory at (its value when repossessed)		$200

If in this example the dealer does not repossess the article, or if it is valueless when recovered, he would be entitled to a bad debt deduction equal to the unrecovered cost of the article (Reg. 1.166-1).

From the above examples we can draw the following recommendations:

1. If the seller retains the title to property until full payment is received, he reports as gain from repossession the cash or other payments received, less any gain on the original sale reported in the year of sale. Also, the seller retains his original basis in the property since the reacquisition is not considered to be a repurchase. This seems to support the recommendation to keep the title to real property sold on an installment basis, until the sale price is collected in full.

2. A dealer in personal property should keep a record of the fair market values of repossessed articles. Switching to the installment method would spread the income from the sale over the actual period of collecting the entire amount of the sale price.

11.10. Splitting the Sale to Qualify for Installment Reporting

Splitting the sale into more than one transaction in order to satisfy the 30-percent test can be applied to the sale of a business and the sale of land in the following manner:

1. A business with the following simplified balance sheet is to be sold for a $100,000 (e.g., note payable in two years) plus the immediate assumption by the buyer of all current liabilities:

SIMPLIFIED BALANCE SHEET

Accounts receivable	$ 90,000	Current liabilities	$ 80,000
Other tangible assets	60,000	Capital investment	70,000
	$150,000		$150,000

The seller can adopt the installment method if he splits the sale into the following two transactions:

a. The first stage is to sell the unrecorded goodwill, all the other tangible assets, and only $10,000 of accounts receivable for the $100,000 note payable in two years. This transaction would produce a $30,000 gain ($100,000 less $60,000, and $10,000) with no portion of the proceeds received in the year of sale. Therefore, the sale would qualify for the installment method.

b. In a separate transaction, the remaining $80,000 ($90,000 less $10,000) of receivables is sold with the only consideration being the purchaser's assumption of the $80,000 of current liabilities. This transaction would not result in any gain or loss. The buyer would be expected to retire all the liabilities before the end of the year of sale.

In this example, by splitting the sale of the business into two separate transactions, the right to use the installment method is preserved.

2. An owner of ten acres of land is offered $20,000 per acre, or a total sale price of $200,000. In the year of sale he may receive $120,000 or an amount in excess of 30 percent of the sale price by splitting the sale into the following two transactions:

a. The sale of five acres at a price of $20,000 per acre and allocation of $100,000 of the cash received to this transaction. The gain from selling the five acres is reported in the year of sale.

b. The sale of the other five acres at a price of $20,000 per acre and allocation of $20,000 of the cash received to this transaction. The installment method may be elected for this transaction.

In this case the seller would enjoy using the installment method in reporting the sale of five acres, instead of losing the election on the sale of ten acres.

11.11. Avoiding the Receipt of a Contingent Selling Price

Sale of property is generally completed when title is conveyed by a deed, or when possession of the property is transferred to the buyer. However, if all or part of the sale price is based on future payments of a contingent nature, the sale is not final for tax purposes, and the installment method may not be adopted (*Burnet v. Logan,* 283US404, 9 AFTR 1453). If the sale price of the property is stated as a minimum selling price plus certain additional amounts, the taxpayer cannot use the installment method for any portion of the sale. For example, if a building is sold for $10,000 plus 10 percent of the net rental income for ten years, the installment method may not be used because the total contract price cannot be ascertained (*U.S. v. Yerger,* 55F. Supp. 521, 32 AFTR 855).

If the contingent obligation can be valued, the gain is taxed in the year of receipt. Otherwise, if it cannot be valued, the sale transaction remains open and additional gain is taxed when received. Therefore, if property is sold at a gain and the installment method is desired in order to spread the gain over a period of years, avoid using a contingent selling price and risking the loss of eligibility for installment sale reporting.

11.12. Transferring Installment Obligations to a Controlled Corporation

Under Code Section 351, no gain or loss is recognized if a taxpayer transfers property to a corporation solely in exchange for its stock or securities, and immediately after the exchange, he acquires control of the corporation. Control means owning at least 80 percent of all classes of stock issued by the corporation. Installment sale by a taxpayer and the transfer of installment obligations to his controlled corporation offer many tax saving opportunities. For example, a taxpayer sells appreciated land for $400,000. Payments received in the year of sale were $60,000. The basis of the property is $50,000. The $350,000 gain ($400,000 sale price less $50,000 basis) is reported on an installment basis. A year later, the taxpayer transfers the installment obligations to a corporation in return for stock which gives him more than 80 percent control of the corporation. The transaction is a Section 351 exchange on which no gain is recognized. The corporation continues collecting payments from the installment note. The gain from future collections is reported by the corporation and taxed separately from the other income of the controlling stockholder.

Notice that the transferor and corporation must report the exchange of installment obligations for a controlling interest in the corporation. Their income tax returns for the year of exchange should describe the transaction (Sec. 1.351-3).

11.13. Installment Selling of Property Received from a Corporation Under Section 333

A corporation may own a greatly appreciated asset (e.g., undeveloped land), and at the same time, has little or no earnings and profits. If the corporation sells the appreciated property, gain from the sale is taxed to the corporation. If the remaining proceeds from sale are distributed to the stockholders, such distributions are taxed to them as dividend or ordinary income. Code Section 333 offers a tax saving opportunity and a solution for a situation like this. The corporation will not sell the property, but instead, is liquidated and the property distributed to the stockholders. The stockholders will sell the property and report the sale on installment basis. This way, they spread the gain from the sale of property over more than one tax period while they liquidate the corporation without recognition of any gain on the appreciation or the increase in value of the property they get (Sec. 333; 1.333-1).

Notice that to secure a tax free liquidation under Section 333 you need to observe the following:

1. The relief offered under Section 333 is not available to collapsible corporations.
2. Within one calendar month from the date of adopting the liquidation plan, the corporation transfers all of its properties to the stockholders.
3. Within 30 days after the adoption of the liquidation plan, the shareholder must file his written election on Form 964 to accept the plan and the corporation files an information return on Form 966 (Sec. 6043; 1.6043-1).

11.14. Drawing into the Sale Contract a Penalty for Advance Payments in the Year of Sale

After selling a property and requesting a down payment plus principal payments in the year of sale not exceeding 30 percent of the gross selling price, the seller usually feels that he is eligible for electing the installment method. The buyer may, in an unexpected way, however, make additional principal payments during the year of sale. This could push the total payments beyond the 30 percent limit, and the seller would lose the right to elect the installment method. In turn, this could result in a substantial tax increase to the seller if the gain from the sale is high, or his other income in the year of sale is in the high tax brackets. In order to avoid this situation, the tax advisor should include in the sale contract a heavy penalty for prepayments in the year of sale only. Such a penalty will usually discourage the debtor (or buyer) from upsetting (intentionally or innocently) the plans of the seller.

Chapter 12

TAX BENEFITS OF THE INVESTMENT CREDIT

12.1. Increasing the Deduction for Annual Depreciation vs. Maximizing the Amount of the Investment Tax Credit

If an asset can be depreciated using a relatively short useful life (e.g., two to five years) the result will be a high depreciation deduction per year. However, the opportunity of increasing annual depreciation should be weighed against the possibility of losing part or all of the investment credit. Whenever the estimated useful life of a depreciable tangible personal property is less than seven years, take into consideration the deduction for depreciation and the investment credit at the same time as one indivisible item. In order to claim maximum investment tax credit on Section 38 property, the estimated useful life of an asset should be seven years or more. Also, no investment tax credit is allowed if the useful life is less than three years.

12.2. Increasing the Amount of the Investment Credit

The 10 percent investment credit can provide a substantial income tax relief. The credit is related to the cost of qualifying property. To maximize the benefit from the investment credit consider carefully the following:

1. Certain types of property may not qualify for the investment credit, but with some care, the treatment can be changed and the property will qualify for the investment credit. For example, a storage area to store

sorted and boxed fruit and vegetables will not qualify for the investment credit. However, if the storage facility is for loose fruit and vegetables, then the investment credit will not be lost. You may save a substantial amount of tax by slightly altering the use of the asset or by changing its description. Sometimes breaking down the cost of a property into its components will lead to saving at least part of the investment credit.

2. A property may qualify for the investment credit, but because of its source of acquisition, you may waste the credit. An example is when acquiring a property as a gift. Also, you cannot claim the credit on property that you buy after you have been leasing it. The credit will be lost if the property is acquired from spouse, ancestor or lineal descendants. Notice that if you acquire a property from your father you cannot claim the credit on it, but, if you acquire the same property from your brother or sister, you can claim the credit.

3. There is no dollar limitation on the cost of new property that may qualify for the investment credit. However, for used qualifying property the cost for each year should not exceed $100,000 (the $100,000 limitation is extended through 1980). The solution is to spread your purchases of used qualifying property over more than one tax period.

12.3. Avoiding Recapture of the Investment Credit

If an asset is disposed of before the end of its estimated useful life, the investment credit which was claimed on this asset must be recomputed (Sec. 47(a); 1.47-1(a)). This may lead to a repayment of part or all of the investment credit previously claimed on an asset. To minimize the chances of such repayment, be aware of the following:

1. The term "disposition" for investment credit recapture purposes is very broad and includes sale, exchanges, abandonment, gifts, trade-ins, the sale of stock by a Subchapter S Corporation stockholder, a sale of interest in a partnership, conversion of business property to non-business use, and involuntary conversion.
2. A property may be treated as one that is disposed of if the taxpayer fails to keep adequate records showing cost, estimated useful life, the date the property was put into use, and the date of final disposition.
3. A change in the use of an asset may affect its classification from a qualifying to a non-qualifying property, such as converting a business property to non-business use.
4. Leasing a property is not considered a disposition. Instead of selling unneeded property and losing part or all of the investment credit, lease it until the end of the estimated useful life you reported for investment

credit purposes when you acquired this property. After the end of this estimated life, you can sell or dispose of the property without fear of recapture of credit.

5. The sale of stock by a Subchapter S Corporation stockholder is considered a disposition for recapture purposes. However, the termination of election to be treated as a Subchapter S Corporation will not result in credit recapture. Therefore, before selling stock in a Subchapter S Corporation, you may consider first terminating the election of a Subchapter S Corporation.
6. Making a gift is considered a disposition, but transfering the property at death is not. Therefore, give as gifts to your beneficiaries, assets which did not qualify for the investment credit, or did qualify, but your actual holding period is not less than the estimated useful life of the property. Notice that transfer upon death will be considered as if the property was held for its entire estimated useful life.

12.4. Maximizing the Benefits from the Carryback and Carryforward of Unused Investment Credit

Under IRC Sec. 46 (b) (Reg. 1.46-2) (and 1976 Act Sec. 802) any unused investment credit may be carried back for three years and carried over for seven years (applied on First-In, First-Out basis in 1976 and later years). An investment credit carryback to a preceding year may result in a tax refund. In order to maximize the benefits from the carryback and carryforward rules, observe the following:

1. Before making any major acquisition of a qualified Sec. 38 property compute the following:

a. Estimated taxable income and total income tax for the current year, and, whether all the investment credit on the newly acquired property will be claimed in the current year.

b. The net income tax paid over the past three years and the amount of tax refund if part of the investment credit for the current year is not used.

2. If you expect a net operating loss in the current year and at the same time you plan to acquire Section 38 property, compute the effect of carrying back both the net operating loss as well as the unused investment tax credit. If any part of the investment credit will not be used, consider acquiring the qualifying property by another business entity, and after that, lease this needed property.

3. Time your acquisitions to fall in the last three months of the tax year. In this way, you will have a better picture of the expected tax liability for the entire year.

12.5. Claiming the Investment Credit on Leased Property

In the case of leased property, the owner usually claims the investment credit if at least one of the following two conditions is satisfied (this applies to individuals, partnerships, and tax-option corporations only):

1. If the period of the lease is less than 50 percent of the useful life of the leased property and the owner's expenses related to the property are more than 15 percent of the rental income from the property, for the first year of the lease, or
2. If the leased property has been manufactured or produced by the owner.

The owner of new property may elect to pass the investment credit to the lessee if the lessee is the original user (Sec. 48(d); 1.48-4(a). However, he cannot pass the credit for used property to the lessee. Also, if the property has a useful life in excess of 14 years and is leased for a period which is shorter than 80 percent of its useful life, the owner may pass through to the first lessee a portion of the investment credit which the lease period bears to the class life of the property. For effective use of the investment credit on leased property, observe the following:

1. Each stockholder in a Subchapter S Corporation claims his proportionate part of the investment in Section 38 property, and takes his credit separately. However, the $100,000 ($50,000 for years beginning after 1980) limit as to used property applies at both the corporate and shareholder levels. Therefore, observe the limit when used property is acquired. If a choice exists between acquiring new or used property, the way to go around the dollar limit is to acquire new property.

2. The lessor of a new Section 38 property should consider carefully whether to claim the credit or pass it on to the lessee. Passing the credit on to the lessee may lead to better terms for the lessor or a more effective use of the credit (e.g., if the lessor cannot use part or all of the credit in the current year and carrying the unused credit backward will not produce a tax refund).

3. Death of an owner of Section 38 property does not result in an investment credit recapture. After acquiring Section 38 property and claiming the investment credit by an individual taxpayer, his estate may sell the property after his death without fear of any tax credit recapture. Therefore, from an investment credit point of view, Section 38 property should be acquired by the oldest member of a family.

4. The investment credit will be claimed by the owner of a leased property if the property is subject to short-term leases. A short-term lease covers a period (including renewal options) less than 50 percent of the property's estimated useful life.

12.6. Electing to Claim Advance Investment Tax Credits for Progress Expenditures

Under Section 302(a) of the Tax Reduction Act of 1975, a taxpayer may elect to claim advance investment tax credits for years before the property is actually placed in service. For tax years ending after 1974, the progress payments rule allows the election to be made if the property takes two or more years to construct (or manufacture) and will have an expected useful life of seven or more years. Credits taken on progress payments, plus the credit for the year the property is placed in service, are equal to the total credit on the full basis of the property. The election to take advance credits applies to the tax year for which it is made and to all later tax years. It may not be revoked without the Commissioner's consent. Also, the election may not be made on a property-by-property basis and must cover all progress expenditure property.

The amount of qualified progress expenditures depend on whether the property is self-constructed or acquired. The following guidelines define progress expenditures:

1. A self-constructed asset should be charged for all its related capital expenditures. Depreciation on machines and equipment used in the construction process may not be capitalized for investment credit purposes.
2. The amount of progress expenditures on acquired property is the lesser of (a) the progress payments during the tax year, or (b) the portion of the basis of construction completed during the tax year.

To maximize the benefit from advance credits for progress payments, observe the following:

1. The Tax Reform Act of 1975 (Sec. 302-a) assumes a steady rate of completion or progress. For example, if the estimated construction period is five years, it is presumed that construction is completed at the rate of 20 percent per year. However, the taxpayer can claim faster progress in certain years if he can prove it with convincing evidence. Realistic certification by an independent engineer can assist in establishing a claim for faster progress.

2. Money borrowed directly or indirectly from a person constructing property for the taxpayer does not count as an amount expended for the construction of that property. This restriction applies to both loans made to the taxpayer by the manufacturer and to loans in connection with property that is treated as self-constructed but is partially constructed (50 percent or less) by the taxpayer. To avoid this restriction and to claim advance credit for progress payments even if they are borrowed: (a) self-construct (50 percent or more) the needed property, or (b) do not borrow from the manufacturer or the party constructing the property, but rather finance the acquisition from other internal or/and external sources.

3. The cost of component parts used in the construction of property qualifying for advance credits may not be treated as qualified progress expenditures until the component parts become irrevocably devoted to use in that property. Since the cost of components will increase the amount of advance credit allowed, it is important to capitalize their cost as soon as possible. To do this, use one of the following solutions: (a) a component is considered immediately devoted to the property being constructed if it is suitable for use only in that property (even if it has not yet become a part of the property), or, (b) if the component has been delivered to the site of construction.

4. Advance credits for progress payments will be fully recaptured if (Sec. 47(a) (3)):

a. The progress expenditure property is sold or otherwise disposed of before being placed in service, or
b. If it becomes apparent that the property will not be a qualified investment oroperty when placed in service.

Notice that disposition for recapture purposes includes sales, exchanges, gifts, trade-ins and involuntary conversions. It does not include transfers at death, transfers to another corporation in a tax-free corporate liquidation or reorganization and changes in the form of doing business.

12.7. Electing the Extra 1 Percent Investment Credit for Contribution to an Employee Stock Ownership Plan

Under Section 301(d) of the 1975 Tax Reduction Act, a corporate taxpayer can elect an 11 percent investment credit for acquisitions and construction of Section 38 property during the 10 percent period, if the extra 1 percent is contributed to an employee stock ownership plan funded by transfers of employer securities. The 1 percent contribution to an employee stock ownership plan (ESOP) must be made upon receiving the 11 percent investment credit. The ESOP must allocate the securities to participating employees as of the end of each plan year. The stock allocation is based on the relative compensation of each employee, disregarding compensation to any employee in excess of $100,000. The stock allocated to an employee may not be distributed to him until more than seven years (or 84 months) after the end of the month in which the stock was allocated to his account, except in case of separation from service, death or disability. Part or all of the extra 1 percent investment credit would be recaptured if the 11 percent credit property is disposed of earlier than expected. The employer cannot, however, withdraw any part of the contribution to the ESOP on account of the credit recapture.

The extra 1 percent investment credit should be claimed by the corporate taxpayer since it does not constitute any extra tax liability or saving. The extra 1 percent is deducted from the tax liability of the corporation and is given in a tax-free transaction to the employees. The extra credit should be claimed (and not wasted), since it contributes towards the welfare of the employees without adding any extra cost to the employer. The employees receive a fringe benefit financed by the government. Also, an extra .5 percent will be granted, beginning in 1977 and continuing through 1980, if the employer's transfer of employer securities equal to .5 percent of the qualified investment is matched by an equal contribution to the ESOP by the employees. Furthermore, the employer could even make the contribution on behalf of the employees.

12.8. Increasing the Basis for Qualifying Cost of Section 38 Property

The amount of the investment credit is based on cost or investment in certain depreciable personal property. Therefore, if the basis or cost that qualifies is high, the resulting credit will be high too. In order to maximize the basis or qualifying cost for the credit, observe the following:

1. If the qualified property is built or rebuilt by the taxpayer (or self-constructed), he may capitalize all of the cost of direct material and direct labor used, and allocate to the self-constructed asset part of the general overhead expenses. There is more than one acceptable method for allocating general overhead expenses. The most widely used methods of allocation are the following:

   a. Allocation based on the number of direct labor hours.
   b. Allocation using direct labor cost (or dollars).
   c. Allocation based on direct material cost.
   d. Allocation using conversion cost (i.e. direct labor and overhead costs).

Exercise great care in computing the cost of a self-constructed asset. Notice that the amount of progress expenditures on self-constructed property that qualifies for advance credit does not include capitalized depreciation on construction assets.

2. An asset is considered self-constructed if more than 50 percent of the total cost is made directly by the taxpayer. The taxpayer through the allocation of part of his general overhead expenses to the self-constructed asset may be able to qualify the property as self-constructed. The part of overhead expenses allocated to the qualifying property will increase the total amount of investment credit.

3. Under Section 201 of the 1976 Tax Reform Act, construction period interest and taxes must be capitalized in the year in which they are paid or incurred. This new rule applies to individuals electing small business corporations and personal holding companies.

a. Circulating expenditures that can be capitalized include mainly the cost of legal fees for acquiring property, cost of conversion of equipment for a different use, and special assessments on the property.

b. Carrying charges and taxes that should be capitalized include interest, taxes, and other finance charges paid or incurred during the construction period.

4. When repairs and improvements are made at the same time, the distinguishing line between a capital expenditure and a deductible expense item is often difficult to draw. If repairs are postponed and timed to occur simultanously with capital improvements, the repair can be shown as a part of the general plan of improvements, and the entire amount spent for both repairs as well as improvements will be capitalized.

5. If a property is purchased with the seller doing the repair, and the exact cost of repair done by the seller is not shown separately, the buyer will be free to allocate part of the total cost to repair services. The exact amount allocated to repairs will depend on the circumstances of each case and the evidence submitted.

12.9. Increasing the Investment Credit on Property Acquired Through an Exchange

The investment credit is based on the amount of investment in qualified Section 38 property. The amount of investment is not too difficult to compute if the property is purchased or self-constructed. More difficulties are encountered if the property is acquired in an exchange or a trade. The general rules are the following:

1. In a non-taxable exchange, the cost of "used" property is limited to boot given.

2. In a taxable exchange, if the property replaces similar (or used) property in a 60-day period before or after the disposition, the "cost" is the basis of the replacement property reduced by the adjusted basis of the property given or replaced.
3. If the property disposed of results in investment credit recapture, the full cost of the purchased property is used to figure the credit.
4. In a non-taxable exchange, the cost of the "new" property is the boot given plus the adjusted basis of the old property.

The general rules mentioned above can be used as follows in order to maximize the credit:

Example One: Taxpayer exchanges a machine with an adjusted basis of $10,000 for a similar used machine, paying in cash $5,000. The tax effect is as follows:

Adjusted basis of old machine	$10,000
Add: Cash Paid	5,000
Basis of received machine	$15,000
Investment credit (10% x 5,000)	$ 500

The same taxpayer can increase the investment credit to $1,500 if the newly-received property is not used:

Adjusted basis of old machine	$10,000
Add: Cash paid	5,000
Adjusted basis of new machine	$15,000
Investment credit (10% x 15,000)	$ 1,500

Therefore, for investment credit purposes, use a non-taxable exchange to acquire "new" property only.

Example Two: A taxpayer sold a machine with an adjusted basis of $10,000 for $10,000 in cash, on August 10, 1977, and bought another used machine on September 20, 1977, for $18,000. The "cost" for applying the investment credit is only $8,000 (i.e., $18,000 less 10,000). However, if this taxpayer waited for a period in excess of 60 days after (or before) August 10, 1977, his cost for applying the credit would have been $18,000. Therefore, time your replacement of a used property with another used property well, in order not to replace it within a 60-day period before or after the disposition. There is another way to avoid the 60-day time limit. Instead of selling the old property, recondition (or reconstruct) it. The full amount or cost of reconditioning without any reduction, qualifies for the investment credit.

12.10. Qualifying an Investment in Property for the Tax Credit

Section 38 property (i.e., eligible for credit) includes mainly depreciable tangible personal property, and depreciable real property except buildings and their structural components, such as central air-conditioning and heating systems, plumbing, wiring, and lighting fixtures. However, in order to qualify real property, it must be used in manufacturing activities, or constitute a research facility. To identify and maximize the cost of Section 38 property, observe the following:

1. In a "basket" purchase, a group of assets is acquired at the same time. Certain items may qualify as Section 38 property, while others will not qualify. When such purchase takes place, allocate in detail the total purchase cost between the various items acquired, having in mind that Section 38 property only qualifies for the credit. Use a professional person to allocate the cost, or include the allocation as a part of the purchase contract. With a great degree of detail, you have a better chance of qualifying portions for the credit.

2. Although apartment houses and properties used predominatly to furnish lodging to non-transients are not Section 38 property, the credit can be claimed on the following:

   a. Coin-operated vending machines, washing machines and dryers in apartment houses, and lodging facilities, and,

   b. A hotel or motel furnishing accommodations predominantly to transients.

3. Generally, the credit applies to investment essential in the manufacturing process. For example, the cost of central air-conditioning or heating systems is not eligible for the credit, but if air-conditioning or heating is needed in the manufacturing process, the cost will be eligible for the credit. Therefore, segregate employee activities so that no activity is conducted in a work area that is not an integral part of the manufacturing process. To do this, restrict the activities of production workers to certain buildings or portions of a building, so that the facilities will be described as essential to manufacturing.

4. The credit applies to depreciable tangible personal property with a useful life of three years or more. An investment in depreciable personal property will qualify as Section 38 property more easily than an investment in real property. Therefore, as much as possible, before

making an investment try to preserve or establish the moveability or portability of the item. If a choice exists between a portable and a fixed item, acquire the moveable one (Department of the Treasury, "Tax Guide for Small Business," 1976 edition, p. 1975).

12.11. Modifying Tax Saving Strategies to Fit the On-Again, Off-Again Nature of the Investment Credit

The investment credit was originally enacted in 1962. The credit was suspended in 1966. In 1967, the credit was restored. The Tax Reform Act of 1969 repealed the credit. Again the Revenue Act of 1971 restored the investment credit. The Tax Reduction Act of 1975 increased the credit rate to 10 percent (or 11 percent). The tax advisor should be fully aware of the on-again, off-again nature of the investment credit. He should keep up to date on any changes in the law in order to modify his strategies or implement new ones.

Chapter 13

MAXIMIZING THE BENEFIT FROM DEPRECIATION DEDUCTION

13.1. Selecting a Method of Depreciation

A basic tax saving idea is to defer a large depreciation deduction to a year when taxable income is high. If taxable income is expected to be stable, the straight line method of depreciation should be used. If cash and additional working capital are presently needed, then a high depreciation deduction will result in lowering the income tax bill. For an effective use of depreciation deduction, you need to take the case of each taxpayer separately and base your recommendations for selecting a specific method of depreciation upon a combination of the following main factors:

1. Eligiblity to use accelerated depreciation vs. straight-line depreciation.
2. Expected future taxable income of the owner of a depreciable asset (i.e., whether it is expected to be higher, lower, or the same as the present level of taxable income).
3. Expected retirement date of the asset under depreciation (to avoid the recapture of depreciation rules).
4. Expected new acquisitions of other depreciable assets (to provide future depreciation deductions).
5. The productive life cycle of the asset (i.e., an asset producing a steady or a fluctuating flow of goods and services).
6. The specific financial conditions of the business using the depreciable asset, (e.g., new business, stable business, growing profitable business, or ailing business.)

13.2. Switching from the Accelerated Method of Depreciation to the Straight-Line Method

If you use an accelerated method of depreciation, you will notice that after a few years it begins to give a depreciation deduction lower than the deduction under the straight-line method. When you reach this point, you should consider switching to the straight-line method.

A change from the accelerated method of depreciation to the straight-line method does not require the approval of the Internal Revenue Service (Sec. 167 (e); 1.167 (e)-1(b)). Periodically check the benefit from such a shift. In the following cases a change to the straight line method is recommended:

1. Lower depreciation deduction will result in higher taxable income that will be used for writing off a net operating loss carryover. Therefore, if you have a net operating loss carryover, and you need to use it before the five-year carryforward period is over, consider increasing the taxable income by reducing the deduction for depreciation through a switch to the straight-line method.

2. If the taxable income of the owner of depreciable assets is expected to increase in future years, the depreciation deduction should be deferred or postponed to these later years. A shift to the straight-line method would slow down the annual deduction for depreciation charges.

3. After the sixth year of a ten-year useful life, or the eleventh of a 20-year useful life, the straight-line method will usually produce a larger depreciation deduction than the accelerated method. To use this proven mathematical concept, start depreciating a newly-acquired asset under the accelerated method. When the annual depreciation deduction declines below the amount that could have been claimed under the straight-line method, change from the accelerated to the straight-line method. Notice that when you switch to the straight-line method, a salvage value would then need to be considered in the computation of the depreciation. Also, the new depreciation is based on both the adjusted basis of the asset as of the date of the change and the remaining useful life at that date.

13.3. Using an Accelerated Method of Depreciation

Deducting depreciation under an accelerated depreciation method results in a larger business expense during the early life of the asset. The depreciation deduction under this method is generally twice the straight-line rate of depreciation. This method gives the greatest amount of depreciation deduction in the first year of use and continues to give decreasing amounts in later years. To use the declining balance method of depreciation, the following requirements should be satisfied (Sec. 167 (c); 1.167 (c)-1):

1. The estimated useful life of the asset is three years or more.
2. The asset was acquired after December 31, 1953.
3. The asset is a tangible, depreciable property.

These requirements to qualify for the declining balance method are easy to satisfy if you are careful enough not to estimate the useful life of the asset below three years. The sum-of-the-years-digits method has the same requirement, except it cannot be used for new or used depreciable real property acquired after July 24, 1969, unless it is new residential rental housing acquired after July 24, 1969.

Depreciation is a matter of timing. It should be claimed when needed most. An accelerated method of depreciation results in higher depreciation charges and a lower income tax bill during the early life of the newly-acquired asset. The decrease in income tax provides additional working capital, especially when coupled with shorter estimated useful lives. If the tax savings offered by the use of accelerated depreciation are set aside and invested at a compound interest rate, we can say that such sums plus the return from their investment would add up to a greater amount than the total deduction allowed under the straight-line method, because of the greater period of compounding. Of course, similar benefits could be achieved by investing the tax savings in your own business. Furthermore, when an asset is new it may require little or no repair and maintenance. In later years when the asset is older, it requires more repair and maintenance.

The accelerated method of depreciation fits the life cycle of most depreciable assets since it claims high depreciation charges when the asset requires no (or little) repairs and lower depreciation charges when the asset requires more (or higher) repair expenses. Adding the depreciation charge to the repair expense for the year would result in almost equal total charges for each accounting period. This effect contributes towards stabilizing the taxable income of the taxpayer. Early recovery of the cost of depreciable property, coupled with the stabilization of taxable income, constitutes the main support for electing the accelerated method of depreciation.

13.4. Maximizing the First Year Additional Depreciation

A bonus is given in the year of acquiring a business asset which is called the first year additional depreciation. It is deductible in addition to regular depreciation in the first year an asset is put into use. This bonus results in a tax saving and should be used if all the qualifications for using it are met. To claim the first year additional depreciation the requirements are (Dept. of the Treasury, "Tax Guide For Small Business," 1976 Ed., p. 92):

1. The asset is a new or used tangible, personal property.
2. The first year additional depreciation deduction should reproduce the basis of the related property (i.e., will reduce the balance of cost available for regular depreciation).
3. The estimated useful life of the asset is six years or more.
4. The asset was not acquired from a related party.

In practical life you need to remember the two major requirements: (1) the asset is a tangible personal property, and (2) the estimated useful life of the asset is six years or more. The estimated useful life requirement may easily be satisfied by adopting an estimated life equal to six years or more. The first year additional depreciation is equal to 20 percent of the cost of qualifying tangible personal property, but only up to a total cost of $10,000. On a joint return, the 20 percent is applied to $20,000 of cost. Therefore, the allowance cannot exceed $2,000 or $4,000 for each year.

To maximize the tax benefit from the 20 percent first year additional depreciation, you can consider one or more of the following ways:

1. Try to spread your purchases of qualifying property between different tax years. For each year try not to exceed the cost limitation of $10,000 (or $20,000 for a married couple filing jointly).

2. When trading an old asset (e.g., a machine) for a new asset, your deduction is limited to 20 percent of the cash difference you pay. To avoid this, try to sell the old asset and use the proceeds to buy the new property. As a result, the entire cost of the newly-acquired asset (up to $10,000 or $20,000) qualifies for the 20 percent first year additional depreciation, without regard to the amount of cash invested in the year of purchase.

13.5. Delaying the Depreciation Deduction to Higher Income Years

If a business is new and future income is expected to be higher than present income, it is advisable to delay the depreciation deduction to the years with the higher taxable income. It may also be advisable to minimize depreciation charges for a year when the net operating loss (NOL) deduction is about to expire. In this case, it is desirable to maximize taxable income and use the net operating loss carry forward. To slow down depreciation deductions, you can use one or more of the following methods:

1. Overstate the useful life of the depreciable property. This way, you spread the depreciation deduction over a large number of tax years.
2. Do not claim the 20 percent first year additional depreciation, since it lowers the basis of the asset available for future depreciation.

3. Elect the declining balance method at a 100-percent rate, then in a subsequent year when more depreciation deduction is desired, switch to the sum-of-the-years-digits-method. This tax planning idea is most suitable in the case of a taxpayer with a net operating loss carry forward.
4. Use a straight line or a reverse of the sum-of-the-years-digits method. Under a reverse of the sum-of-the-years-digits with an asset having a five-year life, the first year's depreciation would be 1/15; the second year's 2/15; etc. Of course, under normal sum-of-the-years-digits method, the first year's depreciation would be 5/15; the second year's depreciation 4/15; etc.

   To show the tax saving opportunities from using a reverse sum-of-the-years-digits, we can assume a taxpayer will fall in a relatively low income tax bracket of 20 percent in the first several years of starting a new business, and a higher income tax bracket of 50 percent in the years to follow. Assume further, that he acquires equipment with a depreciable basis of $27,000 and an estimated useful life of five years. Using the reverse sum-of-the-years-digits would result in saving $3,240 figured as follows:

REGULAR SUM-OF-THE-YEARS-DIGITS:

Year	Depreciation Deduction	Tax Rate	Tax Savings
1	$ 9,000	20%	$1,800
2	7,200	20%	1,440
3	5,400	50%	2,700
4	3,600	50%	1,800
5	1,800	50%	900
	$27,000		$8,640

REVERSE SUM-OF-THE-YEARS-DIGITS

Year	Depreciation Deduction	Tax Rate	Tax Savings
1	$ 1,800	20%	$ 360
2	3,600	20%	720
3	5,400	50%	2,700
4	7,200	50%	3,600
5	9,000	50%	4,500
	$27,000		11,880
Total tax savings during five-year period			$ 3,240

If you want to use the reverse sum-of-the-years-digits method, it might be a good idea to enter into an agreement with the Internal Revenue

Service regarding the useful life, rate, and method of depreciation (on Form 2271; prescribed under Section 167 (d)).

13.6. Changing the Estimated Useful Life of an Asset

Useful life is the estimated period over which a property is expected to be of service to the taxpayer. Usually, there is no definite and precisely measurable useful life inherent in a tangible asset. The estimated useful or service life of an asset is influenced by the following main factors:

1. Physical causes, including wear and tear due to operating use, and unusual events such as accidents, floods, etc.
2. Functional or economic factors, including obsolescence (or the effect of innovations and technical improvements) and inadequacy (or the effect of changes in the needs of the owner of the asset).

The estimate of service life should be related to the cause of service exhaustion. The most practical procedure, however, is to start with an estimate of the maximum physical service life and modify it because of the possible effects of obsolescence and inadequacy. The estimate of service or useful life cannot be overemphasized, since it is one of the three variables on which the entire estimate of periodic depreciation is dependent. (The other two variables are the cost of the asset and the method of depreciation.) Because of the direct relationship between the useful life of a depreciable property and the allowable depreciation charge, the tax advisor should observe the following:

1. If you expect to use an asset for a period shorter than the asset's regular economic life, support the need for the shorter period by showing your own experience or special operating conditions. Mere evidence of accelerated use of the asset is important, but not enough. The claim for an abnormally shorter life should be supported with detailed information about the conditions of the asset itself, and if possible, the prior experience with this type or kind of asset. For example, if a taxpayer usually trades in his taxis after using them for only three years, he may use for depreciation purposes a useful life of three years. The fact that similar taxis normally average a life span of five years should not supersede the special circumstances of this taxpayer (Sec. 1.167 (a)-1(b)).

2. The taxpayer and the Internal Revenue Service may enter into a binding written agreement on Form 2271 as to useful life. However, despite this agreement, if the experience of the taxpayer supports a shorter useful life, he may serve a written notice by registered or certified mail, claiming the shorter life and stating all the facts and circumstances supporting his claim.

3. If the reason for the decrease in estimated useful life is not related to a stepped-up use of property, or is due to conditions other than wear and tear, increase the annual charge for deprecation by claiming an allowance for obsolescence (Sec. 1.167(a)-9). If the physical conditions of the asset are kept well, it is advisable to use technological improvements and economic changes as causes for claiming an abnormally short life.

13.7. Using the Component Method of Depreciation

To compute the amount of deductible depreciation, the taxpayer is given a choice between itemizing each asset separately or combining more than one asset into one account. Therefore, an election should be made to use single item accounts, or multiple asset accounts.

If the single item accounts are used, each individual item of property is treated as a separate account. Components of a real property (heating, air-conditioning, wiring, elevators, etc.) can be depreciated separately from each other and from the building. This can result in assigning shorter useful life to certain items (e.g., elevators, roofs, heating system, etc.), and as a result, claiming a larger depreciation deduction in the early period following the acquisition of an asset. When a real property is acquired, tabulate in the purchase contract the various components and assign an acquisition (or purchase) price to each item separately from the land and building.

If multiple asset accounts are used, the taxpayer can adopt group accounts (for assets similar in nature and life), classified accounts (for assets similar in nature but not life), or composite accounts (for dissimilar items with differing useful lives) (Department of the Treasury, "Tax Guide for Small Business," 1976 Ed., p. 96). In the case of group accounts, the rate of depreciation is based on the average useful lives of all the assets included in the group. In the case of classified or composite accounts, the rate of depreciation is figured by computing first the total amount of one year's depreciation for each item or each group of similar items. The total depreciation amount is then divided by the total cost (or basis) of the assets in the account. The result is an average rate which should be used as long as subsequent additions or retirements do not materially alter the relative proportions of different types of assets included in one account. The classified accounts consist of assets classified according to their application or use, such as furniture and fixtures, transportation equipment, machinery and equipment, etc. This method is widely used for depreciating personal (not real) property.

Using a method of depreciation where separate basis, useful life, method of depreciation, and salvage value are assigned to each component of a real property would usually result in claiming a higher depreciation charge in the year of acquisition, as well as several years hence. A real property (other than land) usually includes the following main components:

Lighting fixtures	Electrical wiring
Partitions	Air-conditioning system
Elevators	Swimming pool facilities
Escalators	Paved parking areas
Leases	Landscaping
Sprinkler systems	Building
Hot water system	Land
Heating system	

13.8. Acquiring Assets During the Tax Year

If assets are acquired (or retired) during the year, a choice is given to the taxpayer to elect any one of the following main methods of computing the partial depreciation period for the year of acquisition (or retirement):

1. Depreciation is computed for the full period on the opening balance in the asset account. Therefore, no depreciation is deducted in the year of acquiring an asset, and a whole year's depreciation is claimed on assets retired during the year. This suggests acquiring assets in the last part of the tax year and retiring the old assets in the early part of the year. This method is peculiar to multiple asset accounting.

2. Depreciation is computed for the full year on the ending balance in the asset account. The result is that a whole year's depreciation deduction is claimed on assets acquired during the year, and no depreciation is deducted for assets retired during the year. This method fits most a new or a growing business.

3. All assets acquired or retired during the year are depreciated for a period of one-half year. Only assets used for a full year will be entitled to a full year's depreciation. This method is peculiar to multiple asset accounting.

4. To compute depreciation using the actual acquisitions and disposal dates. A popular practice is to figure depreciation for a partial period, on a monthly basis. If an asset is acquired on or before the middle of the month, it is given one full month's depreciation. If an asset is retired after the middle of the month, depreciation for a full month is claimed. This method is recommended if single item accounts are used.

5. Acquisitions and retirements take place or are effective on the first day of the following month. Therefore, a new asset acquired during the month would not be depreciated for the month of acquisition. However, an

asset retired during the month, would be allowed depreciation for the entire month of retirement. This suggests retiring assets in the first half of the month and acquiring new assets in the second half of the month.

Since there is more than one acceptable practice for determining the depreciation allowance for the first year (and last year) of service, a special analysis of the specific situation of the taxpayer should be used as a base for adopting one of the above mentioned alternatives. This suggests that the depreciation for the year of acquiring (or retiring) an asset should consider the total taxable income for the year, and the need for a higher depreciation deduction in that specific year.

13.9. Adopting a Class Life Asset Depreciation Range System

A taxpayer may elect the class life asset depreciation (ADR) system for a tangible personal or real property acquired after 1970. The election is made by filing Form 4832 along with the federal income tax return. Adopting the ADR system would reduce the disputes between the taxpayer and the Internal Revenue Service as to estimated useful life, salvage value, repairs, and other matters. The main advantage of the ADR system is that the useful lives are generally shorter than under the normal methods of depreciation. A taxpayer may reduce the estimated useful life of eligible assets by as much as 20 percent less than the useful life specified in Treasury Depreciation Guidelines. Also, salvage value is not considered in computing the annual depreciation deduction, and as a result, higher depreciation charges are claimed. However, the total amount of depreciation taken cannot reduce the basis of the eligible asset below estimated salvage value. The ADR system may be used only for property depreciated under the straight-line, declining balance, or sum-of-the-years-digits (Department of the Treasury, "Tax Guide For Small Business," 1976 Ed., p. 97).

If the volume of business fluctuates from year to year, the taxpayer electing the class life asset depreciation range system would realize an added tax advantage. The system allows an electing taxpayer to decrease his depreciation deduction by increasing the estimated useful life of eligible assets. This results in claiming smaller depreciation deductions in years when income is low. The effect of "stretching" the useful life is to retain a higher basis for future depreciation deductions. Furthermore, the class life depreciation system allows the creation of a "repair allowance." With qualifications, certain non-deductible capital expenditures may be claimed as if they were a deductible repair. This special provision would increase the amount of deductible repairs and reduce the disputes between the taxpayer and the Internal Revenue Service over whether or not an item is a repair or a capital expenditure (or improvement). The "repair allowance" establishes a percentage of cost as a deductible repair expense. Expenses below this established limit are fully deductible even if they consitute capital improvements. However, expenses in excess of the established limit cannot be claimed as repair expenses even though they constitute amounts incurred for actual repairs.

Usually, the asset depreciation range system is not recommended if:

1. The taxpayer can support using lives shorter than the lower limit allowed under the ADR system.
2. The taxpayer feels that compliance with the ADR record-keeping requirements outweighs the benefits to be gained through the ADR election.

13.10. Retiring a Depreciable Property

The decision of retiring a depreciable asset should have a direct relationship with the other tax-related activities of the taxpayer, as well as the factors dictating the retirement decision. Retiring an asset one day earlier or later than the best retirement date may make a difference in a half year of depreciation, or an undesired recapture of investment credit or depreciation. Special tax rules relate the effects of retirement to deterioration, destruction, abandonment, obsolescence, and idleness. Before retiring an asset, observe the following special situations and their related tax rules:

1. Gradual deterioration from normal use, e.g., steady weakening of a foundation by normal winds, is not a casualty loss. Cost of repairing the damage is treated as a capital or repair expenditure, depending upon the nature of the expense. Progressive deterioration may have an effect upon the useful life of the property or its estimated salvage value. However, retiring a property because of deterioration through a steadily operating cause will not entitle the taxpayer to any special tax treatment as in the case of retirement due to a casualty or abandonment. Gain from sale and ordinary retirement is subject to Section 1231 and the recapture rules. Loss from the sale and ordinary retirement of a business asset is a Section 1231 loss.

2. Retirement due to complete or partial destruction or accidental loss of property results in a casualty loss. The amount of deductible loss is the excess of the adjusted basis of the property over the total of any salvage value, insurance proceeds, or other compensation received or recoverable from the loss. Casualty losses of business property are deducted as ordinary losses. When casualty losses exceed income for the year, the excess is

claimed as a net operating loss and may be carried back or carried over to offset income of prior or future years. A casualty loss resulting in a net operating loss may lead to a tax refund through the carryback rules. The proceeds from the tax refund may be used to replace the retired business property.

3. Retiring a business asset through abandonment results in an ordinary loss equal to the difference between the adjusted basis of the asset when it is abandoned and the greater of its salvage value or fair market value at the time of retirement. Abandonment consitutes an abnormal retirement, since an asset is permanently withdrawn from use in a trade or business at an earlier time, or before the end of years used in computing the rate of depreciation for the abandoned asset. A loss from demolition of a building is the adjusted basis of the demolished building, increased by the net cost of demolition (or decreased by the net proceeds from demolition).

Notice that if a building is demolished with the intention to demolish it formed at the time of purchase, the loss for the demolition cannot be claimed and must be added to the basis of the property. The same rule of adding the loss for the demolition to the basis of property applies to demolishing a building under the terms of a contract to sell or lease the land (e.g., if the landlord must demolish a building on the property under the terms of a lease or other binding agreement).

4. If an asset is temporarily idle, a deduction is allowed for depreciation charges and such an asset is treated as being used in trade or business for income tax purposes. However, if the idleness is permanent, the asset is treated as retired under the rules of ordinary retirement.

5. An asset may suddenly lose its value as a result of abnormal (or unexpected) obsolescence due to technological improvements, progress in the arts, economic changes, shifting of business centers, prohibitory laws, or other causes. Apart from physical wear and tear, obsolescence may actually diminish the value of the property or shorten its useful life. If management decides to discontinue the use of an asset because of obsolescence, the gain or loss from its sale is subject to the rules of Section 1231. However, if the equipment is unique, and it is constructed to the taxpayer's own needs and specifications, the machine may be dismantled in order not to fall into the hands of competitors. In such a case, the loss is considered as an abandonment, or ordinary loss. To claim the abandonment loss, the asset should not be dismantled and stored by the taxpayer. It should be dismantled and disposed of or junked.

13.11. Stepping-Up Use of Property

Stepped-up use of property may warrant a higher deduction for depreciation than in a year of normal use. The increase in the amount of depreciation deduction for the year, should not be related to more than normal income in that year. Claiming a stepped-up depreciation in a specific tax period should be based on the facts about the actual use of the depreciable property and the definite effect of such accelerated use on shortening its useful life (Treasury Department booklet "Tax Guide for Small Business," 1976 Ed., p. 92). The burden of justifying the increase in depreciation charges is on the taxpayer desiring the modification. The original estimated useful life of the property should be redetermined if the effect of stepped-up use is significant enough. Also, if you redetermine the useful life of an asset, you should at the same time redetermine its salvage value (if the salvage value was determined at the time of acquisition).

13.12. Deducting Estimated Salvage Value

Salvage value is the estimated value of an asset when it is no longer useful in the taxpayer's business. For tax saving purposes, observe the following:

1. Either salvage or net salvage (i.e., salvage reduced by the cost of removal) may be used in determining depreciation. However, negative net salvage is not allowable, and the net salvage is zero when the estimated cost of removal exceeds salvage value.

2. If you acquire new or used personal property (other than livestock) with a useful life of three years or more, you may reduce the salvage value by an amount up to 10 percent of the full basis (or cost) of the property when acquired. For example, if the taxpayer purchased a new taxi having a useful life of five years for $6,500, and the estimated salvage value of this taxi at the end of its useful life to him is $600, he may disregard salvage value and increase his depreciation deduction by computing it on the entire $6,500 cost. However, in this example, if the estimated salvage value is $1,000, the taxpayer may disregard up to $650 of salvage value (or 10 percent of cost) and compute depreciation on $6,150 (or cost less $350 remaining balance of salvage value) (Sec. 1.167 (a)-1(a)).

3. If it is the policy of the taxpayer to retire assets that are still in good operating condition, salvage value may represent a relatively large portion of the basis (or cost) of the asset. The solution could be to use an accelerated method of depreciation, since salvage value is not subtracted in figuring declining balance depreciation. Although salvage value is ignored in computing the depreciation under the declining balance method, do not depreciate an asset below its salvage value (Regs. 1.167 (b)-2, 1.67 (e)-1 (B)).

4. Salvage value is not considered in figuring the 20 percent additional first-year depreciation allowance. However, in computing normal depreciation, the basis of the property must be reduced by both salvage

value, if it is a factor, and the additional first year depreciation (Sec. 1.179-1 (d)).

5. A taxpayer electing the Class Life Asset Depreciation Range system may disgregard salvage value completely even though it exceeds 10 percent of the cost. But, a vintage account should not depreciate assets included in the account below their salvage value (Sec. 1.167 (a)-11 (d)).

13.13. Converting Personal Use Property into Business Property

Gain from the sale of property used for personal (or non-business) purposes is taxable, while a loss from the sale of such property is not deductible. Furthermore, no depreciation deduction is allowed for property used for personal purposes. To offset this tight income tax treatment of personal use assets, a taxpayer may consider converting part or all of an item of such property into a capital asset or put it into use in his trade or business. Whenever a personal use asset is converted into a capital or business asset status, observe the following:

1. When property held for personal use is converted to business use, the basis of such property must be determined. For depreciation purposes, the basis is the lesser of (1) the fair market value of the property at the date of conversion, or (2) the original cost (or other basis) of the property plus the cost of permanent improvements since the acquisition of the property (and minus deductions for claimed casualty losses).

For example, if a taxpayer converted his personal residence into a rental property, his original cost is $25,000, the added permanent improvements to the house $3,000, and he claimed a $500 deduction for a casualty loss to the house. His adjusted basis at the time of conversion would be $27,500 ($25,000 plus $3,000 minus $500). At the date of conversion, part of the $27,500 should be allocated to the land (as an unlimited life asset) and the remaining balance to the building (as a limited life asset).

2. After converting a property to non-personal use, the basis to be used for determining gain or loss from its sale or other disposition depends upon whether or not there is a gain or loss from the sale. The basis for gain purposes is the original cost (or other basis), plus any permanent additions, minus allowed depreciation, and minus deductions for claimed casualty losses. Furthermore, the basis for loss is the lesser of (1) the basis for gain (as explained above), or (2) the fair market value of the property at the time of conversion, adjusted for improvements, casualty loss deductions, and allowed depreciation charges.

3. If the taxpayer converts a personal use asset into business or rental property, and he was the original purchaser as well as user of the

property, he may select the declining balance or sum-of-years-digits method of depreciation. However, before selecting any accelerated depreciation method, check first whether or not all the requirements for using the method are satisfied. Then, decide whether or not an accelerated method of depreciation would result in tax savings.

13.14. Avoiding the Minimum Tax on Tax Preference Items

Under the 1969 Tax Reform Act, a minimum tax is imposed on tax preference items in excess of $30,000 ($15,000 for a married person filing a separate return), plus the Federal income tax liability for the year. The 1976 Tax Reform Act increased the minimum tax rate from 10 percent to 15 percent. Also, in place of the exemption from the tax of $30,000 plus the regular income tax for the year, individual taxpayers are allowed an exemption of the greater of $10,000 or one-half of the regular income tax for the year. For example, Mr. Richard Smith filed a joint return reporting a taxable income of $110,000 and paid on it an income tax of $60,000. He had tax preferences totaling $80,000. His minimum tax is $7,500, figured as follows:

Tax preference income	$80,000
Less one-half of $60,000 income tax	30,000
Income subject to minimum tax	$50,000
Minimum tax (15% of $50,000)	$ 7,500

The excess of accelerated depreciation over straight-line depreciation on personal property subject to a net lease is a tax preference item. Also, accelerated depreciation on real property in excess of depreciation that would have been claimed had the straight-line method of depreciation been used is a tax preference item (Sec. 1.57-1 (b), (c)). Therefore, to reduce the minimum tax on tax preference items, observe the following:

1. Accelerated depreciation on personal property is not a tax preference item unless the property is subject to a net lease. A net lease is one where business expense deductions are less than 15 percent of the net rent, or the taxpayer is guaranteed a specific return, or guaranteed against loss. Therefore, use an accelerated depreciation method for personal assets and be careful only when the asset is subject to a net lease arrangement as defined above.

2. The excess of accelerated depreciation over straight-line depreciation on real property is a tax preference item. To avoid the

minimum tax, watch for the total preference items for the year and compare it with the greater of $10,000 or one-half of the regular income tax for the year. If liability for the minimum tax may occur, consider switching from the accelerated to the straight-line method of depreciation. Such a change does not require the approval of the Internal Revenue Service.

3. Time the transactions resulting in tax preference items (mainly the one-half net long-term capital gain of an individual) for the purpose of spreading them over more than one tax period. For example, electing the installment method for reporting a large gain from sale would result in spreading the gain from sale.

13.15. Creating Multi-Asset Vintage Accounts

If the taxpayer elects the Class Life Asset Depreciation Range system, he may use more than one vintage account for assets acquired during the year. Each vintage account includes only one asset or a group of assets within a single guideline class. The same depreciation method must be used for all assets included in each separate vintage account. Setting up a number of vintage accounts for assets acquired in a particular year provides a larger degree of flexibility. Also, separate vintage accounts are required for new and used property (Sec. 1.167 (a)-11 (b)(3)(ii)). In the same way, a separate vintage account must be used for property that qualifies for the first year additional depreciation, or 10 percent reduction in salvage value. The concept of multi-asset vintage accounts is illustrated in the following example:

In 1975, a taxpayer bought and placed in service the following machines:

	Cost
Machine A	$30,000
Machine B	30,000
Machine C	36,000

The taxpayer elects the Class Life ADR, so there is a three-to-five-years depreciation range (Asset Guideline Class 30.11). The choices available to him are: (1) to put each machine in a separate vintage account; (2) to put Machines A and B in one vintage account and Machine C in a separate account; (3) to put Machines A and C in one vintage account and Machine B in a separate account; (4) to put Machine A in a vintage account and Machines B and C in a separate account; or (5) to put Machines A, B, and C in one vintage account. Assume that choice (1) or the use of multi-asset vintage accounts is used. A three-year life under the Class Life ADR would result in the following deduction for depreciation in 1975:

	Cost	Depreciation Method	Depreciation
Machine A	$30,000	Straight Line	$10,000
Machine B	30,000	Declining balance	20,000
Machine C	36,000	Sum of years digits	18,000
		Total	$48,000

Assume further, in the same example, that the taxpayer selects instead choice (5) or using one vintage account with all assets depreciated under the straight line method:

	Cost	Depreciation Method	Depreciation
Machine A	$30,000	Straight line	$10,000
Machine B	30,000	Straight line	10,000
Machine C	36,000	Straight line	10,000
		Total	$30,000

In this example, creating multi-asset vintage accounts results in a net increase in depreciation deduction for the year 1975 of $18,000 (i.e., $48,000 less $30,000).

Chapter 14

MINIMIZING THE EFFECTS OF DEPRECIATION RECAPTURE

14.1. Using the Straight-Line Depreciation Method for Section 1250 Property and Holding It for at Least One Year

Code Section 1250 applies to depreciable real property but not to any parts of the building covered by Section 1245 (e.g., elevators). If depreciable real property is held for one year or less, Section 1250 requires recapture of all depreciation taken since 1963. However, if the holding period of depreciable real property exceeds one year, only excess depreciation is subject to recapture as ordinary income. Excess depreciation is the amount of depreciation taken that exceeds what would have been taken by straight-line depreciation. Excess depreciation taken after 1969 is recaptured first, and after that, additional depreciation taken after 1963 and before 1970 is recaptured.

The 1976 Tax Reform Act introduced new rules for the recapture of excess depreciation taken on residential real estate and government subsidized housing. Under the new rules all post-1975 depreciation in excess of straight-line depreciation will be 100 percent recaptured in the case of residential real estate. In the case of government subsidized housing, there will be a full recapture of post-1975 excess depreciation for the first 100 months and a reduced recapture for the second 100 months of holding the government subsidized housing. If such property is held for more than 200 months, there will be no excess depreciation recapture. From all of these complicated rules, the following observations can be drawn:

1. There is no recapture of depreciation taken prior to 1963.
2. If the straight-line method of depreciation is used, there is no depreciation recapture unless the property is held for less than one year.
3. There is no recapture of excess depreciation taken after 1963 and before 1970 on property held for more than 120 months, or ten years.
4. The following events may cause a recapture of depreciation under Section 1245 and/or Section 1250, and therefore, when you deal with them proceed with special care:

Event Which May Cause Depreciation Recapture	Recapture Under Code Sec. 1245 and/or Section 1250
1. Sale:	
(a) Regular sale of a Section 1231	Yes
(b) Sale with a lease-back	Yes
(c) Sale under the installment method	Yes
(d) Sale of a business	Yes
2. Leases:	
(a) Assignment of lease by the lessor	None
(b) Sale of the lease where prior depreciation was taken	Yes
3. Distribution of assets by a corporation:	
(a) Regular liquidation (Sec. 341; 1251; 1252)	Yes
(b) Distribution of Assets (Sec. 1245 (a))	Yes
4. A partner selling depreciable property received from a partnership (Sec. 735)	

5. The following events would not result in depreciation recapture:

Event Which Would Not Cause Depreciation Recapture	Recapture Under Code Sec. 1245 and/or Section 1250
1. Involuntary Conversions Under Section 1033	None
2. Tax-free exchanges Under Section 1031	None (unless gain is recognized)
3. Transfer of property to a controlled corporation under Section 351; 357(c)	

(the corporation not assuming liabilities in excess of basis of transferred property) — None

4. Liquidating dividends under Section 335 — None
5. Retirement of a Section 1231 asset — None
6. Abandonment of a Section 1231 asset — None
7. Giving depreciable property as a gift (Sec. 170(e)) — None
8. Transfers at death (Sec. 691) — None
9. Giving depreciable property to a charity (Sec. 170(e)) — None
10. Transfer of property to a partnership in return for a partnership interest (Sec. 721) — None
11. Distribution of Section 1231 property to a partner — None

14.2. Using Multiple Asset Vintage Accounts

If the taxpayer expects to sell or dispose of depreciable property before the end of its useful life, he may avoid depreciation recapture by using multiple asset vintage accounts under the Class Life ADR. Each separate vintage account includes different assets of the same guideline class. A separate reserve for depreciation is also used for each vintage account. The amount of deduction for depreciation for a tax year cannot exceed the difference between the adjusted basis of all assets in the vintage account and the depreciation reserve plus the salvage value of the account (if any). The reserve for depreciation is adjusted for any retirement of assets included in a vintage account (Sec. 1.167(a)-11 (c)(1)).

The sale or physical abandonment of an asset included in a vintage account is considered as an ordinary retirement (Sec. 1.167(a)-11 (d)(3)(ii)). All proceeds from ordinary retirement are added to the account's depreciation reserve. The only time gain is recognized, and as a result depreciation recapture takes place, is when the balance of the reserve for depreciation at the end of a tax year exceeds the account's unadjusted basis (Sec. 1.167(a)-11 (d)(3)(iii)). To avoid the recognition of such a gain, the solution is fairly simple: whenever an ordinary retirement of an item included in the vintage account takes place and gain, as defined above, takes place, acquire a new asset of the same guideline class and add it to the vintage account.

For example, a taxpayer's vintage account has an unadjusted basis of $2,000 and a depreciation reserve of $1,800. During the tax year, he sold an item included in the vintage account for $500. The proceeds from the sale must be added to the reserve for depreciation. Thus, the total balance of the reserve account will show $2,300, or $300 in excess of the unadjusted basis of $2,000. The $300 would be recognized as a gain, and part of it, or all of it, may end up being taxed as ordinary income under the recapture of depreciation rules. However, if the taxpayer in this example, acquires in the same tax year an asset of the same guideline class, no gain would be recognized, if the cost of such an asset was $300 or more. Thus, continued acquisitions will prolong this deferment process.

14.3. Electing the Installment Sale Method

Reporting a gain from the sale of property under the installment method can spread the gain from such a sale over more than one tax period. Postponement of tax on the capital gain has another application. If the installment method is used for reporting a sale or other disposition of Section 1245 or Section 1250 property, any ordinary income from depreciation recapture may also be reported on the installment basis (Sec. 1.1245-6(d), 1.125-1(b)(6)). Using the installment method would not alter the nature of the gain. It would only spread the total amount of gain over several tax periods. Notice that when the installment method is used for reporting the sale from any Section 1231, the ordinary income from depreciation recapture under Sections 1245, 1250, 1251, and 1252 must be reported first, before any Section 1231 gain is taxed.

For example, a taxpayer sold a building in 1975 for $50,000 and reported the sale on the installment basis. The adjusted basis of the building is $40,000, and the total gain from the sale is $10,000. He had used an accelerated method of depreciation and has determined that the total gain is composed of:

Ordinary income under Section 1250	$ 6,000
Section 1231 gain	4,000
Total gain from sale	$10,000

Through the use of the installment method, he has determined that he must report a gain of $2,000 in 1975 and $1,000 each year thereafter as payments are collected. In this case, the $2,000 gain in 1975 must be reported as ordinary income under Section 1250. The $1,000 gain for each of the following four years must be reported as ordinary income, until the entire $6,000 of ordinary income is reported. After that, Section 1231 gain would be reported as collections are made. In this example, the taxpayer did not escape from the recapture of depreciation. Through the use of the installment method, he reduced the impact of recapture on his tax liability in the year of selling the greatly appreciated property.

14.4. Reducing the Effects of Recapture Through Income Averaging

In the year of selling Section 1245 and/or Section 1250 property the income of the taxpayer may become substantially greater than that of the four preceding years. Electing the income averaging method has the effect of taxing the income of a high income year as if it were spread over a total five-year period. Both ordinary income from depreciation recapture, as well as Section 1231 gain, are eligible for income averaging (Sections 1301-1305). Electing the income averaging method will usually produce an immediate tax saving. However, notice that a taxpayer who adopts the averaging method is not entitled in the year of income averaging to the following special provisions of the code:

1. Computing the tax under the optional tax tables.
2. Computing the tax using the 50 percent maximum rate on earned income (for 1977 and later years the maximum tax applies to personal service taxable income instead of earned taxable income).
3. Computing the tax on long-term capital gains under the alternative method.
4. The exclusion of foreign source earned income (Sec. 911).
5. The exclusion of the income from sources within the U.S. possessions (Sec. 1304(b)).

14.5. Selling Capital Stock Instead of Corporate Property

If a corporation sells its own Section 1245 and/or Section 1250 property, it may become subject to the rules of depreciation recapture. Also, if the corporation sells Section 1245 or Section 1250 property to an individual shareholder for less than its fair market value, the excess of the fair market value at the date of sale over the amount paid for the property by the shareholder is considered as dividend distribution. Furthermore, if a corporation distributes as a dividend property subject to depreciation recapture, any ordinary income on the disposition is taxed to the corporation as if the property was sold for its fair market value at the date of distribution (Sec. 312(c)(3)). Therefore, under Section 312(c) the distribution of appreciated property would increase the earnings and income tax liability of the corporation, and at the same time, increase the taxable dividend income of the stockholder.

Instead of selling or distributing Section 1245 and/or Section 1250 property and reporting ordinary income from depreciation recapture, the corporation should consider the sale of its own capital stock. Usually, no gain or loss results from the sale of capital stock by the issuing corporation. The appreciation in value of property owned by the corporation would be reflected in an increase in the fair market value of its capital stock. Therefore, the new shareholder would be paying a higher price for capital stock without either the corporation or the old stockholders reporting such amounts as capital gains associated with property appreciation. Notice that if a taxpayer owns a corporation with appreciated Section 1245 and/or Section 1250 property, he will bypass the depreciation provisions by selling part or all of his stock in the corporation. On the other hand, the buyer of the capital stock will find himself in the unenviable position of having acquired potential tax headaches, since the corporation still owns the greatly appreciated Section 1245 and/or Section 1250 property. The buyer could, however, bypass the recapture of depreciation through a subsequent sale of his capital stock.

14.6. Timing the Date of Putting Property into Service and the Date of Retirement or Disposition

The amount of depreciation recapture under Sections 1245 and 1250 depends primarily on the method of depreciation used and the length of period during which the asset was held. The holding period used to find the applicable percentages for computing depreciation recapture begins the day after the property is acquired. For property built or rebuilt by the taxpayer, it starts the first day of the month that the property is placed into service (Sec. 1250(e)). Therefore, when construction is nearing completion and the end of the month is approaching, it may be worthwhile to push hard to put the property into use before the end of the month. This way, a whole month would be added to the holding period, since it begins the first day of the month that the property is placed into service.

Another timing recommendation is related to the date of sale or disposition of the depreciable property. All gains and losses from Section 1231 assets are segregated and netted. If the net from all Section 1231 assets is a "gain," all of the gains and losses are treated as long-term capital gains and losses. On the other hand, if the net from all Section 1231 assets is a "loss," all of the gains and losses are treated as ordinary income and loss items. Therefore, there is a significant tax saving opportunity if the net from all Section 1231 assets is a loss. Such a loss would be used to offset ordinary income on a dollar-for-dollar basis. To use this tax break effectively, consider the following tax saving plan:

> Through proper timing, sell all Section 1231 properties with a gain in one year, and sell all Section 1231 properties with a loss in a different year. With a net gain from Section 1231 assets, one-half of the gain is exempted from tax since it constitutes a long-term gain, while the net loss from Section 1231 properties is fully deductible as an ordinary loss.

14.7. Passing Property Through Inheritance

Holding a greatly appreciated Section 1245 and/or Section 1250 property until its transference due to death, has the following two favorable tax effects:

1. The longer a taxpayer holds depreciable property, the less depreciation recapture there will be. When the amount of depreciation deductions taken under the accelerated method equals those that may have been taken under the straight-line method, the "excess" or "additional" depreciation is eliminated, and the amount available for recapture is reduced or eliminated too.

2. The recapture rules do not apply to transfers at death (Sec. 1245(b)(2); 1250(d)(2)). The only exception to this rule is in connection with income that would have been taxed to the decedent if he had remaind alive and received it, e.g., decedent's uncollected installment obligations as of the date of his death (Sec. 691).

14.8. Making Upward Tax-Free Exchanges

Arranging an exchange of a depreciable personal or real property for a like property affects both the possibility of depreciation recapture and the basis of the newly-received property. The results of a tax-free exchange depend upon the following events:

1. A like-kind exchange of Section 1245 personal property does not result in depreciation recapture unless boot is received. If gain from a tax-free exchange is recognized, the Section 1245 gain is the lesser of: (i) gain to the extent of depreciation taken after 1961, or (ii) the gain recognized in the exchange, plus the fair market value of any property received which is not a Section 1245 property. Therefore, unless boot or property other than

depreciable personal property is received in the transaction, no depreciation recapture will result.

For example, on January 10, 1975, a taxpayer acquired a new machine for $7,000 cash, plus his old machine for which he was allowed a $1,000 trade-in. The old machine cost him $6,000 on January 6, 1970. For 1970 through 1974, he claimed depreciation of $2,400, $1,440, $864, $518, and $311. Even though a total of $5,533 has been claimed for depreciation after 1961, the $533 gain on the transaction (i.e., $1,000 trade-in allowance less $467 adjusted basis) is not recognized as a taxable gain, and no depreciation recapture is reported.

2. A like-kind exchange of Section 1250 real property does not result in depreciation recapture unless boot is received. If gain is recognized in the exchange, Section 1250 gain cannot exceed the greater of the following: (i) the total amount of boot received, or (ii) the amount of Section 1250 gain that would be recognized if the exchange was fully taxable, less the fair market value of any depreciable real property received. Therefore, if no boot or other than real property is received in a tax-free exchange, no gain or depreciation recapture needs to be reported on the transactions.

3. The basis of Section 1245 or Section 1250 property received in a tax-free exchange is cost, reduced by the Section 1245 or Section 1250 gain not recognized on the exchange. For example, a taxpayer acquired a new commercial building with a fair market value of $90,000 in exchange for an old building that had an adjusted basis of $75,000. No boot was given or received on the exchange. The additional (or excess) depreciation taken on the old building after 1969 is $10,000, and the additional depreciation before 1970 is $15,000 for which the applicable percentage is 40 percent:

> The total or realized gain from the exchange is $15,000 (or $90,000 less $75,000). Under the rules of Section 1250, the taxpayer would report $10,000 (less of $10,000 additional depreciation after 1969 or his $15,000 realized gain), plus $2,000 (lesser of 40 percent of $5,000 remaining gain or 40 percent of $15,000 additional depreciation before 1970), or $12,000, as ordinary income because of the additional depreciation. However, since the transaction is a tax-free exchange, no depreciation recapture is needed, and the basis of the new building is its fair market value of $90,000 less the $15,000 gain on which the tax is postponed, or $75,000. The $12,000 or ordinary income that the taxpayer would otherwise be required to report is carried over to the new building as additional depreciation. Also, the new building has a new holding period beginning at the date of its acquisition.

14.9. Reinvesting the Proceeds from Involuntary Conversions

If a taxpayer receives payment for property condemned or destroyed by casualty, and he replaces it with property similar or related in service or use, no gain is recognized, but a loss is deductible (Sec. 1033). Since no gain is generally recognized in an involuntary conversion, the rules of depreciation recapture are limited to the unexpended conversion proceeds (Sec. 1245(b)(4), 1250). The following rules and examples relate involuntary conversion to gain under Sections 1245 and 1250:

1. Gain (or ordinary income) under Section 1245 cannot exceed the gain recognized in an involuntary conversion, plus the fair market value of qualified replacement property that is not Section 1245 property. Therefore, if the taxpayer did not recognize any gain from the involuntary conversion, no depreciation recapture takes place. For example, on January 11, 1975, a taxpayer purchased a machine for $2,000. On his 1975 income tax return he claimed $400 additional first-year depreciation and $320 ordinary depreciation computed under the declining balance method. On January 3, 1976, a fire destroyed the machine and he received $1,800 as a result of his insurance claim. If it costs him $1,800 or more for replacement with another machine, no gain is recognized from the involuntary conversion and no Section 1245 gain is reported. However, if it costs him only $1,000 for replacement, he would report $520 as ordinary income, figured as follows:

Cost of old machine	$2,000
Total depreciation taken ($400 plus $320)	720
Adjusted basis of old machine	$1,280
Insurance proceeds	$1,800
Realized gain	$ 520
Recognized gain:	
Insurance proceeds	$1,800
Cost of replacement	1,000
Unexpended insurance proceeds	$ 800
Recognized gain equal to unexpended insurance proceeds but not exceeding realized gain	$ 520

Gain under Section 1245:

Since recognized gain is less than the $720 of depreciation deductions, the ordinary income is limited to	$ 520

2. An involuntary conversion of depreciable real property would not result in Section 1250 gain. However, if gain is recognized from an involuntary conversion, the gain under Section 1250 cannot exceed the greater of the following two limitations: (i) the total amount of the uninvested conversion proceeds increased by the value of the controlling shares acquired in a corporation to get replacement property; or (ii) the amount of Section 1250 gain that would be recognized if the proceeds were fully taxable, less the cost of Section 1250 property acquired (Sec. 1250(d)(4)). Therefore, if all the proceeds from involuntary conversion are invested in replacement of real property, no gain from depreciation recapture is reported. For example, a taxpayer received $80,000 from the condemnation of his depreciable real property. He purchased a similar property for $82,000. No gain under Section 1250 is recognized since no gain from the involuntary conversion is reported.

14.10. Transferring Property to a Controlled Corporation

If property is acquired by a corporation for the issuance of its stock in an 80 percent-control transaction, and if no gain or loss is recognized to the transferor, the basis of the property to the corporation is the same as it was in the hands of the shareholder. However, if the transferor receives other property or cash in addition to the corporation's stock, and gain is recognized to the transferor, the basis of the property to the corporation is the same as it was in the hands of the shareholder, increased by any gain recognized. When a corporation acquires a property by the issuance of stock, other than in an 80 percent-control transaction, the basis of the property to the corporation is usually the fair market value of the stock at the time of exchange. If the stock has no established value, evidence as to the fair market value of the exchanged property may be used to establish the value of the stock. Therefore, if property is exchanged for capital stock, the exchange is usually non-taxable to both the corporation, and the transferor (Sec. 351(c); 351(a)). Notice that, if the corporation acquires the property subject to a liability or assumes transferor's liability, the assumption or acquisition does not prevent the exchange from being tax free (Sec. 357(a)). However, when the corporation assumes liabilities in excess of the basis of property transferred, the excess is taxable gain to the transferor (Sec. 351; 357(c)).

The rules governing the transfer of property to either a controlled or non-controlled corporation can lead to major tax saving opportunities. Instead of selling a Section 1245 or Section 1250 property and reporting part of the gain as ordinary income from depreciation recapture, the owner of the property should consider transferring it for stock of a corporation. Such a transfer is usually tax free. After completing the exchange, the transferor may sell his stock and report any gain from the sale as short-term or long-term capital gain or loss under Section 1221 (ie., as gain or loss from investment property). Be sure to avoid the rules of collapsible corporations, since the stockholder's gain can be taxed as ordinary income, even though the gain would otherwise qualify as capital gain (Sec. 341(a); 1.341-1). A sale of stock will escape the unfavorable tax treatment as a collapsible sale under any one of the following avenues:

1. If the stock is sold within six months from the date of filing a consent by the corporation to recognize gain on all future disposals of assets owned or held under option on the date of the sale.

2. Gain from sale or redemption of stock within a three-year period, beginning with the date of holding the property, is a capital gain if the collapsibility was not intended or foreseeable, and not based on financial considerations. For example, a sale of stock for reasons of death or poor health may be a sound basis for escaping the rules applicable to collapsible corporations.

14.11. Distributing Partnership Property to Partners

When a partnership is formed, each partner contributes money, services, or other property in return for his interest. No gain or loss is recognized on a contribution of property. Also, no Section 1245 or Section 1250 gain is recognized on the transfer of depreciable property to a partnership in return for a partnership interest. Therefore, whenever a partnership is formed to succeed one or more sole proprietorships, inquiry should be made into the composition of the assets owned. Assets which will produce a loss should be sold or disposed of rather than transferred to the partnership, since the individuals may use the loss to offset their high personal incomes. Also, if the enterprises being ransferred have depreciable property that appreciated in value, such property should be transferred to the newly-created partnership without recognition of any gain from the transfer. Of course, the partnership adopts the partner's basis for any contributed property (Sec. 723; 1223(2)).

When a partnership distributes property other than money, no gain or loss is recognized until the property is disposed of. Except in a complete liquidation of a partner's interest, the basis of property (other than money) distributed to a partner is its adjusted basis to the partnership. However, the basis of the property to him may not exceed the adjusted basis of his interest in the partnership reduced by any money he received in the same transaction. If a partner disposes of depreciable property distributed to him, all or part of the depreciation deducted by the partnership may be recaptured as ordinary income to him. Therefore, if he receives the depreciable property and keeps it or arranges its exchange in a tax-free transaction, no depreciation recapture needs to be reported. To report the basis of property received as a distribution from a partnership, let us assume that the adjusted basis of a taxpayer's interest in a partnership is $50,000. He receives a distribution of property (other than money) with an adjusted basis of $40,000 to the partnership and $5,000 cash. His basis for the property is $40,000. If in this example the adjusted basis of the taxpayer's interest in the partnership is only $30,000, and he receives a property with an adjusted basis of $40,000 to the partnership and $5,000 in cash, his basis for the property would be limited to $25,000 ($30,000 less $5,000, the cash he received).

14.12. Converting a Business Asset into Personal Use

The sale or disposition of depreciable personal or real property may result in a depreciation recapture. However, conversion of such property from business to non-business (or personal) use does not constitute either a sale or a disposition. Notice that the conversion to non-business use would postpone the depreciation recapture, but at the same time, no depreciation deduction is allowed on the property, beginning with the date of conversion. Converting a business property to personal use is quite often both convenient and desirable. An example is the conversion of a rental property into a personal residence, or a business car to an auto used solely for pleasure and commuting. Also, if a property used solely for business purposes is converted to a property used for both business and personal purposes, no depreciation recapture is required. Meanwhile, the taxpayer continues deducting depreciation only to the extent that the property is used in his trade or business. Notice that if property is converted from business to personal use, its basis is the original cost, less total depreciation taken.

14.13. Selling a Business and Allocation of the Sale Price

The sale of a going business is not a sale of one asset. Rather, it is the sale of all the individual assets which constitute the business, e.g., receivables, inventories, machines, furniture, fixtures, etc. The assets sold must be classified into:

1. Section 1231 assets (or mainly real and personal depreciable property used in trade or business and held for more than six months).
2. Capital assets (or investment property, such as investments in stocks and bonds as well as goodwill).
3. Other property (including mainly merchandise inventory, and property used in trade or business and held for six months or less).

The nature of the gain or loss from the sale of a business depends upon the nature of the assets sold. The sales agreement should show the allocation of the total price over the various assets involved. To maximize the tax saving opportunities available upon the sale of a business, observe the following:

1. Show a higher sales value for capital assets on which there is a long-term capital gain.
2. Show a lower sales value for assets on which there is ordinary income or a short-term or long-term capital loss. The sale of both merchandise inventory and depreciable (personal and real) property held for more than six months should be observed carefully, since it usually leads to the recognition of ordinary income.
3. The price assigned to depreciable personal and real property should be based upon independent appraisals and/or a written agreement accepted by the buyer and seller.
4. Assets which will produce a material loss should be disposed of under a separate sales agreement or handled with extra care, so that the loss can be defended in the event of tax examination.
5. Any assets retained by the seller create no tax, since the income tax applies to the gain on the sale or other disposition of assets. Therefore, keeping greatly appreciated Section 1245 and Section 1250 properties would postpone the recognition of ordinary income from depreciation recapture.

14.14. Donating Depreciable Property Without Fear of Realizing Income

A taxpayer can donate business property which he had depreciated and achieve the following two tax saving opportunities:

1. Depreciation recapture under Section 1245 and Section 1250 does not take place if depreciable property is donated to a charitable

organization. However, the taxpayer's charitable contribution deduction is reduced by any Section 1245 or Section 1250 income that would have been realized had he sold rather than contributed the property (Sec. 170(e); 1.170A-4(b)(4)).

2. The taxpayer is entitled to a deduction for contributions made to qualified organizations. The deduction for the contributed depreciable property is usually measured by the property's fair market value at the date of the contribution. However, if the property appreciated in value (or with a fair market value in excess of its adjusted basis) the deduction for contribution is the property's fair market value, less the amount of ordinary income that would have been recaptured (or taxed) if the property had been sold (Sec. 170(e)(1)(B)(ii)).

Chapter 15

TAX SAVING OPPORTUNITIES ON THE SALE OF A PERSONAL RESIDENCE

15.1. Converting a Personal Residence into Rental or Business Property

Any gain from the sale of a property used for personal purposes is subject to taxation. On the other hand, any loss from the sale of such a property is not deductible for income tax purposes. Therefore, the gain from the sale of a personal residence is taxable, while the loss is not a deductible loss (Sec. 1.165-3). To avoid losing the loss deduction, the private residence should be converted to a business property before selling it (i.e., home converted into a rental or business property). Notice that the mere listing for rent does not constitute sufficient evidence that the property was converted to a business property. A home, for example, should be rented and actually used as a rental property prior to the date of sale, if a possible loss is expected. An item to pay special attention to is the basis of the home converted into a rental property. For tax purposes, if a loss is expected from the final sale of the property, the basis for loss when sold is the lesser of (*Heiner V. Tindle,* 276 US 582, 48 Sct. 326, 6AFTR 7366):

(a) The fair market value at the time of conversion, or

(b) The adjusted basis or cost of the property on the conversion date.

An integral part of this plan would be to find out what the fair market value of the property is at the date of conversion, through the services of a professional appraiser. The cost of any improvements or additions after the date of conversion should be added to the basis (as of date of conversion). After converting the property into rental or business property, depreciation would be claimed starting with the actual date of conversion.

15.2. Using a Home for Business Purposes

The use of a home for business purposes would result in the following deductible expenses:

1. A pro rata portion of rent, light, heat, taxes, and interest on a mortgage. Any expense which is not purely personal and attributable to family household purposes can be apportioned and claimed as deductible expense (e.g., telephone expense).
2. The cost of repairs and maintenance that benefit the portion of home used for business purposes, is deductible (e.g., costs of painting and repairs to rooms used for business). The cost of painting the outside of the home or repairing the roof should be prorated.
3. Depreciation is allowed on the portion of the residence used for business. Also, depreciation would be claimed on any furniture in the portion of home used for business purposes, (e.g., chairs, lamps, desks, curtains, filing cabinets, etc.).

For taxable years beginning after 1975, the deduction for business use of home is subject to new rules. In order to claim a deduction for business use of his home, the taxpayer should be prepared to show the following:

1. His home is used a a principal place of business, or
2. It is a place of business which is used by patients, clients, or customers in meeting or dealing with the taxpayer in the normal course of business (1976 Tax Reform Act, Sec. 280A).

In the case of an employee, to claim the deduction for business use of a home, he should satisfy the above conditions and in addition show that the use of his home as office is for the convenience of his employer.

15.3. Deducting Theft and Casualty Losses

Theft and casualty losses (from fire, storm or any sudden and unexpected cause) are deductible whether business, investment or personal property is involved (Sec. 165 (c)(3); 1.165-7). For tax purposes, total casualty loss is the lesser of (Sec. 1.165-7(b)):

1. The sustained loss which is equal to the value of the property immediately before the casualty loss, less its value immediately afterward, or

2. The adjusted basis of the property (computed as if a loss is expected from its sale).

The total of theft and casualty loss should be reduced by the following items in order to determine the amount of deductible loss:

1. Recoveries from insurance policies,
2. Amounts received from disaster relief agencies or an employer,
3. Any other compensation for lost or damaged property, and
4. $100 per single event.

The tax advisor should realize that the time to deduct a casualty loss is in the year in which the loss took place (in case of theft, deduct in year of discovery). However, if the extent of damage cannot be determined in the tax year in which the loss was actually sustained, then the deduction would be taken in a later year. If the loss or a portion of it is covered by insurance, it would not be a deductible loss until it could be determined with reasonable certainty whether the reimbursement will be received.

As a general rule, the net operating loss provisions apply to a taxpayer in business. However, a casualty on theft loss can produce a net operating loss, even if the casualty or theft is related to a personal use asset (e.g., personal residence and its contents) (Sec. 1.172-3). If the casualty loss deduction exceeds taxable income for the tax year, the excess is considered a net operating loss and may be carried back for three years and carried over for seven years. A refund claim on Form 843 amending a prior year tax return may generate some relief from the loss.

15.4. Minimizing the Tax on Gain from Condemnation

If a personal residence is seized in condemnation proceedings or threatened by condemnation, and the condemnation award is more than the basis of the residence, the excess is considered as a capital gain. The taxpayer has a choice to report the capital gain and pay the tax on it as if the home had been sold, or, postpone part or all of the capital gain tax by replacing the property with another home within three years after the end of the tax year in which the gain is realized (1976 Tax Reform Act Sec. 2140, amending Code Sec. 1033 (g)). If the condemnation award exceeds the cost of replacement, gain is recognized to the extent of the excess. If the condemnation award is less than the basis of the residence, a loss should be claimed.

When there is a gain from condemnation, the gain must be reported in the year the gain is realized. If replacement is made or is expected to be made, details of the replacement must be reported too. The tax advisor should consider the other items of income and losses sustained by the taxpayer during the year of condemnation before recognizing the gain from condemnation or electing to postpone it. In all circumstances, the Internal Revenue Service must be informed of an actual replacement, or of an intention to replace or not to replace, or of a failure to replace within the required period.

15.5. Postponing Part or All of the Tax on Gain from Sale of a Personal Residence

A taxpayer may postpone part or all of the gain from sale of a personal residence by replacing it with another residence within 18 months before or after the sale of the old residence. (The replacement period is two years if he builds the new residence). In order to obtain this tax break the following items should be considered carefully:

1. All of the gain from sale of the old residence will not be taxed in the year of sale if replacement within the required period takes place and the cost of replacement exceeds the net proceeds from the sale.
2. Part of the gain from sale of the old residence will be taxed if the cost of replacement is below the net proceeds from the sale (provided that replacement is made within the required period) (Sec. 1034 (a), 1034 (c) (5)).
3. Fixing-up expenses for work done to improve the chance of selling the old residence are deducted from the amount realized on sale. This deduction will reduce the price of the old residence and reduce any amount of taxable or recognized gain, since the recognized gain is the excess of adjusted sale price over the cost of replacement, and the adjusted sale price is figured by deducting the fixing-up expenses from the net proceeds from sale (Sec. 1034 (b)).
4. After selling the old residence at a capital gain and replacing it with a more expensive home and postponing all the tax on the capital gain, the taxpayer may purchase a home constructed or under construction before March 26, 1975, and qualify for a tax credit equal to 5 percent of the purchase price of the new residence (not to exceed a maximum of $2,000). This tax credit will not affect the basis for the new residence or the amount of gain realized or recognized from the old residence.
5. A special replacement period is allowed for the members of the U.S. Armed Forces. The replacement period is suspended while taxpayer or spouse is on extended duty. Usually, the suspension cannot exceed four years from the date the old residence is sold.
6. Stove, refrigerator, drapes, furniture, etc. are not a part of real property, even if they are sold with the house. A separate value should be assigned to them. Their value will not be added to the buyer's basis and will reduce the seller's contract price. Such items would normally

result in a non-deductible personal loss. Any gain from their sale would be a taxable capital gain.

For example, if a taxpayer sold his residence for $40,000 and the cost of the residence was $30,000, he realized a $10,000 gain. Within 18 months, if he purchased another residence for $45,000, which is more than what he received for the old one, the gain will not be taxed in the year of sale. The $10,000 gain must be subtracted from the $45,000, making the basis of the new residence $35,000. However, if he sells (later) the new residence for $50,000, and does not acquire and occupy a replacement residence within the required time, he must pay tax on the $15,000 gain in the year of sale ($50,000 less $35,000).

If a property is partially used as a personal residence, only that part of the selling price allocable to the residential portion needs to be reinvested in the new residence to have the tax on that part of the capital gain postponed. For example, a taxpayer owns a three-unit apartment house. He occupies one unit and rents two units. He sold the apartment house, and purchased (and occupied) a new home. His records show the following:

Apartment house:

Cost	$50,000
Add: Capital improvements	4,000
	$54,000
Less: Depreciation (on rented 2/3 only)	8,000
Adjusted basis	$46,000
Selling price	60,000
Selling expenses	3,600
New home: Purchase price	30,000

Since 1/3 of the apartment house is his personal residence, the gain on which tax is postponed is figured as follows:

	Apartment house	
	Residence part (1/3)	Rented part (2/3)
Selling price	$20,000	$40,000
Selling expenses	1,200	2,400
Amount realized (adjusted sales price)	$18,800	$37,600
Basis (including improvements)	$18,000	$36,000
Depreciation		8,000
Adjusted basis	$18,000	$28,000

Realized gain	800	9,600
Adjusted sales price	$18,800	
Gain on which tax is not postponed		$ 9,600
Gain on which tax is postponed	$ 800	
Basis of new residence ($30,000 cost less $800 postponed gain)	$29,200	

15.6. Minimizing the Tax on Gain from Sale of Residence if the Taxpayer Is 65 Years of Age or Older

If the taxpayer is 65 years of age or older at the time of sale of his residence, he qualifies for a once-in-a-lifetime exclusion. His old residence must have been used as a principal residence at least five years out of the eight years before the sale (Sec. 121 (a); 1.121-1). The gain on sale of such residence is completely tax free if the adjusted sale price is $35,000 or less (for taxable years beginning after 1976). If the adjusted sale price of the residence is over $35,000, only part of the capital gain is treated as tax free. The ratio of exemption is $35,000 divided by the adjusted sale price. For tax saving purposes the following items should be considered:

1. An involuntary conversion is treated like sale of residence by a taxpayer 65 years of age or older.
2. This exemption of gain from sale of residence is a lifetime exemption. An election should be made to use the exemption or to save it for use in a future sale of residence.
3. If the sold residence is replaced with a more expensive residence (during the required replacement period), it would be wise not to use this lifetime exemption and elect to postpone the recognition of gain under the replacement of residence rules.

For example, a taxpayer (age 68) sold his home in 1977 for $60,000 and purchased a new home for $45,000 within an 18-months period. He is eligible and elects to exclude from his gross income for the year of sale the gain related to $35,000 of the adjusted sale price of his old residence. His gain exclusion is figured as follows:

Selling price of old residence	$60,000
Less: Selling expenses	2,400
Amount realized	$57,600
Less: Adjusted basis of old residence	31,000

Total realized gain	$26,600
Amount realized (from above)	$57,600
Less: Fixing-up expenses	800
Adjusted sales price	$56,800
Gain attributable to $35,000 of adjusted sale price:—	
Total realized gain (from above)	$26,600
Less: Gain he elected to exclude from gross income $26,600 X $35,000 / 56,800 =	16,391
Gain that he may not elect to exclude	$10,209

15.7. Postponing the Tax on Gain from Sale of Residence Using the Installment Method

When a residence is sold at a gain, the gain is subject to tax. If this gain is reported under the installment method, however, the general effect would be to postpone the recognition of part of the gain until future years. The installment method is very important to the taxpayer who has sold a residence at a substantial gain. To qualify for the installment method, total payments received in the year of sale must not exceed 30 percent of the selling price. Under the installment method, payments received in the year of sale include the down payment, all other cash payments, and property other than evidences of indebtedness of the buyer received in that year. Any earnest money or option payments or deposit received in any preceding year are included if, under the contract, they become part of the down payment in the year the sale becomes effective. Liabilities of the seller such as taxes, accrued interest, and liens that are assumed and paid by the buyer are not generally included in the total payments received in the year of sale. Selling price, under the installment method, is the entire cost of the property to the buyer. Selling price or total contract price cannot be decreased by the amount of any commissions or selling expenses. For tax saving purposes the following items should be considered carefully:

1. To use the installment method, an adequate record of payments received, selling price, and dates must be maintained.
2. The installment method is elective. For each sale, the taxpayer may elect either to report all the profit in the year of sale or to report it on the installment method. Once the installment method is elected for reporting the gain from a specific asset, the election cannot be revoked

unless there has been a material mistake in the data used for reporting the sale.

3. The election to use the installment method should be made in the tax return for the year of sale. Even if no payment was received during the year of sale, the seller still should report his election in the return for that year.
4. The tax advisor should take into consideration all the other capital-gain and capital-loss transactions of the tax year before advising the taxpayer to elect the installment method or to report the entire amount of capital gain in the year of sale of residence.

15.8. Selling Expenses that Qualify for the Deduction as Either a Moving Expense or an Adjustment to Sale Price

Expenses of selling the old residence and purchase of a new residence can be claimed as part of moving expenses or treated as adjustments to the sale and purchase price of the old and new residences (Sec. 217 (e), 1001 (f); 1.217-2). Selling expenses that qualify for the deduction as either a moving expense or an adjustment to sale price include real estate agent's commission, escrow fees, expenses of advertising the property for sale, preparing the deed, other legal services related to the sale and "points" paid by the seller to obtain an FHA mortgage for the buyer, and any state transfer taxes on the sale. Purchase-related expenses that qualify for the deduction as either a moving expense or an adjustment to the cost or basis of the new residence include legal fees, title costs and appraisal fees. For tax saving purposes observe the following:

1. If the expenses of selling the old residence and purchase of new residence are claimed as moving expenses, they are subject to dollar limitations under the moving expense rules (for more details see **2.18** of Chapter 2). However, if the expenses of selling the old residence and buying the new residence are claimed as adjustments to sale and purchase prices, no dollar limit is imposed on their total amount.
2. Part of the selling and purchase expenses can be claimed as moving expenses (up to the dollar limit for moving cost) and the remaining balance can be used as adjustment to sale or purchase prices.
3. Claiming the expense of selling the old residence or buying a new residence as a moving expense is more favorable for income tax purposes. Each dollar of a moving expense deduction offsets one dollar of ordinary taxable income. If, however, the selling and purchase expenses are used as adjustments to the sale or purchase price of residence, the effect will be to decrease a possible capital gain or to increase a possible capital loss. If the gain is a long-term capital gain, it will be taxed at a special, and generally, lower tax rate. If a loss takes

place, such loss is not deductible since it results from the sale of a personal use asset.

4. Take into consideration the dollar amount of the other moving expenses (e.g., transportation, meals, lodging, house-hunting expenses), whether such expenses are reimbursed (usually by an employer), and, whether the old residence is sold at a gain or a loss, before making the election to claim the sale and purchase-related expense as moving cost or adjustments to sale or/and purchase prices.

15.9. Protecting the Right to Postpone the Tax on Gain from Sale of Residence Under the Replacement Rules

The favorable treatment of postponing the tax on gain from sale of residence under the replacement rules, could be lost in either of the following situations:

1. If another residence is purchased and sold before the old residence is sold.

2. If more than one residence is purchased and used as personal residence within one year after the old residence is sold. In this case, only the last residence acquired will be considered a replacement, qualifying under the replacement of residence rules. Only one sale or exchange per tax year can enjoy the special treatment under the replacement of residence rules (Treasury Department booklet "Your Federal Income Tax" (1976 Ed.), p. 121). Postponing the gain from sale of residence under the replacement of residence rules would lead to immediate tax savings. The amount of tax saved depends on the cost of the replacement home. For example, a taxpayer sold his residence on March 10, 1977. The basis of the old residence is $35,000. Selling expenses were $2,500 and the selling price is $50,000. During the 90-day period ending March 10 he had the following work done, which he paid for on April 4, 1977 (i.e., within 30 days after the date of sale):

Painting and wall papering	$1,000
New water heater and new air conditioner	500

Within the required period he purchased another home for $55,500. The amount of gain on which tax is postponed is $12,000 and the basis of the new home is $43,500, figured as follows:

Selling price of old home	$50,000	
Less: Selling expenses	2,500	
Amount realized		$47,500

Basis of old home	35,000	
Add: improvements (heater and air conditioner)	500	
Adjusted basis of old home		35,500
Gain on old home		$12,000
Amount realized on old home	$47,500	
Less: fixing-up expenses (painting)	1,000	
Adjusted sale price		46,500
Cost of new residence		55,500
Gain to be taxed in 1977		0
Gain not to be taxed in 1977		$12,000
Cost of new home	$55,500	
Less: Gain not taxed in 1977	12,000	
Basis of new home	$43,500	

15.10. Claiming the Tax Credit on Purchase of Residence

Under the Tax Reduction Act of 1975, a special tax credit is offered. The buyer of a new home constructed or under construction before March 26, 1975, qualifies for a tax credit equal to 5 percent of the purchase price, not to exceed a maximum of $2,000. If a taxpayer sells his old residence and qualifies under the replacement of residence rules, and at the same time if the newly acquired home qualifies for the new tax credit, then the taxpayer will be making a double-benefit tax move.

15.11. Taking Insurance on a Personal Residence

A good home insurance coverage is both necessary and costly. An insurance premium paid by an individual against fire, burglary, storm and accidents, is not deductible if it covers a personal residence (Sec. 1.262-1). To make the best possible usage of home insurance, observe the following:

1. On a periodic basis, photograph each of the four sides of every room in the house. Keep the photos in a safe-deposit box. A comparison between photos taken before an accident with those taken after the accident provide the best evidence for decline in property value. Items of special value (e.g., art objects, antiques, jewelry), should be listed in writing with the insurance company. Their estimated market value may be

questioned by the insurance company only before and not after an accident occurs.

2. Insurance on property converted to rental or business use is deductible for income tax purposes. If part of the property is used for business and part for pleasure, the insurance premium should be apportioned. Observe the following sub-rules:

a. Insurance premiums paid before the business use of property or after its business related use are not deductible.

b. Converting a part of a personal residence for business storage or use will convert part of the insurance premium into a deductible item.

c. Usually, if a personal residence is converted into rental property, the premiums paid are deductible. However, any premiums paid after the property's business use is over, and the property is offered for sale, must be capitalized.

3. A sudden, unexpected or unusual damage to a personal residence results in a deductible loss. However, if the loss is due to a lack of repair and maintenance or is caused by a steady effect of weather and time, then, the loss is not deductible (*Fay v. Comm.* 120 F.2d 253, 27AFTR432). For example, a roof damage caused by ceaseless winds is not deductible. Therefore, after the occurrence of a major rain, wind, or snow storm, inspect the property, since any sudden damage is deductible.

15.12. Repair vs. Improvement of Home

The cost of repairs to a personal residence is not deductible. However, in the following two cases the cost of repairs would not be completely lost:

1. Repair to a personal residence can be timed to occur with general improvements. While the cost of repair is not deductible, the cost of improvement cost will increase the cost (or basis) of the residence. The increased cost will be felt eventually when the taxpayer sells his home. The capitalized cost of improvement will result in decreasing the reported gain (or increasing the loss) from the sale of property. Notice that when general improvements are made, a detailed description of work made under the improvement plan should be kept. Time your improvements to occur when repairs are badly needed. Request separate bills for the cost of repair and improvements.

2. If a personal residence is converted into rental property, the cost of repair is completely deductible as a rental expense. After deducting repairs, the re-conversion of the property back to a personal residence will not result in the recapture of any repair cost previously taken. Therefore,

while a personal residence is used as rental property, any needed repairs should be incurred. For example, a university professor accepts a visiting professorship for a year. While away from home, he converts his residence to rental property. During this period, he schedules all the needed repairs to his home, and claims the cost as a deductible rental expense.

15.13. Assuming the Monthly Payments of a Wife's Residence After Divorce

A lump sum payment of alimony to a wife is neither taxable to her nor deductible by the husband. Installment payments of a fixed amount of alimony are also not taxable to the wife unless the principal sum is to be paid to her over a period of more than ten years. Therefore, only "periodic" payments of alimony are taxable to the wife and deductible by the husband (Sec. 71; 1.71-1). In certain cases, the husband may assume the monthly payments of a house (or apartment) furnished to the wife (*Pappenheimer v. Allen*, 164F.2d 428, 36AFTR 406). In cases like this, special care should be exercised, since these monthly payments may constitute "periodic" income to the wife.

If it is not desired by the wife to report the monthly payments on the residence furnished to her as periodic income, adopt either one of the following two methods:

1. Relate the monthly payments to a "fixed" amount of alimony which is being paid on an installment basis with the principal sum to be paid over a period of ten years or less. The total "fixed" amount should not vary because of certain contingencies such as reduced earnings or remarriage.
2. Relate the monthly payments for the residence furnished to the wife to child support. Any payments for the support of minor children of the husband are not includable in the wife's gross income (Sec. 71 (b); 1.71-1(e)).

15.14. Avoiding the Tax on Gain from Sale of Home and Deducting the Capital Loss

Gain from sale of a personal residence is taxable, while loss from the sale of a home is not deductible. Therefore, in order to avoid the tax on the capital gain, or, to deduct the capital loss, consider the following two techniques:

1. A donor has no taxable gain if he transfers appreciated property (or property worth more than its cost) to a donee. After giving a home to a

donee, if he in turn sells it at a gain, its basis to him is the same as if it was in the hands of the donor. However, if the home is sold at a loss, its basis to the donee is the lower of the fair market value of the property at the time of the gift, or its basis to the donor. Giving an appreciated home as a gift is a safe way to avoid the tax on expected capital gain. Be sure that the gift is not deemed a transfer in contemplation of death.

2. Any loss from the sale of an asset used in trade or business is deductible. If a property is worth less than its original cost, convert it to business or rental property. After the conversion, sell it and claim the loss as a deductible loss. Notice that when a personal-use property is converted to business or income-producing property, the basis (in case of sale at loss) is the lower of the fair market value or its adjusted basis on the conversion date. Therefore, when you convert a home to an income producing property, observe the following:

a. Compute both the fair market value and the adjusted basis on the date of conversion. To support your computations you may acquire (in writing) the professional opinion of a real estate agent or property appraiser regarding the fair market value.

b. The basis of converted property is adjusted for any improvements or additions. You may consider, therefore, making improvements to the converted property and claiming a depreciation deduction for the period prior to the sale. Upon sale, if the sale price is below the adjusted basis, the loss is deductible.

Chapter 16

ESTATE TAX SAVING TECHNIQUES

16.1. Planning Before Death and Minimizing Legal Problems Related to the Will

Estate tax planning should start before the date of death. A major part of an estate plan is a well written and up-to-date will. Adopt either a will distributing all property of the testator upon his death, or use a "will-trust" combination. It is probably advisable to use a "will trust" instrument if the testator wants to set aside part or all of his property until a specific future date or event before the properties included in his estate are distributed to the beneficiaries. For minimizing legal problems related to the will, observe the following:

1. Identify the testator in a consistent way and use his name as written on the title to properties. Avoid inconsistency in writing the middle name. Use an abbreviation or the full middle name, but be consistent. The same applies to married women; use either the married or maiden names.
2. State clearly that the will revokes all wills made before.
3. Direct the will to pay all the debts and expenses of the estate. This clause will support the deductibility of such items.
4. If the testator made certain gifts prior to the will, do not mention the gifted items in the will. If such items are mentioned in the will, the IRS may take the position that they were not effectively transferred.
5. Define clearly the powers of executors and trustees.
6. The signature of the testator should be witnessed by at least two (or three depending on the requirements in each state) attesting wit-

nesses. Write clearly the name and home address of each attesting witness.

7. The new rules of the 1976 Tax Reform Act make it advisable that all existing wills and estate programs be promptly reviewed.

16.2. Combine the Gift Tax Exemptions with the Estate Tax

The specific exemptions for estate and gift taxes of $60,000 and $30,000, respectively, are repealed under the 1976 Tax Reform Act. In their place, a unified tax credit against both the gift and estate tax is provided. The amount of the unified tax credit is phased over a five-year period as follows:

Year	Tax Credit	Equivalent in Taxable Amount
1977	$30,000	$120,667
1978	34,000	134,000
1979	38,000	147,333
1980	42,500	161,563
1981	47,000	175,625

In general, any portion of the unified tax credit used against taxable gifts made during the lifetime of an individual will reduce the credit available for use against his estate tax. The present gift tax annual exclusion of $3,000 per donee is retained unchanged. Also, the estate tax marital deduction is increased to the greater of $250,000, or one-half of the decedent's adjusted gross estate. In addition, a gift tax marital deduction is allowed for lifetime gifts to a spouse. Under the gift tax marital deduction, a donor will be allowed to deduct the first $100,000 of lifetime gifts and, thereafter, a deduction for one-half of the aggregate lifetime gifts made to a spouse in excess of $200,000. Therefore, no deduction is allowed for the second $100,000 of gifts to spouse.

For example, Mr. Robert K. Smith (with no history of prior gifts) may give to his son in 1977 the amount of $6,000 and to his wife $100,000 without either paying a gift tax or reducing the amount of unified credit available against his future taxable gifts and estate. The $6,000 gift to the son can be claimed by Mr. Robert K. Smith and his wife and thereby the amount per donee per year is reduced to $3,000. The gift to the wife qualifies under the unlimited marital deduction for the first $100,000 of lifetime gifts to a spouse. If the annual exclusion of $3,000 per donee and the $100,000 lifetime gifts to a spouse deduction are not used, the taxable estate of the taxpayer will be higher and, consequently, his estate tax could be higher too.

16.3. Greatly Appreciated, Depreciated, and Income-Producing Properties

The federal estate tax is imposed on the net worth of a person, computed as of the date of his death or at an alternate valuation date which is ordinarily six months after death. The values used for computing net worth are current market values. Therefore, the balance sheet or statement of financial position prepared by the accountant differs greatly from the statement of net worth needed for federal estate tax purposes. The accounting balance sheet will classify assets and liabilities in terms of liquidity into current and non-current items. Also, the accounting balance sheet is basically a listing of value based on original or historical cost. On the other hand, the federal estate tax requires a listing of all properties owned at death without regard to classification as to current and non-current items. Also, the valuation for estate tax purposes is based on fair market values. The estate tax advisor should modify the statement of financial position prepared by the accountant in order to adopt current market values.

Besides preparing a statement of net worth based on fair market values, the tax advisor should prepare the following schedules for each client (i.e., during the lifetime of the client):

1. A schedule of greatly appreciated property with columns for the type of property, original cost or adjusted basis, fair market value, and expected (long- or short-term) capital gain, should be prepared. The tax on capital gain can be postponed by retaining the property until death takes place. A transfer upon death will not result in a realization of capital gain. Therefore, as a general rule, retain, or do not give as gifts, properties with greatly appreciated values. Keeping such properties is better than selling them and paying part of the proceeds as a capital gain tax. Notice that retained properties will be updated in value upon death of the owner, and the beneficiary receiving them will use the fair market value at date of death or alternate valuation date unless such a property constitutes real property used in a family farm or a trade or business. Real property used for farming or other trade or business may be valued on the basis of its "actual" use instead of the "highest and best use."

2. A schedule of depreciated property should be prepared. The owner of such properties will realize a loss by selling or disposing part or all of them. Therefore, instead of losing a chance for loss deduction, a careful analysis should be made in order to determine when to realize a loss and the amount of loss that can be effectively used (and not just wasted in whole

or in part). Generally, a depreciated property should be sold claiming a loss (ordinary or long-term capital loss) deduction against other taxable items.

3. Income-producing properties should be listed separately. The decision to retain or sell such a property should be evaluated in the light of its combined effect on the liability for income tax, gift tax, as well as, estate tax. Generally, giving an income-producing property as a gift will produce a tax saving since it removes taxable income from the donor's high tax bracket to the donee's relatively lower income tax bracket. For more details on giving income-producing items, see **16.4** in this chapter.

4. Special valuation rules apply to a family farm or a real property used in a trade or business. Real property used for farming or some other trade or business may be valued on the basis of its "current" or "actual" use instead of the "highest and best use." This special valuation may not reduce a gross estate by more than $500,000. For the "actual" use standard to apply, the adjusted value of real and personal property used in the trade or business comprises at least 50 percent of the adjusted value of the decedent's gross estate. However, only 25 percent of this adjusted value should consist of qualified real property. Therefore, for estates consisting of farms or closely held business, examine carefully the requirements for avoiding the "highest and best" use standard of valuation.

16.4. Main Types of Income-Producing and the Decision of Giving or Keeping an Income-Producing Property

The area of giving or retaining income-producing properties should be considered carefully because of its effect on the income, gift and estate taxes of the present owner of such properties as well as the prospective owner or owners. Giving an income-producing property will shift its income to the donee. However, the basis of property acquired by gift depends on whether the ultimate sale of the property results in a gain or loss. If the sale results in a gain, the basis is the same as in the hands of the donor. If the sale results in a loss, the basis is the lower of the basis in the hands of the donor, or the fair market value at the time of the gift (Sec. 1015(a); 1.1015-1). On the other hand, retaining an income-producing property will not lead to any income-shifting and if the property is kept until death, the basis to the beneficiary is the value reported for estate tax purposes.

The decision of giving an income-producing property as a gift, or keeping it until it will be transferred to the beneficiary through inheritance should take into consideration the nature of the income-producing property. The following is an analysis of the major types of income-producing assets and their possible tax-related effect:

1. If depreciable property is included in the gross estate, the basis of the property is the value used for estate tax purposes. Usually, it is desirable from an estate point of view to understate the federal estate tax. However, if the highest value is used, the beneficiary will claim larger depreciation deduction and eventually will report a smaller capital gain (or larger loss) upon disposition of the inherited property. If the property is fully depreciated, the owner should consider the possibility of selling it. The sale proceeds could be used for acquiring another property with a depreciation deduction. Notice that, the 1976 Tax Reform Act (Sec. 2005(a)(2)) introduced a new rules for appreciated property passing from a decedent. The beneficiaries receive a "stepped up" basis in the property for income tax purposes. After December 31, 1976, the basis to a beneficiary is the greater of the value of the inherited property (except securities with market quotations) on December 31, 1976, his share of the $60,000 minimum basis per estate, or the original purchase price. Therefore, for purposes of determining gain, but not loss, the basis of all assets will be stepped up to their market value on December 31, 1976. As a result, no appreciation in value occuring before January 1, 1977, will be subject to the capital-gain tax between the hands of the beneficiary. If the property is not fully depreciated, the decision of giving it as a gift or retaining it depends mainly on:

(a) the annual net income or loss from such property

(b) the income tax bracket of the owner and prospective donee

(c) current fair market value of the property and the amount of expected capital gain or loss from its sale or disposition

(d) the expected estate tax rates of the owner of property. In the area of giving or retaining a real property, there is no constant formula. A checklist of the taxable income and gross estate of both the owner and beneficiary is needed. Such a list should be designed to cover the possible effects on the total liability for income, gift, and estate taxes.

2. In case of stock and bonds producing dividend and interest income, the basis of such securities must be determined. Then, the periodic income and expected capital gain or loss are computed before making any decision to give, sell, or keep all such securities or part of them. If the securities are issued by a controlled corporation, the question of keeping an effective control should be raised.

3. An interest in a partnership is considered as a business property. However, the value of such interest may vary depending upon the partner's rights in the partnership. For example, the partnership agreement may specify a flat dollar amount the deceased partner's estate would receive for his interest. In such a case, the agreed-upon amount measures the interest to be included in his gross estate. On the other hand,

if the partnership agreement is silent, various problems will rise regarding the share of the partner in each asset owned by the partnership including "goodwill." Therefore, the partnership agreement is very important and may provide that:

(a) a deceased partner's estate is to receive a percentage of the partnership's profit over a specified period of time in lieu of other amounts to which it would otherwise be entitled, or

(b) a deceased partner's estate will be paid a flat dollar amount for his interest, or

(c) a deceased partner's estate will have a proportionate share of each asset owned by the partnership, or

(d) a deceased partner's estate will receive either a share of profits or a fixed dollar amount in addition to the value of the proportionate interest in the partnership's assets.

The estate tax advisor should check if a partnership does not terminate at the death of a partner, and the rights of a partner's estate. Notice, that the value of interest in a partnership should be added to the gross estate of the deceased partner, but the right of his estate to continue as a partner and receive such a share of profit or loss is not a right to be included in the gross estate. The right to own part of a business should be distinguished from a right to receive a portion of future profit or loss. Therefore, the estate of the deceased partner will benefit from receiving both a fixed dollar amount for his interest and, in addition, a share of earnings of future years. Do not specify the number of future years. Show the estate as a continuing partner which may not only share in profits but also must be charged for losses.

4. Interest in a private or closely-held corporation, and also interest in a sole proprietorship, will lead to valuation problems since there is no established market for such properties. As in the case of all valuation questions, the burden of proof rests on the estate. If there is a price offered by a willing buyer and accepted by a willing seller, it must be used. Otherwise, a combination of net worth, prospective earning power, and the dividend-paying capacity will determine the value of such ownership. This will give a larger degree of freedom to the estate tax planner, although his final recommendation will depend greatly on both estimates of value as well as periodic taxable income.

16.5. Gifts Within Three Years of Death

Any transfer of interest in property or rights made within three years of death without adequate consideration is presumed to have been made in contemplation of death (Sec. 2035; 20.2035-1(d)). Section

2001(a)(5) of the 1976 Tax Reform Act requires unconditional inclusion in a decedent's gross estate of all transfers made within the three-year period prior to his death. Whether a transfer made within that period is not "in contemplation of death" is irrelevant. In determining the amount of the gross estate, the amount of the gift tax paid on transfers within three years of death must be included or "grossed-up" in the decedent's gross estate.

In general, it is better to make a transfer before death even if there is a chance that the transfer will be added back to the gross estate. The following reasons support making a gift despite the contemplation of death rule:

(1) The donor may live more than three years after the date of transfer.

(2) The income (if any) from the transferred property will be subject to relatively lower income tax rates in the hands of the donee.

(3) If the transfer is made as if full consideration was received, the contemplation of death rule will not apply since it does not include sales.

(4) The executor is not required to report all gratuitous transfers of value of less than $1,000.

(5) Donors remain entitled to an annual gift tax exclusion of $3,000 per donee.

(6) The estate tax is avoided on any appreciation in the value of the donated property if such increase in value took place after the gift of the property but before the death of the donor.

16.6. Inter Vivos and Testamentary Transfers to Charity

A deduction from the gross estate is allowed for the value of properties transferred for public, charitable, educational, health, religious, or other related uses (Sec. 2055; 20.2055-1). Also, a charitable deduction is allowed for property transferred to a charitable use because it was refused by the distributee. However, to claim this added deduction, the distributee should file an absolute and unqualified refusal (or disclaimer) to accept any rights in the property. If the distributee dies before filing the disclaimer in the probate court, the deduction still may be claimed. Giving gifts to charitable organizations can serve one or more of the following objectives:

1. To reduce the estate tax.
2. To reduce the gift tax on transfers.
3. To reduce the income tax.
4. To avoid tax on gains from greatly appreciated property.
5. To aid a charitable purpose.

Gifts to charity can take an *inter vivos* or testamentary (i.e., a bequest) form. Periodic inter vivos gifts will reduce the annual income tax. If the savings in income taxes are used to purchase life insurance, the proceeds from the insurance will provide more liquid funds for use by the estate. The extra feature of saving income taxes (by claiming a charitable contribution deduction) makes an inter vivos gift more advantageous than a bequest. Also, if the owner of property is paying income tax at a high bracket, adopting a system of giving annual charitable gifts will result in an annual income tax saving that will increase available liquid funds during the life of the taxpayer.

A special type of inter vivos gifts is to give a charitable remainder interest (Sec. 642(c)(5), 664; 2055(e)(2)). The donor will reserve to himself the right to an annuity for the duration of his life. Upon his death, the remainder is given to charity. Notice, a charitable remainder interest is not deductible for income tax, gift tax, or estate tax purposes unless the transfer is in the form of a charitable remainder annuity trust, a charitable remainder unitrust, or a pooled income fund. Creating an inter vivos charitable remainder annuity trust and transferring greatly appreciated property to it, will give the combined effect of more than one saving. The capital-gain tax is saved. A deduction for income tax purposes is claimed. In addition, the donor will enjoy the security of an income from the trust property for the rest of his life. The estate planner should observe very carefully the differences between (1) charitable remainder annuity trust, (2) charitable remainder unitrust (i.e., the trust's governing instrument does not prohibit additional contributions to the trust after the initial contribution), and (3) pooled income fund (i.e., property transferred to such a fund is commingled with that of other donors and the charity entitled to the remainder controls the fund (I.R.C. 642(c)(5)(e)).

Guaranteed annuities or bequests of a fixed percentage, distributed yearly, of the property's fair market value (determined annually), constitute the only deductible charitable income interest (Sec. 2055(e)(2)(B)). This inter vivos gift should provide irrevocable annual payments from property to go to charity, with the remainder going to beneficiary of the donor, either at the end of a specific number of years or at the time of the donor's death. The donor will not be taxed on the income from this type of trust. He will claim as an annual deduction (for income tax purposes) the fixed annual payments to charity. By giving to the trust an appreciated property, he will save the capital-gains tax. In addition, since the transfer of property is irrevocable, the value of the property is removed from his gross estate.

Testamentary gifts to charity, like inter vivos gifts, may take the form of an outright testamentary gift, or a gift through a testamentary trust. A testamentary trust for the life of an individual beneficiary with remainder interest to charity may produce certain tax and other benefits. The value of the remainder interest is deducted from the gross estate as a charitable contribution. At the same time, the beneficiary of the testator is provided with periodic payments in stated amounts for the rest of his life. By saving the estate tax, the funds available for use by the testamentary trust will be greater.

16.7. Claiming a Payment as an Income Tax or Estate Tax Deduction

Certain expenses and deductions may be claimed on the fiduciary income tax return (Form 1041), or on the estate tax return (Form 706). The tax planner should compare the relative advantage of claiming such items as an income tax deduction or a deduction against the gross estate. Of course, the amount of the expense and the effective income and estate tax rates will determine the outcome of the comparison. Those deductions (also called double deductions) include mainly accrued business expenses such as interest, deductible taxes and expenses related to the production or collection of income. Business and non-business expenses of the decedent, can be claimed on the estate tax return (Form 706) if the estate pays them or is liable for them. The following special items of income and deductions are subject to their own rules:

1. A deduction for depletion is claimed by the person who receives the income to which the depletion relates. Depletion is not connected with ownership of the property from which the income is derived.
2. There is a definite advantage in paying medical expenses before a decedent's death, especially where costly illness has prevailed. If an individual pays the medical expenses before his death, the payments will reduce the funds left for inclusion in his gross estate. At the same time, the medical expenses paid are claimed as itemized deduction on his final income tax return. However, if the payments for medical expenses are not made until after death, the funds used to pay the bills are included in the gross estate, and the liability for the payment is deducted as a claim against the estate. However, the medical expense deduction for income tax purposes will be lost.
3. Administration expenses and casualty and theft losses can be deducted from the gross estate or deducted for income tax purposes on Form 1041. However, in order to claim them as income tax deductions, a waiver of the estate tax deduction should be filed with the income tax return (Sec. 2054).
4. A liability for periodic payments under a divorce decree will result in a double deduction on Form 706 and Form 1040.
5. Under Section 2009(d) of the 1976 Tax Reform Act, expenses related to selling a property by the estate may not reduce the taxable gain on

the sale reported by the estate (or trust) if they have also been deducted for federal estate tax purposes.

6. The gain on the sale or exchange of a property by an estate must be included in the gross income of the estate. A special rule allows the long-term capital treatment to assets sold by the estate within six months of the decedent's death (Sec. 1223 (11)). Also, any part of the capital gain paid, credited or required to be distributed during the year to the beneficiary is deductible in the income tax return of the fiduciary (Form 1041).
7. The loss on the sale or exchange of a property by an estate is deductible by the estate. Such loss is either a short-term or long-term capital loss. However, under a special rule all losses from sale or exchange of assets by the estate within six months of the decedent's death are treated as long-term capital losses. Therefore, it is advisable not to sell such assets (at a loss) by the estate. Instead, title should be passed from the decedent to his heirs. After passing the title, any loss from disposition will be reported by the heir. If the holding period of the heir is less than six months, the loss will be deducted by him as a short-term loss.

An estate is an income-tax-paying entity. As such, it is entitled to certain deductions from its taxable income. At the same time, such deductions may affect the determination of the estate tax liability. The estate planner should handle each group of expenses separately in the light of the special rules and restrictions imposed on the use of the deductions. The facts and circumstances of each situation will determine whether it is more appropriate to claim an item as an income tax or estate tax deduction. However, in making the election, the tax planner should try to treat all the beneficiaries equally. For example, election of an income tax deduction will favor the income beneficiary while increasing the estate tax burden on the remaindermen.

16.8. Maximizing the Marital Deduction

The estate tax advisor should take full advantage of the marital deduction if the deceased has a surviving spouse. The marital deduction was introduced in the Revenue Act of 1948 to give the residents of non-community property states the same estate tax advantages available to residents of community property states. The marital deduction under the 1976 Tax Reform Act (Sec. 2002(a)) is limited to a maximum of one-half of the adjusted gross estate with respect to adjusted gross estates of $500,000 or more. If the adjusted gross estate is less than $500,000, the maximum marital deduction is the greater of $250,000, or one-half of the decedent's adjusted gross estate. Of course, the marital deduction still is limited to the value of any amount which is passing or has passed from the decedent to the surviving spouse. Therefore, the amount claimed as a marital deduction can not exceed the value of property that passes through at death to the surviving spouse.

Property for which the marital deduction is claimed must be included in the gross estate of the decedent, and the surviving spouse must receive the property or interest in it. The most common types of transfers to a surviving spouse which qualify for the marital deduction are the following:

1. An outright bequest or transfer to the surviving spouse.
2. Transfer to the surviving spouse by the decedent at any time.
3. The property was held by decedent and surviving spouse as joint owners with right of survivorship.
4. Transfer consisting of proceeds of insurance on decedent's life.
5. Transfer consisting of an annuity receivable by the surviving spouse.
6. Transfer of property to the surviving spouse because of the disclaimer of another person.
7. Interest passing under a testamentary trust qualifying for marital deduction.
8. Life-time transfers included in gross estate (e.g., gifts within three years of death).

Taking full advantage of the marital deduction may require a careful observation of all or part of the following rules and suggestions:

1. The careful drafting of a will can ensure achieving all the benefits of the marital deduction.
2. A prerequisite of the marital deduction is that the decedent must have been a citizen or resident of the U.S. at the time of his death (the surviving spouse can be a nonresident alien).
3. The decedent must be survived by a spouse. A bequest to a divorced wife will not qualify for the deduction. But, if the divorce decree has not become final and local law recognizes the husband-wife relationship until the decree is final, the status of "surviving spouse" is met.
4. The marital deduction is mandatory and is not an elective. If two spouses die within a short period of time, waiving the marital deduction for the first one to die would reduce the estate of the survivor. The Internal Revenue Service will not approve a waiver of the marital deduction for any purpose (Rev. Rul. 59-123, 1959-1 C.B. 248). However, a surviving spouse may disclaim property left to her

and such disclaimer may produce tax results similar to a waiver of marital deduction.

5. If interests passing to a surviving spouse share the burden of any death taxes (state or federal) the value of such interests will be reduced and may lead to a reduction in the maximum deductible marital deduction. This problem can be avoided by not paying any taxes out of the value of interests passing to spouse. Nevertheless, if the interests passing to the spouse are in excess of the maximum marital deduction, such interest may be charged for any death taxes. The estate tax advisor should compute the effect of paying tax out of interests passing to spouse in order not to reduce such interests to less than the amount of the maximum marital deduction. Of course, the problem is that the amount of the tax burden and the marital deduction are interrelated. The solution could be on a trial-and-error basis, by assuming different amounts for the maximum marital deduction, then checking to see whether the marital deduction is reduced by allocating death taxes to the value of interest passing to spouse.
6. If interest passing to a spouse is subject to a claim or mortgage and if the decedent was personally liable for the claim against the property, the net value of the property (or the net equity passing to a spouse) qualifies for the marital deduction. This is important for tax saving purposes since the liability for the claim is charged in full against the value of property passing to the spouse. Also, the same applies if property passing to the surviving spouse is subject to her assumption of an obligation. The obligation assumed by the spouse will reduce the value of interests passing to her and may reduce the maximum marital deduction. As in the case of charging death taxes to interests passing to the spouse, a mortgage (whether assumed by the spouse or not) must be computed carefully in order to receive a maximum marital deduction. If liability against property passing to a spouse is discharged out of other assets of the estate, the payments made are treated as additional interests passing to the surviving spouse (Reg. 20.2056(b)-4(b)).

16.9. Generation Skipping and Transfers to Minors

If a person has a child (or children) and grandchildren in his family, generation skipping may produce definite estate tax savings. Property may be transferred to the grandchildren since they have a longer life expectancy and a family would pay estate taxes only once every several generations. The 1976 Tax Reform Act imposed a generation-skipping tax equivalent to the estate or gift tax that would have been imposed if a property was subject to an outright transfer. The value of the property subject to the generation-skipping tax is added to transfers made by the transferor. A tentative unified estate and gift tax is computed on the total value of these transfers. Then the tax on all transfers other than the generation-skipping transfer is subtracted to leave, as a balance, the new tax imposed on generation-skipping transfers.

The generation-skipping tax does not apply to transfers under irrevocable trusts in existence on April 30, 1976, or to transfers under a will or revocable trust in existence on, and not amended after, that date if the grantor dies before January 1, 1982. If the grantor or testator is incompetent to change the will or trust, the 1982 date is extended for two years after the disability is removed. Therefore, before making any transfer to children or grandchildren after April 30, 1976, consider carefully whether the new tax on generation-skipping applies or not. To avoid the new tax on generation-skipping transfers observe the following:

1. Within a family, the grantor, his wife and his brothers and sisters are in one generation. Their children are in the first younger generation and their grandchildren are in the second younger generation. Therefore, a generation-skipping inside the family occurs if a transfer (usually through a trust) is made to two or more generations of beneficiaries belonging to a younger generation than the grantor. But a trust for the grantor's spouse for life with remainder over to the grandchildren would not be a generation-skipping trust.

2. In case of transfers outside the family, generations are measured from the grantor. Beneficiaries not more than 12 1/2 years younger than the grantor are treated as members of his generation. However, beneficiaries more than 12 1/2 years but not more than 37 1/2 years younger than the grantor are considered members of his first younger generation. Individuals more than 37 1/2 years younger than the grantor are considered members of his second younger generation. Therefore, transfers to individuals not more than 37 1/2 years younger than the grantor are not taxable generation-skipping transfers. Also, a transfer to a trust for more than one individual within one generation group is not subject to the tax since no transfer is made to two or more generations of beneficiaries.

3. Transfers to grandchildren within a family are not subject to the tax to the extent that the total transfers do not exceed $250,000 through each deemed transferor. The grantor's child is considered the deemed transferor. Therefore, the $250,000 exclusion is limited by the number of the grantor's children and not by the number of the grandchildren. For example, if the grantor has three children and ten grandchildren, up to $750,000 can be transferred to the grandchildren tax free.

Instead of making an outright transfer or gift to a minor grandchild, the transfer can be made under a custodianship arrangement under the terms of the applicable Gifts to Minors Act. The major disadvantage of utilizing custodianship arrangements is that property must be turned over to the minor when he reaches age twenty-one. Also, if the minor dies prior to reaching the age of 21 years, his estate will be taxed on such property. The tax advisor should help in the comparison between the advantages of trusts for minors and custodianship arrangements. If the amounts involved are small the custodianship arrangement may be used. For larger sums, the trust arrangement may provide a better protection to the rights of the minor. Also, a trust arrangement will allow property to be held after the minor reaches the age of 21 years.

16.10. Installment Payment of Estate Tax

If the decedent owns interest in a farm or other closely-held business, a special rule will allow the executor of the estate to pay the estate tax over 15 years (new Sec. 6166 A). Payment under the installment method is elective. Interest at 4 percent a year on the estate tax that is attributable to the first one million dollars of farm or other closely-held business property is payable on the unpaid balance. The regular 7 percent a year (present rate) applies to the excess.

To qualify for the new 15-year installment payment of estate tax, the following conditions must be satisfied:

1. The value of a decedent's farm or other closely-held business interests included in his gross estate must exceed 65 percent of the adjusted gross estate (i.e., gross estate less expenses, debts, and losses).
2. If the decedent had more than one business, the estate can meet the 65-percent test if he had more than a 20-percent interest in each business or he is an owner in a partnership or corporation with 15 or less partners or stockholders.
3. Disposition of one-third of the value of an interest in a farm or other closely-held business accelerates the due date of all deferred tax.

The tax advisor may suggest making a "protective election" if he is not certain that an interest in a business qualifies the estate under the installment method. If a notice of "protective election" is filed, and it is found later that the interest does not qualify, the timely notice will be treated as an application for an extension of time to pay tax (Sec. 20.6166-1). Without the special rules of the installment payment, the estate tax is due and payable in full nine months after the decedent's death.

16.11. Redemption of Stock Under Section 303

Generally, when stock is redeemed, the redemption may result in taxable dividend (treated as ordinary income), or may be treated as sale of stock with the shareholder paying only a capital-gains tax on any gain. When a corporation acquires its stock from a shareholder for cash or other property, the redemption may be examined carefully by the IRS in order to treat it as sale or actual payment of dividend. Nevertheless, a special relief is provided under IRC Sec. 303. The redemption of stock to pay death taxes, funeral and administration expenses, will qualify for the capital-gain or loss treatment. For taking cash out of a corporation, the following terms should be met:

1. The value of the stock is included in the decedent's gross estate.
2. The stock is redeemed after death and within 4 to 15 years after filing the estate tax return.
3. The stock is redeemed for an amount not more than death taxes (federal and state), funeral and administration expenses (including interest). Any excess of redemption proceeds over the allowable amount is treated as dividend.
4. The value of stock in the corporation exceeds 50 percent of the decedent's adjusted gross estate (i.e., gross estate less expenses, debts and losses).
5. The stock must be redeemed from shareholders whose interest in the estate is reduced (directly or through a binding obligation to contribute) by the payment of the death taxes and funeral and administration expenses.

For tax saving purposes, it must be remembered that any cash taken from a corporation under Section 303 should not exceed the death taxes, funeral expenses, and administration expenses. Any excess will be taxed as dividend (or ordinary) income. A stockholder may wish to redeem part or all of his stock in order to improve his own liquidity. However, proper timing through the postponement of stock redemption until after death, will provide the estate of the deceased stockholder with the desired liquidity. Still, an estate should consider carefully if it prefers to distribute the stock rather than to redeem it.

16.12. Selecting the Taxable Year of the Estate

An estate tax advisor should be familiar with the rules related to a short taxable period. When an individual dies, his income from the first day of the year to the date of death is reported in his individual income tax return. Upon his death, a fiduciary is created and called the "estate." Any income from the estate is subject to the federal income tax after deducting an exemption of $600. An estate is entitled to the full $600 exemption even if the return is for a short period or a fractional part of the year. However, the $600 exemption can not be claimed for the year when the estate distributes its assets to the beneficiaries and terminates. Therefore, the tax planner should try to maximize the benefit from the $600 exemption.

Example: Mr. Brown dies October 10, 1975, and his executor expects that administration will take 15 months. The executor may adopt one of the following alternatives:

1. A short taxable period from October 11, 1975, to December 31, 1975, and claim an exemption of $600. A regular year for the period January 1, 1976, to December 31, 1976, and claim another $600 exemption. A short taxable period from January 1, 1977, to January 11, 1977, and no exemption can be claimed since it is the year when the estate terminates, or
2. A full taxable year from October 11, 1975, to October 10, 1976, and claim an exemption of $600. A short taxable year from October 11, 1976, to January 11, 1977, and no exemption can be claimed for the year when the estate distributes its assets to the beneficiaries.

Of course, in this example, alternative (1) will result in claiming the $600 exemption twice, while alternative (2) will give only one $600 exemption.

Selecting the taxable year of the estate has another serious tax effect. The income of the estate is taxed at the same rates applicable to a married person filing a separate return. The tax rates are progressive and the proper selection of the tax period may lead to a lower taxable income and as a result a lower top-tax bracket. Also, in each tax period, the estate is allowed a deduction for the income included in its gross income that is currently distributable to the beneficiaries. The tax advisor should be aware of the possibilities of this allowable deduction for distributions to beneficiaries.

The combined effect of all these rules related to the taxable period of an estate seems to lead the tax advisor (or executor) to take into consideration all of the following data before making a decision regarding a taxable year for the estate:

1. The total expected period to distribute the assets to the beneficiaries and terminate the estate.
2. The estimated income and deductions of the estate.
3. The anticipated taxable income and deductions of each one of the beneficiaries.

16.13. Selecting the Date of Decedent's Death or an Alternate Valuation Date

The executor may elect to value property as of the date of decedent's death or as of an alternate valuation date (a special evaluation rule applies to farms and closely-held business realty). This alternate valuation date is six months after decedent's death, or the date of sale or disposition of property, whichever occurs first. The election to use an alternate valuation date may be made within nine months after a decedent's death or within the period of any extension by the District Director of the time for filing the estate tax return. If the alternate valuation date is elected, it applies to all the property included in the gross estate. It cannot be used selectively for part of the estate only. Selecting the date of decedent's death or an alternate valuation date is very important since it will influence the following three areas:

1. *Total federal estate tax:* the value of the property included in the gross estate directly affects the amount of taxable estate and as a result the estate tax that is payable.

2. *The basis of property distributed to the beneficiaries:* the value assigned to property acquired from, or passing from, a decedent before December 31, 1976, is the same as value assigned to property for estate tax purposes. This rule provides a stepped-up value for such property. Section 2005(a) of the 1976 Tax Reform Act ended this treatment and introduced instead the "fresh start" rule. Under the new rule, the basis of inherited property (except marketable bonds or securities) is the same as the decedent's basis immediately before his death, with an adjustment for appreciation in value attributable to the period decedent held the property before January 1, 1977. For example, depreciable property was acquired on January 1, 1971, at a cost of $40,000 and was depreciated under the straight-line method claiming a depreciation deduction of $1,600 per year. The fair market value of the property at date of death in 1982 is $80,000. Therefore, the depreciable property was acquired 11 years before the decedent's death and 6 years before January 1, 1977. The addition to the decedent's basis under the "fresh start" rule is $30,520, figured as follows:

Fair market value at date of death	$80,000
Adjusted basis at date of death ($40,000 - $16,000)	24,000
Excess of market value over adjusted basis	56,000
Depreciation up to date of death	16,000
Appreciation of value until date of death (56,000 - 16,000)	40,000

Number of days in holding period of asset before January 1, 1977 (6 years X 365 days)	2,190
Number of days in total holding period of asset (11 years X 365 days)	4,015
Fraction composed of 2,190 over 4,015=	0.545
Appreciation of the property before January 1, 1977 ($40,000 X 0.545)	21,800
Depreciation attributable to holding period before January 1, 1977 ($16,000 X 0.545)	8,720
Addition to basis ($21,800 + $8,720)	30,520

Notice that the "fresh start" rule applies for computing gain (but not loss) on eventual disposition of property passing from a decedent. Also, any substantial improvements to the property made by the decedent or his predecessor will be treated as a separate property.

3. *Relation to income tax:* after the date of decedent's death and during the period of administration, a casualty loss to estate property may take place. The executor will have a choice to reduce the gross estate (for estate tax purposes) or to claim the casualty loss as a deduction from the taxable income of the estate (for income tax purposes). However, the executor cannot claim the deduction for casualty loss for both estate tax as well as income tax purposes (Sec. 2054; 20.2054-1). If the decision is made to claim the casualty loss as a deduction for income tax purposes, a statement must be filed (with the estate tax return) that the loss has not been claimed as an estate tax deduction.

Notice that if an asset is destroyed by fire or other casualty during the six months after the date of decedent's death, and if the loss is not compensated for by insurance, the alternate valuation date cannot be used for estate tax purposes, if, at the same time, the loss deduction is claimed for income tax purposes. The use of the alternate valuation date in a case like this will lead to a double deduction for the casualty loss: first, through reducing the gross estate; and, second, reducing the taxable income of the estate. This double deduction is not permissible.

16.14. Maximizing the Deductions from Gross Estate and Waiver of Executor's Fee

A deduction from the value of the gross estate is allowable for administration expenses, funeral expenses and claims enforceable against the estate. Maximizing the deduction for expenses and claims is related to two main factors: (1) whether to claim medical expenses as a deduction from the gross estate or an income tax deduction; and (2) whether to pay compensation or commission to the executor, or exercise a waiver of executor's fees if he is a beneficiary of the estate. The following rules and observations may assist advisor in using effectively the deduction for these items:

1. A claim against the estate for large amounts of medical expenses from the last illness of the decedent can be deducted from the gross estate. However, if such expenses are paid by the estate within one year after the date of decedent's death, they may be claimed as income tax deductions on the decedent's income tax return. The income tax deduction is allowed only upon filing a statement with the estate tax return that a deduction was not taken for unpaid medical expenses in order to claim them on the decedent's final income tax return. A waiver of an estate tax deduction is irrevocable (Sec. 213(d); 1.213-1(d)). Notice that if these medical expenses are not paid within one year of death, they are deductible only as claims against the gross estate, and the election will be lost.

2. Any amount paid to the executor of the estate as fees or commissions is deductible from the gross estate. However, such amounts should be added to the gross income of the executor and subjected to the income tax. If the executor is also a beneficiary of the estate, he may wish to waive his right to commissions, if his own income tax savings would exceed the estate tax. Notice that if the will provides that the executor would receive a bequest or devise in lieu of his commission, no deduction from the gross estate would be allowed for the value of such a bequest or devise.

16.15. Suggestions for Reducing the Tax on Income Derived After the Death of the Decedent

Usually, the income of an estate is taxed at the same rates as married taxpayers filing separate returns. In figuring the taxable income of an estate, a deduction is allowed for amounts paid, credited, or required to be distributed to the beneficiaries. In addition, the estate is allowed a personal exemption of $600 per year except in the year the final distribution of assets is made. There is no double taxation imposed on the income of an estate. The income tax is imposed on the estate or the beneficiaries. Therefore, as long as the estate is not closed, the estate planner would have the opportunity of income splitting between the beneficiaries and the estate. To a certain extent, the executor may either delay or accelerate closing the estate. Usually, the beneficiaries of an estate favor closing it as quickly as possible. However, they may reconsider their request for a quick termination of the estate if the potential income tax savings are well understood and secured by them. Suggestions for reducing the tax on income derived after the death of the decedent and before the final closing of the estate, include the following:

1. Where the income of the estate is expected to be high, arrange for it to be distributed between as many beneficiaries as possible.
2. Assets giving rise to high income and distributed to charitable organizations will reduce the impact of both the estate tax and the income tax.
3. It may be desirable to distribute more income to a beneficiary in a comparatively low income tax bracket.
4. If income from the estate is to be paid to a surviving spouse, a substantial amount of this income should be distributed to her when she still has the privilege of filing a joint income tax return.
5. Where the income of the estate is expected to be high, spread it over an extended period of time and slow down the process of closing the estate. The executor may delay the closing of an estate by using one or more of the following reasons:

(a) claims by creditors or beneficiaries may be contested and litigated,
(b) values of assets included in gross estate may be questioned by the IRS,
(c) questions may arise as to gifts made in contemplation of death,
(d) better offers may be solicited for the sale of estate properties,
(e) winding up the business activities of the decedent requires extra time in order to protect the best interest of the beneficiaries.

16.16. Use of Renunciations and Disclaimers

Estate tax planning should take place before the date of decedent's death. An estate which is not planned well may resort to emergency measures taking effect after the decedent's death. One of these emergency tools is the use of renunciations and disclaimers. A beneficiary's renunciation of his share in an estate can be made within "a reasonable time" after he learns of the existence of his inheritance rights. The IRS contends that a renunciation will transfer rights in a tax-free way if the following three conditions are satisfied:

1. The written renunciation should take place before acceptance of inheritance rights.
2. A right should be rejected in full not later than nine months after the day on which the transfer creating the interest is

made. The right cannot be accepted in part and renounced in part (Reg. 20.2041-3(d)(6)).

3. The interest must pass to a person other than the person making the disclaimer as a result of the refusal to accept the property.

If a renunciation is unequivocal and effective (Sec. 2518), it can be used in one or more of the following ways:

1. A beneficiary (other than the surviving spouse) may disclaim his rights, and as a result increase the amount of property passing to the surviving spouse. With an increase in property passing to the surviving spouse, the marital (charitable) deduction claimed by the estate will increase too.

2. A beneficiary paying income tax at a high rate, or with a large estate on his own, or suffering from ill health, may decide to disclaim his inheritance rights. Such disclaimer may shift income-producing property to another beneficiary or at least decrease the income and estate taxes of the beneficiary exercising the disclaimer.

Notice that under IRS Sec. 2056(d)(1), if the surviving spouse refuses to take the property or interest passing from the decedent, the marital deduction for the disclaimed property will be lost. Also, making a qualified disclaimer is not regarded as making a gift. As a tax advisor, use renunciations and disclaimers only for the rearrangement of a poorly planned estate.

16.17. Methods of Eliminating Life Insurance Proceeds from Gross Estate

The area of life insurance is very important for estate tax purposes. The tax advisor may suggest the purchase of life insurance for one or more of the following objectives:

1. To provide needed liquidity to pay the estate tax.
2. To provide the liqudity to pay claims against the estate, such as a mortgage on property.
3. To provide financial security for the beneficiaries and the surviving spouse.

Usually, the proceeds from a life insurance policy are included in the gross estate if such proceeds are receivable by the executor or administrator, payable to the estate, or receivable by or for the benefit of the estate. The tax advisor should be familiar with the following related areas:

1. The methods of eliminating life insurance proceeds from the gross estate.
2. How to qualify life insurance proceeds for the marital deduction.
3. The methods of distributing life insurance proceeds.
4. The tax benefits of a life insurance trust.
5. The use of annuities for estate planning purposes.

In the following summary each one of the five above mentioned areas will be reviewed:

1. Insurance payable to beneficiaries is not included in the estate if the decedent did not possess at death any incidents of ownership, such as power to change the beneficiary, or power to assign or borrow on the policy. The most popular methods of eliminating life insurance proceeds from the estate of the insured are: (a) irrevocable assignment of insurance policies to others; (b) irrevocable assignment of policies to the insured's business or business associates. Notice that after an assignment of life insurance, if the insured continues to pay the annual premiums on the policy, the IRS will impose a gift tax on the premiums and also will include in the gross estate of the insured a portion of the insurance proceeds. This portion included in the estate of the insured is in the same proportion as the premiums paid in the last three-year period (before death) bears to the total premiums paid on the policy (Rev. Rul. 67-463, I.R.B. 1967-52, 15). Therefore, to eliminate life insurance proceeds from the estate of the insured completely, the policy should be transferred more than three years before his death and the beneficiary should pay all the premiums that subsequently become due.

2. To maximize the marital deduction, the estate advisor should ensure that the insurance proceeds will qualify as interest "passing" to the surviving spouse. To qualify life insurance proceeds for the marital deduction, one or more of the following requirements must be met:

(a) The insurance proceeds are payable to the surviving spouse in a lump sum.

(b) The proceeds are payable to the surviving spouse in installments and for life. After the death of the surviving spouse, any remaining installments are payable to her estate.

(c) The interest on insurance proceeds is payable to the surviving spouse for life, and upon her death, the principal amount is payable to her estate.

(d) The proceeds are payable to a trust and the trust provisions meet the requirements for the marital deduction.

3. The most popular methods of distributing life insurance proceeds, are the following:

(a) Lump sum payment to the estate of the insured, his beneficiaries, or to a trust.

(b) Installment payments for a certain number of years.

(c) Proceeds are payable to the beneficiary in installments and for life. After the death of the beneficiary, the remaining installments are payable to his estate or to another beneficiary.

4. If insurance proceeds are received by a trust, an insurance trust would be created. Insurance trusts are used in any one of the following forms:

(a) A revocable insurance trust where the trust corpus is a part of the settlor's gross estate. This type of trust is recommended to qualify for the estate tax marital deduction.

(b) An irrevocable insurance trust would save estate tax if the settlor did not retain any incidents of ownership.

(c) A funded insurance trust will receive from the settlor other assets to be used for the payment of premiums during the life of the insured.

(d) An unfunded insurance trust will receive either a paid-up insurance policy or another person, usually the settlor, will pay the premiums during the life of the insured. If the insurance is not paid-up, the payment of the premiums may create a gift tax liability.

5. An annuity purchaser may invest a certain amount of money in an annuity. In return he would receive periodic payments for the balance of his life with or without a survivor's benefit. The money paid to purchase the annuity would reduce the amount available for inclusion in the purchaser's gross estate. Also, if the annuity terminates at death of the purchaser, the annuity will have no remaining interest to be added to the gross estate upon his death. However, if the annuity has a survivor's benefit, the value of the benefit is added to the estate of the purchaser if such benefit is payable to his estate.

16.18. The Credit for Tax on Prior Transfers

When property passes through more than one taxable estate within a ten-year period, a credit for tax on prior transfers is allowed (Sec. 2013(a), 2013(d)). This credit is the lesser of the following two amounts:

1. The prior decedent's adjusted federal estate tax, multiplied by the ratio of the value of transferred property, divided by the prior decedent's adjusted taxable estate, or
2. The estate tax on the present decedent's estate, multiplied by the ratio of the value of property received (from the prior decedent), divided by the total estate of the present decedent.

The credit for tax on prior transfers is allowed in full if the present decedent dies within two years after the death of the prior decedent. Otherwise, the credit is reduced by 20 percent. for every two years. Therefore, no tax credit is allowed if the present decedent dies after ten years from the date of death of the prior decedent. The estate planner should examine the possibilities for claiming this credit and at the same time should be aware of the various limitations on the credit.

16.19. Business Agreements as Liability Against the Estate, and Whether to Sell or Continue Business Interest

The following two areas can not be separated from estate tax planning:

1. Business agreements as liability against the estate, and
2. Whether to sell or continue the family business after the death of its founder.

In the following review we will examine the possibilities under each one of these two issues:

1. Under IRC Sec. 2053(c) an enforceable claim against the estate is deductible in full. Let us assume that prior to his death the decedent promises to pay his son $20,000 and gives his son an enforceable instrument to that effect. Upon his death the IRS will try to deny the deduction for the claim on the ground that the decedent did not receive something of a monetary value in exchange for the obligation undertaken by the decedent. The son in this example will take the position that the claim is enforceable and the consideration requirement is satisfied. Satisfaction of the consideration requirement may deal with the question of what constitutes an adequate and full consideration. Interfamily debts can reduce considerably the amount of taxable estate if they can stand the scrutiny of the IRS. The estate planner may suggest to the client to endorse the note of a family member, instead of making an out-right promise to pay the family member a specific amount of money. Endorsing a note of another person would satisfy the consideration requirement, when the borrower receives the money (and not the endorser). In this case, if the endorser dies, the claim against the borrower is deductible from the estate of the endorser, if the right against the borrower is worthless.

2. A businessman should make the decision whether to sell or continue the business after his death. The estate advisor should help in reaching this decision. If the business is to be continued, it can be bequested to an adult beneficiary willing and capable of assuming the

managerial functions. Another method or vehicle for continuation of the family business is to incorporate it and make periodic gifts of shares of stock to family members. This method allows the continuation of the business, and at the same time the donor would utilize his gift tax annual exclusions. Also, after such gifts are carried out, the gross estate of the founder of the business may be reduced considerably. Still another possible avenue, if the beneficiaries are minors, is to transfer interest in the business to a trust and the created trust will continue under the management of a trustee until the beneficiaries are capable of caring for the business on their own.

The founder of a business may leave the decision of whether to sell or continue the family business without any definite stand on his part. In this case, the beneficiaries must reach the final decision. On the other hand, the businessman may decide to discontinue the family business upon his death. In this case, he may direct in his will that the business will discontinue through direct sale or liquidation. The executor, in a case like this, should be given a flexible time table to carry on the sale or liquidation. Another common method of selling a business is under a buy-sell agreement. Such agreements are covered in greater detail in the next section of this chapter (i.e., 16.20).

Under the 1976 Tax Reform Act, a special evaluation rule applies to farms and closely-held business realty. However, if within 15 years after the decedent's death the heir sells or transfers the property to a non-family member, or the property is not used for farming or other closely-held business purposes, the special valuation benefits are recaptured either in full or in part. There is no estate tax recapture if the heir holds the property for 15 years or more or dies without converting it to a non-qualified use.

16.20. The Use of Buy-Sell Agreements

The value of a decedent's interest in a business is, of course, a part of his gross estate. In the case of a sole proprietorship, the interest of the owner refers to all the various assets of the business. The estate of the sole proprietor will have no problem dealing with a legal entity standing between the deceased and his business assets. However, the situation is different if the decedent owns an interest in a partnership or a closed corporation. Disposing of a business interest in a partnership or a closed corporation may not be as easy as expected. Also, the surviving partners or stockholders may not accept a stranger to the business. A happy solution, usually, is to adopt a buy-sell agreement. The common advantages of a buy-sell agreement include the following:

1. The surviving owners will not fear that interest in the business will pass to an undesirable or uncongenial person.

2. The estate of the deceased is spared the uncertainty of disposing of an interest in a closely-held business since not many investors may be interested in this kind of close business association.
3. Through the buy-sell agreement, the estate will have an access to a needed source of liquid funds. Such funds can prove to be handy for paying funeral expenses, legal and administration fees, estate taxes, etc.
4. The cost of the buy-sell agreement to the surviving business associates, may be minimized through the purchase of proper life insurance.

The estate advisor should examine carefully the possibilities of a buy-sell agreement. If such an agreement is desired, he should ensure that it covers well all of the following major areas:

1. Identity of the purchaser or purchasers (surviving partners, surviving stockholders or corporation).
2. The buy-sell agreement may give the estate the option to sell and the surviving business associates the option to buy, or it may make the buy-sell agreement as an absolutely binding contract.
3. The agreement should establish clearly the purchase price and the method of payment.
4. The buy-sell agreement may be funded from the proceeds of acquired insurance. If insurance is used for funding purposes, the agreement should cover the following:
   (a) Whether the insurance proceeds will pay for part or all of the purchase price.
   (b) Who would pay the insurance premiums.
   (c) Whether the insurance proceeds would be added to the value of the business.
5. If the business interest is in a partnership, the buy-sell agreement should release the estate of the deceased partner from present, as well as, future claims against the partnership.

16.21. Tax Benefits of IRA and H.R.10 Plans

Certain estate and income tax advantages could be achieved through the creation of an IRA or H.R.10 plan. Under the plan, the periodic contributions of the employer (or self-employed) are not taxed as income to the employee (or self-employed). Payments from the trust to the survivors of the employee or self-employed are not included in the gross estate to the extent of employer contributions. However, the gross estate exclusion does not apply to all lump-sum payments from qualified pension, profit-sharing and other retirement plans (Sec. 2009(c), 1976 Tax Reform Act). Notice that the qualified plan may, instead of making an outright payment to the employee and his survivors, purchase annuity contracts under which payments are to be made to the employee and his survivors. Such employee annuities also enjoy the same exemption from the estate tax.

The estate tax exemption under Section 2039(c) would be realized without creating employees' trust, if the employer purchases under a qualified plan a retirement annuity for an employee. The value of the survivor's rights under the annuity contract is exempt from the estate tax if the benefits are due to employer contributions. The exclusion under Section 2039(c), as amended in 1976, includes any trust or annuity payments attributable to contributions made by the employee or the self-employed if the decedent's payments into the account were deductible for income tax purposes. Contributions made by the self-employed are treated, for the purpose of this special exclusion measure, like the contributions of an employer. Therefore, the self-employed is treated under Section 2009(c) of the 1976 Tax Reform Act like an employee. As a result of the new rules of Section 2009(c), even a lump-sum payment to the beneficiary may not produce any estate tax liability (even though such payments are included in the decedent's gross estate). For example, a lump-sum payment to a wife who is the beneficiary of the qualified plan will qualify for the $250,000 marital deduction plus an equivalent exemption of $120,000 in the year 1977. In 1981, a lump-sum payment to the wife, as beneficiary, up to $425,000 would not be taxed (i.e. $250,000 marital deduction plus $175,000 exemption).

To use the exemption under Section 2039(c), the employee (or self-employed) should avoid permitting his estate (or executor) to be the beneficiary of any death benefits from employees' trust or a qualified plan. Instead such benefits should be made payable to the survivors of the employee or to an inter vivos (or living) trust. If an inter vivos trust is created and would be the beneficiary of such death proceeds, the living trust may even lend money to the estate to solve any problem with liquidity. Furthermore, in a community property state, this estate tax exclusion also applies to the community property share of a taxpayer's spouse in benefits accumulated under an IRA or H.R.10 plan when the spouse dies before the taxpayer.

16.22. Custodianship and Trust Arrangements for Transfers to Minors

Both transfers in trust for the benefit of a minor and making a gift to a minor under a custodianship arrangement qualify for the annual gift tax exemption under the Gifts to Minors Act. Beside the gift tax saving feature, the donor would reduce his gross taxable estate through life-time gift giving. Also, if the subject of the gift is an income-producing asset, the income from it is removed from the income tax return of the donor. The tax advisor should be aware of the following merits and demerits of giving gifts to minors under the custodianship vs. trust arrangement:

1. A gift to a minor under the custodianship arrangement would result in the following:

(a) The custodianship arrangement is easier to establish than the trust arrangement.

(b) Property can not be held for the minor beyond age 21 and must be turned over to him at that time.

(c) If the donor is also the custodian, the IRS will include the property in the donor-custodian estate.

(d) On death of the minor, the property may return in whole or in part to the donor through intestacy.

(e) The annual gift tax exemption is available to the donor. Also, the income from the custodian property is taxed to the minor.

2. A gift to a minor under a trust arrangement would result in the following:

(a) Property may be held in trust for the minor until after he reaches the age 21.

(b) The trust instrument may specify, in case of death of minor, how to distribute his properties in order to avoid an undesirable return of property to the donor.

(c) If the donor is also the trustee, the IRS will not add the property of the trust to the gross estate of the donor-trustee if he dies while serving as a trustee. This advantage of the trust arrangement will be achieved if the trust is not revocable and the donor does not retain any rights over the gifted property.

(d) Giving to a minor under a trust arrangement qualifies under the Gifts to Minors Act for the available annual gift tax exemption. Also, the income from trust property is taxed to the minor or the trust itself.

16.23. Annuity Contracts and Estate Tax Planning

Annuities can serve as an effective estate planning device. The estate advisor should be familiar with the rules regarding the taxation of annuities and the advantages of the purchase of an annuity contract. Generally, the taxation of an annuity depends on the special features of the annuity contract. Annuity contracts take a variety of forms, and the most popular types are the following:

1. A single life annuity without any refund feature where an amount is paid to the annuitant for his life. Upon his death, all rights under the annuity contract terminate. There is no estate tax on this type of annuity because no property right or interest remains at the time of the annuitant's death.

2. A single life annuity with a refund feature, under which if the amount paid to the annuitant during his life does not equal the cost of the annuity contract, the difference will be paid to his estate or a certain survivor. If the survivor's benefit is payable to the annuitant's estate, it should be included in his gross estate. However, if the survivor's benefit is paid to named persons, the value of the survivor's benefit is included in the gross estate only in proportion to the decedent's contribution to the total cost (or purchase price) of the annuity contract.

3. A self and survivor annuity where payments are made to the annuitant during his life, and the same will be paid to the survivor for his life. Under Section 2039, the value of amounts receivable by beneficiaries is to be included in the decedent's gross estate.

4. A joint and survivor annuity, under which a specified sum would be paid to two annuitants jointly during their lives, and after their death a specified sum is payable to the survivor for his life. Section 2039 applies to this type of annuity contracts, too, since a beneficiary would receive benefits by reason of his surviving the decedents.

5. The value of an annuity receivable by a beneficiary of an individual retirement account will be excluded from the decedent's gross estate to the extent the decedent's payments into the account were deductible for income tax purposes. For the purpose of this exclusion, any payments under an H.R.10 plan by a self-employed person will be considered the same as contributions by an employer (1976 Tax Reform Act Sec. 2009(c)). However, this special exclusion from the gross estate is lost if the payments from qualified pension, profit-sharing and other retirement plans are made directly to the estate of the decedent or if the payment constitutes a lump-sum amount.

The rules of Section 2039 do not apply to two specific situations: (1) amounts receivable under life insurance policies and payable in the form of annuities; and (2) annuity contracts entered into before March 3, 1931. Special care should be exercised when dealing with employees' annuities and employment related contracts since they are subject to their own rules.

Purchasing an annuity contract may lead to one or more of the following advantages:

1. The annuitant removes from his gross estate the money used to purchase the annuity. In return, he receives, on a periodic basis, a steady flow of income.
2. If the annuitant is disabled or advanced in age, he may not be able to carry the burden of managing and investing the assets used to purchase the annuity.
3. Because of the predictable and steady nature of the annual income from the annuity contract, the annuitant may then feel more relaxed about meeting his revenue needs after reaching a certain age.

The issue of taking an annuity should be examined by each individual in the light of his own needs and objectives. Some individuals may prefer not to deal with an insurance company, and instead would like to use a "private annuity" or a non-commercial annuity agreement. An elderly parent may sell property to a child and require the sale price to be paid over the balance of the parent's life. Under Rev. Rul. 69-74, IRB 1969-8, 8, if the decedent has transferred property reserving the right to the income for the rest of his life, the value of the property should be added to his gross estate. On the other hand, if the annuitant transfers property to another person who accepts to pay him, periodically, amounts equal to the purchase price or the anticipated income from the property, for the rest of his life, the property would be removed from the gross estate of the annuitant for estate tax purposes. The private annuity appears to be a device that would avoid the estate and gift taxes if used well according to the rules summarized in Rev. Rul. 69-74, IRB 1969-8, 8. The effect of the private annuity on the income, estate, and gift taxes of both the annuitant and transferee must be taken into consideration in determining whether to use it as a tax saving device or not.

16.24. Use of Sale-Leaseback Agreements

All property owned by an individual would be added, upon his death, to his gross estate. To reduce the total amount of gross estate, a property may be sold and still enjoyed and used through a lease-back arrangement. No general rule can be given as to when to use the sale-leaseback arrangement. Each case must be decided on its own facts. However, generally, the sale of a property to a related person and the leaseback of the same property, would result in the exclusion of the property from the gross estate of the original owner (or the seller) if he does not retain any equity in the property. The following three tests are applied before giving full effect to a sale-leaseback agreement:

1. The relationship between the sale price and fair market value of the property,

2. Whether the rental is realistic, and
3. Whether the sale-leaseback is at arms length.

A sale-leaseback agreement would influence both the income and estate taxes of the buyer and the seller. Also, its objective could be one or more of the following:

1. To transfer income from a property to the new owner.
2. To remove the value of a property from the estate of the selling taxpayer.
3. To realize a deductible loss on the transaction by the seller.
4. To create a rent expense deduction for the user of the property.
5. To transform a fully depreciated property between the hands of one owner, to a property with depreciable basis in the hands of the new owner.

A word of caution, before entering a sale-leaseback agreement between a husband and wife, or an individual and his controlled corporation: be sure to check the rules under I.R.C. Section 1239. Gain from sale of such depreciable property must be treated as ordinary income (Rev. Rul. 69-109, 1969-1 CB202, see also, *10-42 Corp.*, 55 TC593; *Miller V. Comm.*, 35AFTR 2d75-714).

16.25. Trusts and Estate Tax Saving

Trusts are traditional and an important media for income, gift, and estate tax saving. Their great value lies in the amount of flexibility they provide for the creator of the trust through the availability of a wide variety of trusts. Each type of trust can be fashioned to serve specific needs while omitting unneeded features. For tax saving purposes, it is essential to exercise a great degree of care in the stage of drawing the trust instrument. Also, of course, it is important to know the special features of each type of trust. In the following summary, trusts are classified into inter vivos and testamentary. Then, each broad classification is subdivided into special purpose trusts, as follows:

1. Inter vivos (or living) trust is established during the lifetime of the grantor or creator. An inter vivos trust is created to achieve any one of the following objectives:

(a) To save income taxes for the settler,
(b) To save estate tax for the grantor, or
(c) To save both income and estate taxes.

Some of the special purpose inter vivos trusts are the following:

(a) Life insurance, irrevocable trust
(b) Life insurance, revocable trust
(c) Reversionary (or Clifford) trust
(d) Trust for minors
(e) Trust for incompetent child
(f) Irrevocable trust for adult relative
(g) Sprinkling trust (e.g., for grantor's children)
(h) Revocable trust utilizing the marital deduction
(i) Trust with income to charity for term of years
(j) Trust with income to donor for life and charitable remainder
(k) Reciprocal trusts

2. Testamentary trusts provide the testator with an opportunity to exercise his influence over an extended period after his decease. This type of trust can be used to reduce the income tax of the beneficiaries, their estate taxes, or both. Some of the popular special purpose testamentary trusts are the following:

(a) Trust for the surviving spouse
(b) Trust for children
(c) Accumulation trust
(d) Sprinkling trust
(e) Will-form trust
(f) Trust designed to provide dollar amounts periodically
(g) Trust designed to invade principal
(h) Form empowering trustee to terminate trust

The tax advisor should acquaint the taxpayer with the purposes served by trusts without confusing him about the boundless variety of trusts. The goals of the taxpayer should be stated and the created trust should be fashioned to serve those goals. The most common purposes of trusts in general, are the following:

1. To save income taxes
2. To save estate taxes
3. To overcome civil disabilities of infants
4. To protect funds against future spouse of widow
5. To protect funds against future child of widow

6. To protect beneficiaries against creditors
7. To overcome age or health disabilities of beneficiaries
8. To arrange for continuity of business interest
9. To protect beneficiaries against financial inexperience.

16.26. Use of U.S. Treasury Bonds, Admitting a Family Member to a Partnership, and Reporting Sale to a Family Member Under the Installment Method

The following three common estate tax saving devices should be considered carefully:

1. The purchase of certain U.S. Treasury Bonds.
2. Admitting a family member to a partnership.
3. Adopting the installment method for reporting a sale to a family member.

The three above-mentioned tools are examined in the following summary:

1. Certain United States Treasury Bonds can be purchased at a discount (or a price below the face or par value) and are acceptable in payment of estate taxes at their face (or par) value (P.L. 92-5, Sec 4). The effect of using such bonds for the payment of estate taxes can be summarized as follows:

(a) Only bonds used for payment of the estate tax will be accepted by the IRS at their par value.

(b) Bonds used for payment of the estate tax must be included in the gross estate at their par value too (*Bankers Trust Co.* (*Ellis*) v. U.S., 7AFTR 2d 1691, 284 F. 2d 537).

(c) The difference between the cost or basis of the bonds used for paying the estate tax and their par value is taxed as ordinary income realized by the estate or the beneficiaries.

An estate advisor should consider the purchase of such bonds by a client in poor health or advanced age. Sometimes, a serious illness is discovered and a substantial saving to the estate and the survivors can be achieved by purchasing this type of U.S. Treasury Bonds. A list showing bond issues available for redemption at par to pay estate taxes, may be acquired from any Federal Reserve Bank.

2. A decedent's interest in a partnership is, of course, included in his gross estate. However, the interest to be included in his estate would vary depending upon the decedent's rights or share in the partnership at his death. Thus, any transfer of rights to a family member and before the

date of death, would reduce a deceased partner's estate. An agreement showing the transfer of certain rights in a business constitutes an evidence as to the remaining interest to be included in the decedent's estate. Under such an agreement the rights of the newly-admitted partner should be defined clearly. Also, the consideration for the transfer and method of payment should be stated. The objective of the estate planner is to reduce the value of interest in a going business before death takes place.

3. A bona fide sale would remove a property from the gross estate of the seller. However, if in connection with the sale the seller receives full consideration in money value (or money's worth), the estate of the seller is not reduced. The sale amounts only to a substitution or exchange of assets. To reduce the seller's estate, the sale should be reported under the installment method, and the periodic due payments are not collected, but reported instead as gifts. The estate advisor should observe carefully all of the following pit-falls:

(a) The transfer of ownership should be based on a bona fide sale and not a gratuitous transfer. In connection with the transfer, the seller receives full consideration in money or money's worth.

(b) Transfers within three years before death would not be subject to the rules of transfer in contemplation of death, if they constitute bona fide sales. If in fact, a question is raised, it would be regarding the adequacy of consideration received in exchange for the transfer.

(c) The seller should not retain any rights in the property sold or any power to revoke the transfer.

(d) If a periodic sale installment is not collected and given instead as a gift, it should be reported properly by the donor. If possible, the entire sale price should be accounted for as either collected or given as gifts before death of the seller takes place.

16.27. Claiming the Orphan's Exclusion

Under Section 2007 of the 1976 Tax Reform Act, an orphan's exclusion is allowed. The new exclusion provides a substantial deduction for amounts which pass to a minor child of the decedent when there is not surviving spouse of the decedent (or other known parent). The amount of orphan's exclusion is equal to $5,000, multiplied by the excess of 21 over the child's age on the decedent's death. For example, a taxpayer died (after December 31, 1976) leaving two children without their surviving mother. The children's ages on the decedent's date of death are 5 and 7. The maximum amount allowable as orphans' exclusion against the gross estate of the decedent is $150,000, figured as follows:

Deduction for first child, age 5:	
21 minus 5 = 16 X $5,000	$ 80,000
Deduction for second child, age 7:	
21 minus 7 = 14 X $5,000	70,000
Total Orphan's Exclusion	$150,000

In order to claim the exclusion observe the following:

1. Any child of the decedent, whether natural or by legal adoption, who has not reached 21 before the decedent's date of death, qualifies as a minor child.
2. The exclusion is lost if the child's interest in the property passing to the minor is terminable (e.g., a life estate).
3. If the decedent was divorced and is survived by the other known parent, the deduction is not allowed.

Chapter 17

THE GIFT TAX AND GIFTS TO FAMILY MEMBERS

17.1. Reasons for Giving Gifts and Establishing a Gift-Giving Habit

The gift tax bears a close relationship to both the estate tax and the income tax. At the same time, it has a basic feature not available in either the estate or the income tax. As far as the relationship is concerned, giving a gift results in reducing the gross estate of the donor, and, if the gift constitutes an income-producing property, income from it will be shifted to the donee. On the other hand, estate and income taxes must be paid when reporting a taxable estate or income. The gift tax may be eliminated completely by not giving any gifts. This very special feature makes many individuals think about the gift tax as an optional tax. Thus, since the gift tax can be avoided completely, it is hard to convince a person to pay the tax voluntarily. The only way to support a suggestion to make gifts of valuable assets is through understanding the following persuasive reasons:

1. Making gifts during the lifetime of a person would reduce the total value of the remaining assets owned by the donor. Upon death of the donor, his gross estate would be smaller and the payable estate taxes lower.
2. Giving a gift may not result in a gift tax liability because of the available annual exclusion, unified estate and gift tax credit, and the marital deduction.
3. If the gift is an income-producing property, an income tax saving results from shifting income from such property from the relatively high tax bracket of the donor to the relatively lower tax bracket of the donee.

4. If the gift is to a family member, the same amount of economic resources remains under the control of the donor and his immediate family. A gift to a family member will result in a transfer in ownership, but for the family as a whole, there is no increase or decrease in total net worth because of an inter-family transfer.
5. Under the 1976 Tax Reform Act, there is an unlimited gift tax marital deduction for the first $100,000 of lifetime gifts to a spouse. Gifts over $100,000 up to $200,000 (to a spouse) are fully taxed and a 50 percent marital deduction is allowed for gifts over $200,000. However, the maximum estate tax marital deduction is to be reduced by the amount of the marital deduction allowed for lifetime transfers in excess of 50 percent of the value of the transfers when lifetime gifts are less than $200,000. For example, if a decedent left an adjusted gross estate of $400,000 and had made a lifetime gift of $100,000 to his wife, the maximum marital deduction for estate tax purposes would have been $200,000 (i.e., $250,000 less 50 percent of $100,000). If the lifetime gift was $150,000, the estate tax marital deduction would have been $225,000 (i.e., $250,000 less 50 percent of the difference between $150,000 and $100,000). Thus, the maximum reduction of the estate tax marital deduction is $50,000, and this will apply only where the donor has made precisely $100,000 in lifetime gifts to a spouse after December 31, 1976. Combining the marital deduction for gift tax purposes with the martial deduction for estate tax purposes would result in a major decrease in the amount of the remaining taxable estate.

For the above-mentioned reasons, whenever a gift is contemplated, it is better to establish a gift giving habit. Giving gifts on a systematic basis is preferred over erratic gift giving for the following main reasons:

1. The annual gift tax exclusion is $3,000 per donee per year. Through proper timing, the annual exclusion could be used effectively to eliminate any liability for a gift tax or at least reduce it considerably. The $3,000 annual exclusion would be increased to $6,000 if the gift is made with the consent of the spouse (Sec. 2513; 25-2513-1).

2. If a gift is made more than three years prior to the death of the donor, it can not be treated as if it was made in contemplation of death (Sec. 2035).

17.2. Gifts to Minors

Under the Uniform Gifts to Minors Act, transfers to minors under both the custodianship and trust arrangements qualify for the annual gift tax exclusion of $3,000. Although a minor is not capable of accepting property until he reaches the legal age, still a gift to him is not considered a transfer of future interest and the annual gift tax exclusion remains available (Sec. 2503 (c); 25.2503-4). A gift to a minor under a custodianship arrangement will result in the following advantages:

1. The custodianship arrangement is easy to establish and usually broad powers of administration are available to the custodian.
2. The annual gift tax exclusion is available.
3. Income from custodial property is taxed to the minor.
4. Custodial property is included in the gross estate of the minor.

A transfer to a minor under a custodianship arrangement may produce one or more of the following disadvantages:

1. Custodial property must be transferred to the minor upon reaching the age of 21. However, the minor may not be mature enough to receive the property when he reaches the age of 21.
2. If the donor is also the custodian, the Internal Revenue Service would include the custodial property in his gross estate.
3. On death of the minor, part or all of the custodial property may return to the donor through intestacy.

Giving a gift to a minor under a trust arrangement is more advisable if the value of the gift is relatively large. Also, giving under a trust arrangement would add protection to the minor from spouse or creditors of the donor. An inter vivos trust to a minor would build up funds for him while the trust's property may be held until after he reaches age 21. Furthermore, by creating a trust, the grantor may specify that the trust property would not return to the grantor upon the death of the minor before attaining the age of receiving property under the trust.

Outright gifts to minors, as well as gifts under a custodianship or trust arrangements, qualify for the gift tax exclusion if the following two conditions are satisfied:

1. The property and the income from it may be expended by or for the minor, and,
2. The property and income not so expended will pass to the donee or his estate.

17.3. Gifts to Spouse and Divorce Transfers Subject to Tax

Gifts to the donor's spouse qualify for both the marital deduction and annual exclusion. Therefore, a husband may give his wife $103,000 free of gift tax by claiming $100,000 marital deduction, and $3,000 annual exclusion. To illustrate, we may say that during the year 1981, a husband may give to his wife $358,000 in lifetime gifts and pay a gift tax of $120 only. The gift tax is figured as follows:

Gross amount of gift	$358,000
Less:	
Annual exclusion	3,000
Marital deduction	179,000
Taxable gift	$176,000
Unified gift tax:	
on the first $150,000	$ 38,800
on the remaining $26,000 X 32%	8,320
Total gift tax	$ 47,120
Less: Unified tax credit	47,000
Gift tax liability	$ 120

As another illustration a husband may give his wife $280,000 in the year 1978 and pay only $900 as a gift tax. The tax is figured as follows:

Gross amount of gift	$280,000
Less:	
Annual exclusion	3,000
Marital deduction	140,000
Taxable gift	$137,000
Unified gift tax:	
on the first $100,000	$ 23,800
on the remaining $37,000 X 30%	11,100
	34,900
Less: Unified tax credit	34,000
Gift tax liability	$ 900

Therefore, in both community as well as non-community property states the marital deduction for gift tax purposes should be considered as a tool in estate tax saving. For example, if the wife enjoys good health while the husband is suffering from a serious illness, he should consider giving gifts to his spouse. By giving gifts to the wife and using a combination of the marital deduction for gift tax purposes and the annual exclusion, the taxable estate of the husband in this example can be reduced considerably.

Another area of transfers between husband and wife is in connection with divorce. Under I.R.C. Section 2516 (25.2516-1, 25.2516-2) property settlements are exempted from the gift tax if the following two requirements are satisfied:

1. The settlement is per a written agreement relative to the marital and property rights of the spouse, and
2. Final divorce takes place within two years after execution of the written agreement.

Therefore, the statutory requirements for exemption from the gift tax under Section 2516 are easy to satisfy if the parties involved are not hasty. If such requisites are met, it is unnecessary to show either that the transfer was for a consideration, or that it was according to a judicial degree.

17.4. Sale on Installment Basis and Forgiveness of Due Payments

A common device used for both estate as well as gift tax saving purposes is installment sales. Through a bona fide sale a property is removed from the gross estate of the seller. The consideration for the property sold is arranged for payment over a specified number of future periods. Each periodic due installment is not collected, but is reported instead as a gift. After deducting the annual exclusion and the unified credit for gift tax purposes, the donor may not even pay any gift tax on the forgiven periodic installment. For more details regarding the use of installment sales for gift and estate tax saving, see **16.26** in Chapter 16.

17.5. Generation Skipping

An effective device for both estate and gift tax saving purposes is known as generation skipping. This means that the grantor selects the youngest members in his family in order to transfer property to them through gift giving, inheritance, or both. Since the life expectancy of the young recipients of property is relatively long, the possibility for making another taxable transfer of the same property is reduced considerably. For example, if the age of a donor is 75 and he transfers through gift giving a property to his grandson who is three years of age, the grandson could possibly own the property for another 70 years without giving it away through either lifetime gifts or inheritance. Of course, giving a gift and generation skipping are more rewarding to a married donor. With the consent of his spouse, the gift to the youngest generation in the family will be claimed as if made by both the husband and wife, and consequently, the liability for any gift tax is minimized. Notice that the 1976 Tax Reform Act added a new tax on generation-skipping transfers. For more details about the new tax on generation-skipping transfers see **16.6** in Chapter 16.

17.6. Transfers to Inter Vivos Trusts

Such a gift would take place through both direct and indirect transfers. An outright gift giving constitutes a direct transfer. Indirect gifts include transfer in trust, gratuitous transfers to private corporations, a creditor's gratuitous discharge of a debtor's obligation, interest-free loans, gift by renunciation, and a transfer by an incompetent's guardian. The most popular type of indirect gift is the transfer in trust. Creating an inter vivos trust may assist in achieving one or more of the following tax and non-tax related objectives:

1. To reduce income tax of the grantor.
2. To reduce estate tax of the grantor.
3. To reduce income and estate taxes of the grantor.
4. To protect the beneficiary from grantor's spouse or creditors.
5. To arrange for continuity of a going business after death of its owner.
6. To protect a minor, elderly, incompetent, or ill beneficiary.

The inter vivos trust device is flexible enough to protect any one or more of the above-mentioned objectives. From a gift tax point of view, a transfer in trust is treated as an indirect gift of separate interests to the beneficiaries. Therefore, the annual exclusion for gift tax purposes applies to each beneficiary. However, a transfer in trust may be a completed gift to some of the trust beneficiaries while not considered as an indirect gift to others.

For example, a transfer in trust subject to outright revocation by the donor is not a completed gift. Only a complete relinquishment by the donor of all his rights and control over the trust constitutes a completed gift of the trust corpus. The gift tax is imposed on completed transfers of property. Therefore, a transfer treated as complete for gift tax purposes is not necessarily similarly treated for purposes of either the estate or the income tax. A special example is the case of income from a revocable trust. Although there is no gift tax liability on the trust corpus, if the donor retains the power of revocation over the trust, any income paid to the beneficiaries of such a trust is a gift of income and constitutes a taxable gift. In this example, it is assumed that the donor or grantor receives the income and then turns it over to the beneficiaries.

Because the annual gift tax exclusion is available in the case of transfers to the trust, the tax advisor should examine the terms of the inter vivos trust, the number of beneficiaries, and the value of annual property transferred to trust. An irrevocable trust may result in a gift tax liability, but, it would lead to definite income and estate tax savings. On the other hand, while a transfer to a revocable trust would not result in a gift tax liability, it does not produce any income or estate tax savings. Therefore, a careful analysis of the gift, income, and estate tax effects should be made before adopting either the revocable or irrevocable form of trust.

17.7. Gifts to Straw Men

A $3,000 exclusion from gifts of present interests in property is allowed per donee per year. To increase the number of $3,000 annual exclusions, the donor needs to increase the number of donees receiving the gifts of present interests in property (a gift of future interest is not entitled to the annual exclusion). In practical life, some donors are using straw men to increase the number of $3,000 annual exclusion for each donee. For example, a donor may give $3,000 each to A, B, and C, but requires B and C in turn to give their gifts to A. Consequently, the donor may claim the transfers to A, B, and C as non-taxable, since they do not exceed the $3,000 exclusion per donee per year. At the same time, this scheme results in giving A the entire total sum of $9,000. In Reg. 25.2511-1 (h)(2), (3) the Internal Revenue Service took the position that transfers to a straw man are not gifts to him and therefore do not qualify for the $3,000 annual exclusion for gift tax purposes. Therefore, two gifts to a single donee, one direct and one through a straw man, result in one annual exclusion only. The tax advisor should be aware of this trap before actually losing the annual exclusion or exclusions.

17.8. Gratuitous Performance of Services and Hiring a Relative for Compensation

Direct and indirect gifts of interest in property are subject to the gift tax. To avoid this tax either one of the following two methods may be used:

1. A person's gratuitous performance of services for another does not constitute a gift of property and, therefore, is not subject to the gift tax. The distinction between property and services is very important for gift tax purposes. For example, the receipt of property is subject to the tax while the receipt of free services wholly escapes tax. Services are subject to the gift tax only if the would-be donor earning the right to compensation, gratuitously shifts that right to another.

2. A transfer of property is subject to the gift tax, while payment of compensation for services does not constitute a taxable gift. Therefore,

instead of making a direct or indirect gift of property, use the services of another person and compensate him for those services. The problem in a case like this is that the recipient of compensation for services should report the receipt for income tax purposes, while a donee is not subject to any income tax on gifts received. Therefore, it is a question of comparing or trading the gift tax on the donor with the income tax on the donee.

17.9. Interest-Free Loans and Cancellation of Debts

Rather than giving a gift to a family member, a person may give a loan and later cancel the debtor's obligation to pay the loan. Giving interest-free loans and canceling debts, causes a wide variety of both income and gift tax problems. In the following summary, the various possible effects of giving business as well as non-business loans to relatives are examined:

1. The Internal Revenue Service insists that a loan for less than normal interest consitutes a gift (Rev. Rul. 73-61, 1973-5 I.R.B. 15). Of course, the $3,000 exclusion per donee per year often would leave no taxable gift. However, even if the IRS continues to assert that an interest-free loan constitutes a gift, non-interest-bearing loans to relatives and friends should still be made for estate tax saving purposes. Interest-free loans tend to reduce the creditor's estate subject to estate tax since the property obviously could have been put into productive use.

2. The IRS has a special rule for measuring a gift due to an interest-free loan. Under this rule, if the loan is payable at the end of a fixed term, the gift occurs at the date the loan is made. Furthermore, if the loan is payable on demand, gifts will occur during each calendar quarter while the loan is outstanding. Therefore, to make more effective use of the $3,000 annual gift tax exclusion, an interest-free loan should be made payable on demand. This would divide the imputed interest and as a result, often lead to no taxable gifts because of the annual $3,000 gift tax exclusion.

3. When a creditor gratuitously forgives a debt, the amount forgiven is considered as a gift. However, if the forgiveness of debt is for consideration, the creditor is not looked upon as a donor, and, the debtor realizes instead an income equal to the amount of the canceled debt (Sec. 1.61-12). Therefore, before canceling a debt to a friend or relative, a comparison should be made between the gift tax effect on an outright foregiveness of debt and the income tax effect on a cancellation for consideration received from the debtor, such as a certain performance of services. In the light of the comparison, the most favorable tax course should be used.

4. Loans to friends or family members do not constitute gifts. If a loan is made to a relative who wishes to make an investment, the credit usually would be paid back if the investment is profitable. However, if the investment is not profitable, or the creditor wishes to cancel the debt, a gift at the time of cancellation occurs. Multiple valid demand notes constitute good evidence that a transfer is a loan and not a gift. Also, they are easy to use as a suitable vehicle for annual cancellation, if cancellation is desired or necessary.

17.10. Investment in Corporation of a Relative

Instead of making a gift to a friend or family member and paying a gift tax on the transfer, invest in a corporation owned by the friend or family member. The following income and gift tax consequences support this tax saving device:

1. The investment in capital stock of the corporation does not constitute a transfer without consideration. Therefore, if the corporation is organized for a business purpose, the investment in the stock is not subject to the gift tax. It is more advisable for income tax and gift tax purposes to transfer property in exchange for stock, rather than making gratuitous transfers to the corporation. The reason for this is the unsettled issue of whether or not a private corporation is an entity separate and distinct from its shareholders for gift tax purposes. Reg. 25.2511-1 (h)(1) considers a gift to a private corporation as a gift to the other individual shareholders of the corporation to the extent of their proportionate interest in the corporation.

2. If the corporation issues stock under Section 1244, any loss from sale, exchange or worthlessness of such stock is fully deductible as an ordinary loss. Any amount of loss not absorbed in the year the loss is sustained becomes part of the stockholder's net operating loss, which is available for carryback and carryover under the net operating loss rules. On the other hand, any gain from sale or exchange of Section 1244 stock is taxed as a capital gain, and, if the holding period is in excess of six months, the gain is eligible for the favorable long term capital gain tax treatment.

17.11. Purchase of Goods and Services Through Relatives

Frequently, a person must acquire goods and services for both business as well as personal use and purposes. For example, a person may buy a life insurance policy through any of several companies or from his son-in-law who happened to be an insurance broker. In a case like this, there is no transfer of property subject to the gift tax. An insurance service is acquired after paying its worth in a free market place. Another method for avoiding the gift tax is to give valuable advice to a friend or relative. Such advice does not constitute a transfer of interest in property and, therefore, is not subject to the gift tax. An example of valuable advice is to suggest to your son that he acquire a vacant acreage next to your vacant acreage because you intend to build a first-class shopping center on your vacant land. If the son followed the advice, he would receive a capital gain and the advisor would not be liable for any gift tax.

17.12. Disclaimers and Constructive Gifts

A person may make a taxable gift through the renunciation of a property he could have had. Usually, an individual cannot make a gift of something that is not his. However, the Internal Revenue Service takes the position that an indirect gift is made when a person knows he may have a property and yet renounces his rights to it (Reg. 25.2511-1 (c)). The area of renunciations and disclaimers is very important for both estate and gift tax saving.

For example, a surviving spouse may renounce her intestate share so that the entire estate would go to her children. Through such a renunciation the surviving spouse is reducing her own gross estate, and yet, paying a gift tax on the value of the renounced property would reduce the benefit from the estate tax saving. The effect of imposing a gift tax on the value of renounced property can be countered through adoption of one or both of the following devices:

1. Under I.R.C. Section 2056 (d), property interests received by the surviving spouse as a result of a disclaimer by the person who would otherwise acquire the property qualifies for the marital deduction. The increase in the amount of the marital deduction would decrease the taxable estate and consequently reduce the estate tax.

2. Under I.R.C. Section 2514 (b), and, Reg. 25.2514-3(c)(5), the renunciation of powers of appointment is tax-free if local rules of law allow it. Also, Rev. Rul. 25.2511-1 (c) acknowledges that a renunciation of property may not constitute a taxable transfer if local law permits refusal. Therefore, if renunciation is "unequivocal and effective under the local law," and, the refusal is made "within a reasonable time after learning of the transfer," the renunciation may not constitute a taxable transfer.

Answers to questions regarding taxation of renunication transfers are not always clear since the present rules of I.R.C. Section 2514 (c) seem to rest on local laws that lack uniformity. To make the best out of this muddy area of taxation, try to check the following issues before making any renunciation transfer:

1. The rules of local law regarding vested rights and the time of gaining vested interest, and,

2. If local law permits refusal of interest in property. Of course, any refusal of property must be made within a reasonable time after learning of the receipt of interest. The new rules of Section 2009 (b) of the 1976 Tax Reform Act require satisfying all of the following four conditions before considering a disclaimer as irrevocable and a "qualified disclaimer":

(1) The refusal must be in writing;
(2) The written refusal must be made not later than nine months after the day on which the transfer creating the interest is made;
(3) The person must not have accepted the interest or any of its benefits before making the disclaimer;
(4) The interest must pass to a person other than the person making the disclaimer as a result of the refusal to accept the property.

If the disclaimer qualifies under the new rules, a person making it will not be considered as having made a gift to the person to whom the interest passes as a result of the disclaimer.

17.13. Gifts to Charity

Gifts to charity can serve one or more of the following tax purposes:

1. To obtain an itemized deduction against gross income and as a result to reduce the income tax.
2. To reduce the taxable estate and the liability for estate tax. With a reduced liability for estate tax, the need to build up liquid funds during one's life is less.
3. To avoid tax on capital gains from greatly appreciated property.
4. If a person buys life insurance and makes it payable to charitable beneficiaries, his gross estate will increase and the amount available for the maximum allowable marital deduction will increase too. With an increase in marital deduction and the allowable deduction for charitable bequests, the amount of taxable estate and liability for estate tax would be less.
5. To avoid gift tax on transfers to charity during one's life.

A popular method to achieve both income and estate tax saving is to set up an irrevocable ten-year inter vivos trust with fixed annual payments to a charitable beneficiary, and the remainder to third persons. The annual payments would give the grantor a periodic charitable contribution deduction. Also, since the trust is irrevocable, the property transferred to the trust would be removed from the estate of the grantor. Another very popular method of giving gifts to charity is to create a trust under which the grantor reserves for himself the right to an annuity for the duration of his life. Upon his death, the remainder would go to charity.

Under this type of trust, the grantor or donor has the right to deduct for income tax purposes the value of the remainder interest at the time of the initial transfer in trust.

Notice that Reg. 1.662-2 (b) requires that in the case of a charitable remainder annuity trust, the trust's instrument must prohibit additional contributions to the trust after the initial contribution. The reason for this restriction is that any such additions would inject further complications into the valuation of the remainder interest. Gifts to charity during the life of a person are recommended for income and gift tax saving purposes, while testamentary gifts to charity are suggested for a person without close family or friendship ties. A testamentary gift to charity may take the form of an outright gift or a gift in trust.

17.14. Gifts of Life Insurance

Life insurance is popularly used for gift and estate tax saving. Frequently, the purchase of life insurance serves one or more of the following purposes:

1. To build up liquid funds to pay estate taxes.
2. To provide financial support and security for the survivors of the insured.
3. To finance any buy-sell arrangement, retire debts, or protect business against death of a key man.
4. To save through the increase in the cash surrender value of an insurance policy.

Usually, the proceeds of life insurance are included in the gross estate of the insured for estate tax purposes. In order to eliminate such proceeds from inclusion in the estate, any one of the following methods could be used:

1. An irrevocable assignment of insurance policies to other persons, e.g., family members.
2. An irrevocable assignment of insurance policies to an inter vivos trust.
3. To arrange for ownership of policies by the insured's employer or business.
4. To arrange for ownership of policies through a qualified employee benefit plan.
5. To elect during the life of the insured to receive the cash surrender value of the insurance policies and to use the funds received.

Therefore, an irrevocable assignment of insurance policies would decrease the gross estate of the insured. The problem with this type of assignment is that an interest in a life insurance policy is considered as property and its transfer constitutes a taxable gift. All of the following insurance transactions constitute a transfer of interest and are subject to the gift tax:

1. A purchase of a policy for the benefit of another.
2. An irrevocable transfer of an existing policy to another.
3. Payment of premiums on an existing policy owned by another.
4. An irrevocable designation of a new beneficiary and the relinquishment of right to change existing beneficiaries.

Notice that a transfer could be incomplete for gift tax purposes and would result in the inclusion of the transferred policy in the insured's gross estate. The degree of control which the insured retained would render a gift as either complete or incomplete for gift as well as estate tax purposes. If the insured retained any "incidents of ownership," the transfer is not complete. Incidents of ownership include mainly the right of the insured or his estate to the economic benefits of the insurance, the power to change the beneficiary, the power to surrender or cancel the policy, the power to assign it, the power to revoke an assignment, the power to pledge the policy or borrow from the insurer against the value of the policy.

Since the annual exclusion, marital deduction and unified tax credit are available for use against any lifetime transfers of life insurance policies, the donor may carry on the transfers without any payment of a gift tax. Therefore, the lifetime transfer of insurance policies should be considered seriously even if their assignment is considered taxable for gift tax purposes. Observe the special limitation imposed by the Internal Revenue Service in case of assignment of a policy and continuation to pay the annual premiums by the donor during the three-year period prior to the donor's death. A proportion of the proceeds from such a policy would be included in the estate of the insured (even though the transfer is considered complete for gift tax purposes).

17.15 Gifts of Annuities

A donor may transfer an annuity contract. Annuity contracts take a variety of forms. The most popular types of annuities are the following:

1. A single life annuity paid to the annuitant for his life and, upon his death, all rights under the annuity contract terminate. A single life annuity could be with or without a refund feature. The refund feature would provide a payment to the annuitant's estate (or a designated party) if

the payments during the life of the annuitant were below the cost of the contract.

2. A self and survivor annuity (also called a survivorship or longer life annuity) would provide payments after the death of one annuitant until the other annuitant dies too.

3. A joint and survivor annuity contact would provide payments to two annuitants jointly during their lives and a similar or reduced amount to the survivor for his life.

For gift tax saving purposes observe the following:

1. The valuation of annuities presents a unique problem. The general approach to valuation of annuities reflects using cost to the donor (or premiums paid on the contract) rather than value (or immediate cash value) to the donee. In case of annuities issued by companies regularly engaged in their sale, actuarial tables are used to estimate their value. These tables reflect the cost principle in determining the value of an annuity (Reg. 25.2512-5, 25.2512-9).

2. The mere purchase of a single-life, non-refundable annuity by a taxpayer and for himself does not constitute a taxable gift. However, the purchase of an annuity for another, the assignment of an annuity, the purchase of a joint annuity, or the purchase of a joint-and-survivor annuity for the purchaser and another constitute taxable gifts.

3. The terms of annuity contracts with survivorship features should be examined carefully by the tax advisor since they may have estate tax consequences.

17.16. Assignment of Income

The gift tax can be related to the income tax in the area of assignment of income. The tax principle of the "fruit and the tree" applies in this situation. While the income tax is imposed on the "fruit," the gift tax is related to the "tree." This makes the area of giving income-producing properties have a special significance for both income as well as gift tax saving purposes. Nevertheless, a taxpayer may not assign or transfer the income-producing property itself. Rather, he may keep the property and assign the periodic income from it (*Holmes,* ITC 508;, *Austin V. Comm.,* 161 F.2d666, 35AFTR 1350). A situation like this would result, in a sense, in the conversion of the well known gift tax "free" into an income tax "tree" into an income tax "fruit." The tax advisor is concerned about when the gift occurs and what is the amount subject to the tax.

Assignment of rental income, interest income, and royalty income without a transfer in property producing the income would lead to income, gift, and estate tax problems which should be solved on a case-by-case basis. The following four major areas should be examined carefully whenever income is assigned:

1. If the lifetime transfer was made in contemplation of death.
2. If the donor transfers all his rights or makes a conditional transfer.
3. If the donor retains any powers of control, and if so, the extent of retention and its effect.
4. If the transfer is made with the donor reserving for himself the income for his lifetime.

17.17. Giving Income-Producing and Greatly Appreciated Property

A donor may transfer all his rights in a property, or transfer partial (or fragile) property interest. He may also transfer present interest in property, present and future interests, remainder interests, terminable interest, tenancy in common, tenancy by entirety or miscellaneous property interests (e.g., gas or oil and mineral rights, stock options, etc.). The liability for the gift tax depends on the value of rights or interests which gratuitously passed to another during the lifetime of the donor. The value of interest in a property, for gift tax purposes, is determined at the date of the gift. Therefore, the fair market value (or estimated sale price) will be used as the basis for valuation. When the donor transfers a property observe the following:

1. Compute the market value at the date of transfer and support the computation (whenever possible) with the appraisal report of a qualified appraiser.

2. Special valuation rules apply to transfer of the following types of properties:

a. stock and bonds,
b. business interests
c. mutual fund shares,
d. property subject to an excise tax,
e. notes receivable, and
f. United States savings bonds.

3. Giving appreciated property would shift the potential capital gain from the donor to the donee. For making the best possible use of a tax preference item such as long-term capital gains, the entire tax situation of

both the donor and the donee should be examined before determining the amount and date of gift.

4. Giving depreciated property (or property with market value below its basis) would shift the potential capital loss to the donee. If the donor has a greater variety of wealth and is in a higher income tax bracket, he may need the tax deduction from such a loss more than the donee.

5. Giving an income-producing property would reduce both the future taxable income of the donor as well as his gross estate.

17.18. Giving Stock in a Closely Held Corporation and Transfers to Private Corporations

Giving stock in a corporation is a popular method of giving gifts. It is easy to endorse a stock certificate to a friend or a family member. However, it is not as easy to determine the tax effects of such gift giving. Prior to a gratuitous transfer of capital stock, observe the following:

1. If a gift is made by a corporation, and the corporate gift is not ascribed to the corporation's shareholders, the gift tax will be avoided completely. The gift tax is imposed only on transfers by individuals and does not apply to transfers by corporations or persons other than individuals (I.R.C. Sec. 2501 (a)(1), and Reg. 25.2511-1 (h)(1)).

2. If a gift is made by a closely-held corporation, and the corporate gift is ascribed to the corporation's shareholders, the gift will be ratably apportioned among the shareholders. After that, each shareholder would report his share of the gift separately. In this way, each shareholder would use his exclusions to offset his share of the corporate gift.

3. An indirect gift, such as a gift to a private corporation, may result in a gift tax liability. For gift tax purposes, and in a case like this, the corporation is not viewed as an entity separate from the entity of its shareholders. The gift to the corporation is viewed as a way through which benefits flow to all of its shareholders. Of course, if a person makes a transfer to a corporation exclusively owned by him, the transfer is for his own benefit and would not be subject to the gift tax. However, a gratuitous transfer to a corporation partly owned by the donor (or donors) would be subject to the gift tax. If a gift is given to a partly owned corporation, the gift is limited to the extent of benefits received by the other shareholders and in accordance with their proportionate interests in the corporation (Reg. 25.2511-1 (h)(1)). Therefore, instead of making a taxable gift to a private corporation, consider first making a transfer in exchange for securities (stock and bonds) of the corporation.

4. A transfer of property by a corporation to one of its own shareholders, is a gift to him from the other shareholders only to the extent it exceeds the shareholder's (or donee's) own interest in such amounts as a stockholder (Reg. 25.2511-1 (h)(1)).

5. Listed stocks or stocks trading over-the-counter are valued at the mean between the highest and the lowest selling price on the valuation date (Reg. 20.2031-2 (c)). Under the "blockage" rule, if the number of shares is so large that it carries with it control of the corporation, the stock's actual value could be more, and sometimes less, than the market quotations. If the stock is not listed on any exchange or otherwise not traded regularly, the concept of the willing seller and willing buyer is used for valuation purposes. This type of corporation is called a "close" corporation and treated like an unincorporated business interest (Rev. Rul. 68-609, 1968-2 C.B. 327, 328). In the case of giving stock of a close corporation, the donor should be prepared to defend his computation of reported value. If value of the stock cannot be based on a price of a willing seller and a willing buyer, the determination of stock value becomes more difficult. Under Reg. 20.2031-2 (f)(2) where no stock selling prices are available, the value of stock is to be determined with reference to the company's net worth, prospective earning power and dividend-paying capacity, as well as any other relevant factors. Giving shares of stock would influence the income, gift and estate taxes of the donor. Therefore, the combined tax effect on both the donor and donee should be evaluated carefully before introducing this significant tax saving technique.

INDEX

D

E

F

G

H

I

J

K

L

M

N

O

P

R